Stanley Leathes

The Christian Creed

Its Theory and Practice, With a Preface on Some Present...

Stanley Leathes

The Christian Creed
Its Theory and Practice, With a Preface on Some Present...

ISBN/EAN: 9783337004033

Printed in Europe, USA, Canada, Australia, Japan

Cover: Foto ©Lupo / pixelio.de

More available books at **www.hansebooks.com**

THE CHRISTIAN CREED:

ITS THEORY AND PRACTICE.

WITH A PREFACE ON SOME PRESENT DANGERS
OF THE ENGLISH CHURCH.

BY THE
REV. STANLEY LEATHES, M.A.,
PREBENDARY OF ST. PAUL'S, PROFESSOR OF HEBREW, KING'S COLLEGE, AND
MINISTER OF ST. PHILIP'S, REGENT STREET, LONDON.

New York:
E. P. DUTTON AND Co.,
713, BROADWAY.
MDCCCLXXVIII.

PREFACE.

THE object of the following pages is at once simple and obvious. I had occasion some time back, in the course of my weekly ministrations, to deliver a series of discourses on the articles of the Apostles' Creed. In doing this I naturally had in mind a somewhat larger gathering than the fluctuating and precarious one of my own Church, and wrote accordingly. The result is now given to the reader, in the hope that the object thus aimed at may, so far as it shall please the Divine Head of the Church, be attained.

The Christian Creed, in its *theory*, cannot fail to come into direct antagonism with the various forms of unrestrained and self-chosen opinion that are rife in the present day, and that attract attention because of their apparent novelty, and elicit sympathy because they are bold in their unrestraint. Under the circumstances it was clearly desirable rather to glance at than to specify them more fully, or to make direct reference to the works in which they are found. It is, in fact, the *tone* of much of our popular ephemeral literature that needs to be corrected. Another standard of thought requires to be presented to the popular mind, and such a standard is afforded by the theory of the Apostles' Creed.

The Christian Creed, in its *practice*, is the secret spring of moral action to every believer, and contains by implication the standard of all Christian conduct. No sound treatment of the Christian faith can deliberately pass by the obligation to Christian practice. While dwelling necessarily on those aspects of the Christian faith which are opposed to very much of the prevalent thought of the day, I have not intentionally overlooked the practical bearing and importance of the Creed.

The Christian Creed, therefore, in its *theory* and *practice* may concisely express the obligation of the Church in all ages in the twofold direction of faith and conduct. The subjects thus suggested can never be obsolete. But there are sundry indications that the due consideration of them is more than ever indispensable at the present time; and under the present aspects which the Church presents it may not be out of place to dwell briefly upon some of these.

In speaking of the Church, however, it must be borne in mind that the meaning of the word is one that varies with the sentiments and predilections of the persons using it. By education, choice, and conviction I myself am a Churchman, and sincerely attached to the Church of England as by law established. Let it, however, not be supposed that in speaking of the Church I have any desire to limit the just application of the term to those who like myself are in communion with that Church. The Church of Christ is something vastly more than the Church of England, and its limits can only be assigned by Christ Himself. Consequently, if these pages fall under the eye of any members of non-conforming denominations, such persons must not be jealous if, for convenience sake, the term Church is at times here used in the restricted sense more familiar to a Churchman. It is not the present aspects of the Church of Christ that I wish to dilate upon, but rather to offer in all humility to my fellow Churchmen some brief observations on the present position of the English Church.

There can no longer be any doubt that a considerable body of persons exists in the Church of England, in open and professed membership therewith, who are deliberately bent upon doing all they can to assimilate it in teaching and practice to the Church of Rome. During the last thirty years, and, indeed, for little short of half a century, this has often been affirmed; but it has of late years, and by the progress of recent events been demonstrated to a degree of certainty, greater perhaps than at any previous time within that period. At the commencement of what is called triumphantly the 'Catholic Revival,' the impulse was communicated solely by the agency of doctrinal teaching. The *Church* was put forward as the great source and depository of grace. The priesthood was invested with functions which had almost entirely been in abeyance in the Church of England since the death of Queen Mary. Those passages in the formularies which gave any colour to them were dwelt upon with greater emphasis and dragged into fictitious prominence; the Sacraments were insisted upon as the chief and the only sure and direct means of personally applying the benefits of redemption, and the character of an elaborate and graduated system was given, not only to the offices of the Christian ministry, but also to the very relations of the individual soul to its God.

There were not wanting many who detected at once the real tendency of this teaching which was so openly inculcated, but the great body of the religious public were incapable of doing so. Many persons hailed the revived system of religion as a promising and an agreeable substitute for much that was naturally distasteful or unattractive in the traditional teaching that was in vogue. The Sacraments had been greatly neglected, but they were manifestly the ordinance of Christ. The Sacramental system had this great merit to the ordinary mind, that it gave something tangible and definite to the perplexed, the enquiring, and the awakened.

And at the first beginning of the movement the elaboration of the Sacramental system in its bearing upon practical conduct, and as the most satisfactory method of cultivating the development of the spiritual life was the main object with its advocates. The treatise of Robert Isaac Wilberforce on the Doctrine of the Incarnation was the most perfect exponent, and the most finished expression of this theory. It was really an expansion of certain famous sections of Hooker which, perhaps more readily than anything else in English theology, lent themselves to this treatment. But here, as in so many other cases, the disciple outstripped the master whose fervid rhetoric was turned into earnest and uncompromising logic.

The effect which the publication of this book had

upon the teaching of the English clergy was undoubtedly very great, and I am very far from insinuating that the influence was only evil. I am very willing to acknowledge my own great obligations to the teaching of that book in many ways. And as a work of pure theology there have been few like it in the present century. But it was doctrinally the highest achievement of the Sacramental theory in the Church of England, both as a work of intellect and as a treatise of systematic theology. When, however, a few years afterwards, its accomplished author was received into the Church of Rome, it became evident that whether or not the teaching therein inculcated was the teaching of the Church of England, it at all events was not essentially antagonistic, but might even be preparatory, to that of Rome. In fact the development of the Sacramental system may be regarded as in some respects more perfect in the Church of England than in that of Rome, for the very reason that the Church of Rome has a far greater wealth of system to present than the existing formularies of the Church of England gave any scope for. Consequently the desire for system was at first obliged to expend itself on the Sacramental theory, and there can be but little doubt that many persons earnestly endeavouring to serve God, found, or seemed to find, all that they wanted in the practical working out of the Sacramental system. They were taught that in the Sacrament of the Lord's Supper there was provided a direct opportunity for coming into personal contact with the Lord Jesus Christ, which had the advantage of leaving nothing to be desired, inasmuch as the union between the soul and the Redeemer therein effected was complete, and assured to the senses by participation in the elements. The peace and joy thus palpably and tangibly given, seemed to be the very fulfilment of all that redemption meant. Earnest and enquiring souls who took refuge in this ordinance had the consolation that they were acting on the express commands of Christ, and were accordingly assured that the path they had chosen was the right one. It followed, however, necessarily, that if the Sacrament of the Lord's Supper was thus a means or direct channel of grace, unto which there was none other like it, then, the oftener the act of participation was renewed the better. And hence the advisableness of increased communions was largely dwelt upon. Whereas the rubric of the English Prayer-Book had ordered that every person should communicate "at the least three times in the year," and exceptional provision was made for " all Priests and Deacons " " in Cathedral and Collegiate Churches and Colleges " to communicate "every Sunday at the least," it rapidly began to be the custom for communions in *parish* churches to be monthly, and then weekly, until at last, as now in the metropolitan cathedral and elsewhere, they were made daily.[1] Let it not be supposed that this is mentioned as being in itself a misfortune or a fault. We owe a debt of gratitude. in this respect, as in so many others, to the pioneers of the 'revival' in stimulating the practice of the Church, and leading it on so many degrees further towards perfection. But, unfortuately, while its practice was improved, the principles of its faith as a reformed and evangelical church were secretly undermined and vitiated. And this in a way that was the least suspected. There is so much that appeals to our higher feelings in the multiplication of communions, that it is difficult to suppose that any danger can underlie it. There is no surer test of vitality in a church than the increase of communions; but I am regarding them now from the side of one who, being anxious about his spiritual welfare, desires to avail himself to the utmost of their increase, and so is misled to seek in the frequency of the act that which alone can be found in a deeper apprehension of the meaning of the act. Very commonly in such cases it is not more frequent communions that are

[1] According to Mackeson's *Guide* there are now thirty-nine churches in London where there is daily communion, and in two of them it is twice a day.

wanted, but a greater degree of simple and childlike faith, and the one is no substitute for the other. The frequent, or even daily, multiplication of communions, though not certainly, was probably a characteristic of the Church's infancy,[1] and, therefore, of the days of her innocence and first love; but it by no means follows that the direct imitation of the early Church in an outward and accidental characteristic of this kind carries with it the energy or exercise of the same motive principle under the present and existing circumstances of the Church. If we suppose that daily communions were the original custom, they were at least a *spontaneous* act then; the same cannot be said of the restoration in the present day of a custom long obsolete, if, indeed, there is any evidence of it in the Reformed Church. The impelling motive in a case of this kind is everything. In the early Church the practice would arise from the intense freshness and power of the newly-learnt faith and the newly-felt love. The practice would flow naturally from the fountain but just opened out in the regenerated heart. It is altogether different now. The desire for daily communions now manifestly arises from the feeling that weekly communions are insufficient. But insufficient for what? For the due performance of the Church's

---

[1] Acts ii. 46, and cf. xx. 7 and 1 Cor. xvi. 2.

ministrations, or for the life of the individual soul? Manifestly not for the former reason, because if so he who said "*Let all things be done decently and in order*,"[1] and made arrangements about the collection for the saints, would not have omitted a direction of this kind, or, at least, an allusion to it would have escaped him in one or other of his epistles had it been part of the original Apostolic order. Clearly, therefore, it must be for the life of the individual soul; but if so then the rubric of the Church, which prescribes as a *minimum* communion three times in the year, is surely incompatible with such a notion, and cannot be reconciled therewith. In short, it is unquestionable that the demand for daily communions can only arise from the felt insufficiency of more infrequent ones to sustain at the requisite height the spiritual vitality of the soul; in other words, the spiritual vitality of the soul is directly dependent upon the frequency of the act of communion. And thus frequent communions, weekly communions, and even daily communions are resorted to as a means of increasing that spiritual vitality, to the abundance and overflow of which they can alone be ascribed in the early Church. Let it, therefore, be distinctly understood that it is not daily communions or weekly communions in them-

[1] 1 Cor. xiv. 40.

selves that are objected to; every Christian must rejoice in every opportunity of meeting his Lord in His own blessed ordinance of breaking of bread; in themselves they are neither right nor wrong, neither good nor bad; when proceeding spontaneously from pure and fervent faith they cannot be otherwise than good; but when resorted to as a means of acquiring the increase, or even as a substitute for the presence of that faith of which the felt deficiency is the very motive impelling to the use of them, they can only be pernicious as leading the soul astray in a false direction and to a delusive result. And this is proved by the fact that the restoration of the early practice of the Church at Troas[1] is found to be so inadequate and insufficient for the spiritual sustentation of the soul, that it has to be multiplied to a *sevenfold* degree in order that the result may be obtained which may be presumed to have been obtained in the case of the early apostolic Christians of the Troad in St. Paul's days. The very great divergence of practice in the two cases is enough to show that the principles predominating in the two cases must be no less different. Monthly communions are found by experience to be insufficient till they have been multiplied *fourfold*, and weekly com-

[1] Acts xx. 7.

munions are found by experience to be insufficient or the wants of the individual life (because the corporate necessities of a largely increased number of communicants proportionate to the extended growth of the Church is not now the question) till they have been multiplied *sevenfold*. What room is there for yet further increase? But is it not obvious, from the analogy of past experience that the actual result desired has not yet been obtained, for if so, why this sevenfold increase? On examination of the gospel history we find nothing that can in any way be conceived to answer to these repeated communions. Christ, on two several occasions, fed four thousand and five thousand men, and when they were filled He sent them away. We nowhere read that He fed them again. He showed significantly by His feeding them that He was the Bread of Life, but with reference to that bread He declared that he that came to Him should *never hunger*.[1] The coming, then, would seem to represent a permanent condition, and not an act which was ever being repeated but was never complete. In the various miracles of healing performed by Christ, the cure effected was an instantaneous and a permanent one. We nowhere read that the same person had occasion to come to Him twice. We

[1] John vi. 35.

are taught, therefore, that when Christ heals, He heals effectually, and once for all. The act needs not oftentimes to be repeated[1]; it cannot be repeated by any series of acts at all answering to the repetition of communions. To suggest, therefore, that for the health of the soul it is indispensable, or even expedient, to repair to the Holy Communion every week, or, in some cases, every day, is to suggest a course which has nothing in common with those incidents in the Gospel, which, if they are designed to teach us anything, are designed to teach us the fulness and the freeness of Christ's redemption, and to show us the mode and method in which it acts.

It seems to follow, therefore, and the history of the repetition of communions serves to show, that the theory expressed by them is different from that which is proposed to us in the historical gospels and in the Apostolical epistles. At all events there is nothing in the New Testament which can be alleged in support of daily communions as a desirable means of grace,—unless it can be assumed that the act of communion is identical with something which is otherwise expressed or implied in the language of it. And if this is not so, it becomes more than doubtful whether the over-repetition of the act of communion

[1] Cf. Heb. vii. 27, ix. 25—28, x. 14—18.

does not argue a confusion between the means and the end, the significant act, and the thing which the act signifies. The act of communion implies a participation of Christ, but upon one condition only, which is that of faith. And this means not that I partake of Christ in the communion because I believe, and by means of my believing that He is present in the communion; but that I partake of Christ when I believe and by means of my believing in *Him*. It is He and He only who is the life and significance of the communion; the act of communion itself, therefore, is invalid unless I see Him, and see Him aright —yea, unless I believe on Him to the saving of the soul, for " the mean whereby the Body of Christ is received and eaten in the Supper is Faith."[1] But clearly to believe in the Holy Communion as *the* means of applying Christ's salvation is something very different from believing in Jesus to the saving of the soul, and is it not possible that the very repetition of the act of communion may be resorted to, because even in the Holy Communion itself there is no saving apprehension of the Lord Jesus. Can the ever-recurrent hunger for the repetition of the means be compatible with that coming to Him of which He said that whosoever so came should never hunger?

[1] Art. xxviii.

It was soon found, however, that even the continual repetition of the act of communion was inadequate to accomplish the end desired unless it was supplemented and corroborated by something else. And hence arose silently, secretly, gradually and insidiously the restoration of the practice of sacramental confession to the priest, which has increased to an unknown and incalculable extent. It must be borne in mind that there is an intrinsic difference between spiritual counsel and advice, and the habit of sacramental confession. This is often forgotten by the advocates of the latter, who maintain that a practice analogous in its essence to the confession of the Roman Church is to be found in those of various reformed and evangelical bodies. The truth is that the two practices are essentially and intrinsically different. When the Ethiopian eunuch asked Philip the Evangelist, *I pray thee, of whom speaketh the prophet this, of himself or of some other man?* and in reply to his question, *Understandest thou what thou readest?* said, *How can I, except some man should guide me?* [1] there was no similarity or relation whatever in the incident recorded to the habit or act of auricular confession as practised by the Roman Church, and of late years revived in our own. When the jailor at Philippi asked, *What must I do to be*

[1] Acts viii. 30, 31.

saved?[1] the question was one of mental perplexity and distress, and bore no analogy whatever to the specific confession of sin. The object of the one act is to seek guidance in perplexity and doubt; the object of the other to obtain the repeated assurance of the forgiveness of ever-recurrent sin. This latter is felt by experience to be the indispensable concomitant even of multiplied communions, and is thus conclusive evidence of the inability of such communions to give peace. And hence, under the principles of the Sacramental system, we are gradually but surely committed to the entire paraphernalia of an organised priesthood, and a complex system of sacerdotalism. And this is nothing less than an elaborate machinery of mediation, and of mediation not between God and the soul, but between Christ and the soul. Instead of the invitation *Come unto Me!*[2] being urged and acted upon, we are assured that the only effectual way of approaching Christ is through the Sacraments of His own ordinance, and the only profitable way of approaching the Sacraments is through the absolution of the priest. Thus fetters, and a chain of insupportable weight and of slavish bondage[3] are forged for the enquiring soul under the vain pretext of facilitating its access to the Saviour.[4]

[1] Acts xvi. 30.
[2] Matt. xi. 28.
[3] Cf. John viii. 32, 36.
[4] Cf. John v. 40.

It may seem as though such language were only the commonplace outcry of Protestantism against the enormities of the Church of Rome. But it is not so. Not a word has now been used which does not equally apply to hundreds and thousands of communicants who boast of their union and membership with the English Church. This is the doctrine and practice which is inculcated upon a very large number of congregations throughout the land. It is unquestionably one of the signs of the times.

But how is it to be interpreted? How is it to be dealt with? There is and can be but one interpretation. Such teaching and practice is significant, and can only be significant of a return to the principles of the Church of Rome. It is not to be denied that a very large portion of the English Church at the present day is not only unduly and extravagantly enamoured of the principles of the Church of Rome (save and except only the dogma of papal supremacy and infallibility) but can find no rest or satisfaction except as those principles are more and more nearly approached, and more and more earnestly embraced. It is not, indeed, everywhere or always that men proceed to the full length of the principles and practices indicated, but they among whom principles identical in essence with those of the Church of

Rome are adopted and acted upon are to be counted by thousands and by tens of thousands. What, then, is to be done? The evil is gone too far to be suddenly checked, but one thing is quite certain, there is no use in any longer concealing the fact. Every minister of Christ who desires to be faithful to his trust is bound to expose and condemn it boldly and unhesitatingly. It is often supposed that the less that is said on such topics the better, but it is too late to hold one's peace, or to affect any ignorance of or indifference to the magnitude of the evil. It is high time to *cry aloud, and spare not, to lift up the voice like a trumpet, to show the Lord's people their transgression, and the house of Jacob their sins!*[1]

The fact of the matter is this: it is of the utmost importance to understand that the principle and essence of the Sacramental system implies and involves sacerdotalism or the mediation of the priest, and the principle and essence of sacerdotalism implies and involves the religion of the Church of Rome; it is virtually and actually identical with it in theory and principle. If, therefore, the English Church owes her very existence as a separate and independent Church to the stand which she made three hundred years ago against the usurpations, enormities, and

[1] Isa. lviii. 1.

errors of the Church of Rome, it is absurd to suppose that we can be loyal children of the English Church if, instead of continuing to make that stand, we begin to obliterate the distinctive difference of *principle* upon which it was based, and throw ourselves heart and soul into doctrines and practices which are altogether identical with those errors and enormities. Nor is it possible that there can be any sound and healthy union between elements and principles in their very nature opposed. If the very existence of the Church of England is a witness that she does abjure and protest against Roman teaching, how is it possible that there should be more than nominal union between those who heartily protest against and those who systematically adopt that teaching? It cannot be for the strength and welfare of the Church that we should endeavour to slur the difference over, or to extenuate and ignore it. Rather to do so will be fraught with imminent peril and with ultimate destruction to the Church.

A wiser plan would be to look it fairly in the face and act accordingly. A house divided against itself cannot stand. Matters have proceeded to such extremities that nothing but strenuous and vigorous action can avail. When insubordination enters an army its doom is sealed. Nor can it be otherwise with the Church. When constituted authority is set at defiance, and every man is content to do only that which is right in his own eyes, the time of dissolution can hardly be far distant. If that day is to be averted, it must surely be by prompt and decisive measures, by bold and faithful utterance. A little leaven leaveneth the whole lump. It is patent that Roman leaven has very largely pervaded the English Church. LET US CAST IT OUT. There can be no peace while it is suffered to work insidiously. There is nothing more wearisome and useless than the cry, *Peace, peace, when there is no peace*,[1] for peace is an impossibility when incompatible antagonistic elements are at work. In every human institution there must doubtless be forbearance and toleration on all sides. It is not desirable that the Church should consist of only one party; but even opposite parties may be loyal to a common head or to a common principle. And those only have no place in the pale of the English Church who are not loyal in the common stand that should be made against the common foes of Romanism and unbelief.

The fundamental principle of the English Church is the recognition of the supreme authority of Scripture, and readiness to be bound by its decisions in

[1] Jer. vi. 14.

every question, as by a court of ultimate appeal. It acknowledges the volume of Revelation to be the sole fountain of the knowledge of eternal life, and believes that by the ministry of the Word the sick may be made whole and the dead be quickened into life, but that in no case can this be brought about but by the operation of the Holy Spirit on the one side, and by the exercise of personal faith on the other.[1]

But when the Sacrament of Christ's body and blood is made the centre of all Christian life and practice, there is always room for grave anxiety lest the *mind should be corrupted from the simplicity that is in Christ*.[2] Under certain limits a Sacramental form of religion is fairly within the scope of the English formularies, but when the Sacrament is made the pivot of all individual life and of all public worship it has unquestionably usurped the place of Christ Himself as the sole sufficient and *sufficing* object of faith. The apprehension, however, of Christ as the simple and sole object of faith is an act too sublimated and transcendental for the natural heart, which, therefore, thankfully takes refuge in a sensuous worship of outward and visible signs. So thoroughly is this the case that the practice has become very common in

[1] Acts xv. 8, 9; xvi. 14; xiv. 1.   [2] 2 Cor. xi. 3.

the English Church of being present at the rite of communion without communicating. As soon as this practice is adopted, the motive for the frequent repitition of communions, derived from a particular interpretation of and inference from our Lord's language about eating His flesh and drinking His blood, is withdrawn, and a custom is introduced for which there is no Scripture warrant whatever, and which is by implication contrary to the intention of the English Communion Service.

Another significant indication of the tendency of a certain phase of religious teaching is the establishment and restoration of duplicate altars in churches; a thing in itself perhaps innocent,[1] and always, probably, to be excused on the ground of convenience or symmetry, and the like; but assuredly only to be explained upon the hypothesis of a Sacramental religion having been confessedly accepted as the expression and agency of the ministry of reconciliation. But this should be distinctly understood in every case, for the ministry of reconciliation is the ministry of the *word*,[2] which operates by *belief of the truth*,[3] and not by participation in any outward rites, be they what they may.[4]

In short, it is undeniable and only too manifest

[1] But cf. Hosea viii. 11.   [3] 2 Thess. ii. 13; John viii. 32.
[2] 2 Cor. v. 18, 19.   [4] Gal. v. 6; vi. 15; 1 Cor. vii. 19.

that great efforts are being made in the English Church to turn the sacrament of the Lord's Supper into the Romish Mass. And it is not too much to say when this is done that the principle affirmed is that of *a different Gospel which is not another*.[1] If we are only saved by Christ's death through receiving its benefits in the Sacrament, then there is an end to the Gospel as proclaimed by Christ Himself, *God so loved the world that He gave His only-begotten Son, that whosoever believeth in Him should not perish but have everlasting life*.[2] And that this is virtually the case is shown by an assertion openly made some years ago by an Oxford divine of the highest note in favour of sacerdotal religion, " There is not one word in Holy Scripture of our applying *to ourselves* the promises of the Gospel;"[3] that is to say, they can only be applied through the machinery of the priest and the Sacraments. This is not the place to argue the abstract question, it is enough to draw attention to the fact that such teaching has very deeply penetrated and permeated the English Church, and is openly advocated in a thousand churches as the true way of salvation, while at the same time it is identical in principle with the teaching of the Church of

[1] Gal. i. 6, 7.
[2] John iii. 16.
[3] See the well-known Sermons entitled *Entire Absolution of the Penitent*.

Rome, and is fundamentally opposed to the whole spirit and principle of the prayer-book.

The entire fabric of the Sacramental system rests upon the fatal theory of post-baptismal sin. In a church in which the great majority of members are baptised in infancy, the question of post-baptismal sin must always be one of the greatest urgency. And it is a question which Scripture has left, comparatively speaking, unanswered, unless the answer which applies to all other sin applies also to *that*. The assumption of the Sacramental theory is that it does not, and hence the opening for the elaborate organisation of the religion of the priest; an organisation, however, which is not even sketched in outline in the writings of the New Testament, nor, indeed, in those of the Apostolical Fathers. Scripture, however, has by anticipation answered and effectually demolished this theory by the Epistle to the Galatians. The whole drift and tenour of that Epistle is absolutely fatal to the Sacramental system. Furthermore, Scripture strenuously refuses to discriminate between kinds of sin. It tells us that Jesus Christ is *the Lamb of God which taketh away the* SIN *of the world*,[1] that the Holy Ghost shall *convince the world of sin*,[2] and that *the blood of Jesus Christ cleanseth us from all sin*.[3] The words

[1] John i. 29.   [2] John xvi. 8.   [3] 1 John i. 7.

must refer in the last case to the Christian Church when past her infancy, and therefore necessarily include post-baptismal sin. We must decide, therefore, whether we will deal with sins after baptism as we should with those before it, or whether they come under another category and must be dealt with otherwise. In the, one, case we meet them with the proclamation of the word of faith, in the other by the religion of the priest and the Sacramental system.

But it is highly important to observe that the two principles are directly antagonistic and mutually destructive. One is the principle of the Church of Rome, the other is that of the Reformed Church of England, as it unquestionably is that of the Gospel itself. The message of the Gospel appeals to faith as the one only indispensable pre-requisite in the heart of man. *Believe on the Lord Jesus Christ and thou shalt be saved.*[1] *If thou believest with all thine heart thou mayest*[2] be baptised. It will doubtless be said by the advocates of the Sacramental system that these were words addressed to the jailor at Philippi and to the Ethiopian eunuch, and not to mankind generally, or at all events to recent converts; but it is hardly possible that the people of England with

[1] Acts xvi. 31.   [2] Acts viii. 37.

their open Bible can have read it thus. They will have received from the book its own message. The laity, however, require to be put upon their guard as to the real principle involved in the teaching which is so attractive and so popular, in order that they may know what it is they choose, and may not think that they are faithful members of the Church of England when they have largely imbibed the essential doctrines of the Church of Rome.

It is, however, not a little remarkable that a movement, which in its beginning was wholly one of doctrine, should after a while have been mainly indebted for its rapid progress to the development of ritual, which was a matter altogether indifferent to the original authors of the movement. The Eastward Position, for example, was a thing utterly unknown to John Henry Newman as vicar of St. Mary's. Vestments not only were not adopted, but were never even thought of for many years after the publication of Tract 90. A movement which was eminently intellectual when it began, has developed into the advocacy of puppet shows and child's play. The popularity which the Eastward Position has acquired in the last thirty years, before which it was rarely if ever practised in the English Church, is simply astounding, and only to be explained by the principle it involves. The churches which have adopted the Eucharistic vestments throughout the kingdom are probably to be counted by the hundred.[1] Are these things, as some would have us believe, of no importance, or are they not much rather of the most profound significance, and of ominous foreboding to the peace and welfare of the Church, not to say her safety? It has no doubt been found, practically, that certain doctrines were far more attractive with the accessories of form and show than in the character of dry theological statement; and so things in themselves as trifling and even trivial, as the position of the priest at the altar and the colour of his robes have been made the subject of the most deperate contention, because they were the convenient instruments and appropriate channels for conveying doctrines which, left to themselves, would have had but small prospect of success. This circumstance, however, is no slight indication of the *natural* drift and tendency of a movement so eminently intellectual as the 'Catholic Revival' was in its origin and first efforts. In view of the remarkable aspect it now presents under the form of Ritualism we have reason to exclaim, with Desdemona,—

"O, most lame and impotent conclusion!"

---

[1] According to Mackeson thirty-five in London and the suburbs.

If the Church of England is to be faithful to her original calling, as a witness for the saving power of God's Word, there can be no doubt that the aspect of affairs at the present time is calculated to give rise to the most serious apprehension, and the more so because there seems to be a general supineness pervading the more influential both of the clergy and the laity. It may be that little can be done, or is desirable to be done, by repression, or by calling into play the machinery of the law. But a vast amount can be done in all quarters by discouragement of the evil, and by the mind of the laity being on the alert and well informed. Is it possible that the people of England will suffer the spiritual heritage of their forefathers, which was purchased for them by the blood of men who were faithful unto death, to become the prey of false teachers, who will infallibly give her over to Romish superstition and to Romish practices? Is it possible that the laity will consent to be beguiled of their reward in possessing the pure and undefiled religion of the true Word of God, by receiving instead a religion of priests and human mediators who will *make merchandise of them with feigned words*,[1] and draw their souls away from the knowledge and practice of the truth ? Is it possible that the bulk of the people of this land and Church can be so blind as

[1] 2 Pet. ii. 3.

not to see the magnitude of the dangers which threaten them; so indifferent or so infatuated as to refuse to take warning against them?

There is something apparently so reverent and so laudable in doing honour to an ordinance of Christ's own appointment, that it is oftentimes difficult to persuade men that any danger can lurk beneath it. But the ordinances of Christ are not more sacred to the Christian than the Divine ordinance of the Sabbath was to the Jew, and yet we know, on the authority of Christ Himself, that a superstitious reverence for the Sabbath had destroyed all its meaning to the Jew. The Sabbath was a sign between him and God, but he had put the sign in the place of God, and so had both shut out God and had also forgotten the message of the sign. Is it impossible that Christians should do the same? When we see the Eucharist exalted to the position it is, or may we not rather say *degraded*?—and societies like the Confraternity of the Blessed Sacrament making it a kind of masonic badge, it is surely time to remind our brethren that it is possible to be very devoted to the blessed Sacrament, and yet wholly ignorant of the benefits which flow from the death of Christ, and of the redemption through His blood. It is quite possible to believe in the Real Presence and yet not believe in *Christ*: yea, even to be prevented from believing in Christ by allowing the ordinances of Christ to come between ourselves and *Him*.

Let it not be thought, however, that what has now been said has been said with any view to depreciate the ordinance of Christ or to discourage the practice of more frequent communions, the restoration of which we undoubtedly owe to the great mercy of God towards our revived Church,—but much rather to utter a seasonable warning against a misapprehension and misapplication of Christ's ordinance, and to suggest to the most ardent votaries of it that belief in Christ is after all something more than belief in the Sacrament; that there is a danger of supposing the two to be the same; that the one is the seal and confirmation of the other; that the Sacrament follows after faith, and is valid only upon faith, while faith is to be sought, not from the Sacrament, but from Him alone of whom the Sacrament speaks. *Lord, increase our faith.*[1] *Lord, I believe, help thou mine unbelief.*[2]

The greatest danger of the Church of the present day is not improbably to be found in the vast amount of machinery by which it is sought to supplement

[1] Luke xvii. 5.   [2] Mark ix. 24.

and prepare the way for faith, whereas faith is rather stifled and overlaid thereby, and the wound of the Lord's people has been healed slightly,[1] because the Great Physician in Gilead has not been sought, and has not effectually applied His balm.[2] A variety of indications show but too plainly that in many quarters the most elaborate development of the Sacramental system has been adopted without suspicion or alarm, while a less pronounced modification of it is now the most fashionable and popular form of religion. The one, however, is nothing more nor less than the preparation for the other, and will inevitably grow into it; and both are alike fatal to the simple enunciation in all its depth and breadth and power of the vital maxim, *Believe and live.*[3]

The danger of the Church, however, arising from the prevalence of Romanising theology and the fascination of Roman practices, great as it is, is not the only one in the present day. Wherever there is superstition there is also unbelief. And side by side with doctrines and customs, which belie the whole character of the Church as a reformed body, there is a spirit of doubt and denial abroad, which tends to sap the very foundation of the Church's existence,

---

[1] Jer. vi. 14.   [2] Jer. viii. 22.   [3] Hab. ii. 4; Rom. i. 17, etc.

and to rob her of her supernatural life and her share in the Divine nature.[1] The authority of Scripture is impugned or rejected as a Divine and supernatural guide. The function of science as a natural revelation of God is exaggerated at the cost of the supernatural revelation in Scripture, and in forgetfulness of the supremacy and permanence of the moral revelation in the conscience. While some are shutting their eyes to the true *light which lighteth every man*[2] in the personal revelation of the living Lord, and are seeking it unadvisedly in outward, albeit Divinely ordained symbols, others are turning away from it altogether for the fatuous light which shines from nature or the scintillations which glimmer from time to time in the merely natural heart. They prefer to walk in the light of their own fire, and in the sparks which they have kindled, rather than in the light of the Sun of Righteousness.

It is certain, however, that superstition affords no protection against unbelief, but is itself unbelief in another form. The Church of Christ at the present day is brought face to face with questions affecting her very life; and to flee from the struggle with these questions, and to take refuge in superstition or in superstitious practices is to surrender the ground to

[1] 2 Pet. i. 4.   [2] John i. 9.

unbelief. The only engine which is capable of fairly dealing with these questions is the Divine revelation of the Gospel. That contains in itself the highest philosophy, because it is based upon an absolute knowledge of human nature. It is the sure word of One *who knew what was in man*.[1] But the Gospel itself is powerless unless it is implicitly believed, and has produced the moral and spiritual regeneration consequent upon belief. It then becomes *invincible*, because, being the very truth itself, it is the touchstone of falsehood; and though falsehood may again and again raise its head in one of its myriad forms, and for a time lead captive many, yet truth will ever ultimately detect, expose, and overthrow it.

An immense amount of harm is done when the revelation of the Gospel is represented, as it too often is, as being so vague and uncertain as to give scope for every variety of opinion. Those who are interested in thus representing, or rather misrepresenting it, certainly do little honour to the human understanding. If the Bible is regarded as a Divine book we can conceive no object in its being given in language unintellible to the human mind, or so expressed as that its broad message should be un-

[1] John ii. 25.

discoverable; and one of the most obscure of the prophets was bidden to write his vision so plain that he who ran might read it running.[1] If the Bible is regarded as a human book then it is still more unwarrantable to assume that its general meaning or message is impossible to be ascertained. Is the general message of " Hamlet," of " Paradise Lost," or of Homer's " Iliad " such that the ordinary mind cannot grasp it ? And can we honestly say that any of these as a *human* production, is more easy of comprehension than St. Mark or St. John ? Can the ordinary mind take in the broad message of Bacon or Hooker, and yet fail to perceive the general drift of one of St. Paul's epistles. Then if so, verily St. Paul cannot have been the great writer we supposed him. But, as a matter of fact, the general impression left by the study of the Gospel is indubitable and unvarying. It only becomes a subject of obscurity or uncertainty when other considerations enter in and confuse our mental vision, or cloud the 'dry light' in which we should regard it if our minds were free from bias and prejudice.

" Knowledge is easy," we are told, " to him that hath understanding," and assuredly it would be doing wrong to the Divine knowledge of salvation

[1] Hab. ii. 2.

imparted by the Gospel to assume the contrary of *that*. But, in point of fact, we may safely affirm that the vast majority of Christians, of whatever denomination—Greek, Roman, Anglican, Protestant, Evangelical—are all agreed on the central elements of their faith. It is not too much to say that the entire body of Christians throughout the world nominally accept the Apostles' Creed as the symbol of their common belief; the exceptions are so inconsiderable that practically they may be disregarded. Christianity is eminently a religion of Divine facts. It is impossible that these Divine facts can be held in their integrity and their simplicity without producing in the mind certain results. It is the philosophy of these results that generates Christian doctrine, at least in certain branches. And then, as a further consequence, doctrine becomes substituted for fact. But fact being the central germ of doctrine has the tendency to unite and combine, whereas the tendency of doctrine is to divide and subdivide. The only way, therefore, in which Christians who have received facts through doctrines, and have become separated in doing so, can be reunited, is by gathering round the central common facts, and learning to view them in the 'dry light' of reality, and yielding themselves to the natural influence of their Divine power.

For example, it must be vastly more essential to believe that Jesus Christ *died*, and that He died *for our sins*,[1] than to believe any one particular theory about the cause, nature, or consequences of His death. Now all Christians are agreed upon the Scripture statement of these facts. It is about the theories invented for them and the doctrines deduced from them that they begin to differ. But surely it is in the simple facts that the Gospel message lies, and in the facts that its vitality is enshrined. If, therefore, we would receive the vital message of the Gospel, it must be by clinging to the reality of the facts rather than by stopping short in the doctrines which are based upon or deduced from them.

It is, therefore, no slight indication of the Divine forethought which kept watch over the Church that in its early manhood, and while it was yet one, the Apostolic Creed of Christendom was framed, we know not how, which yet survives as the recognised symbol of our faith. In that we breathe the atmosphere of fact rather than of doctrine, and assuredly if its witness is accepted in all its length, and breadth, and depth, and height, its fulness, meaning, and vitality, it will be found to be not only a rallying-point for all who *love the Lord Jesus Christ in sincerity*,[2] but also will supply the truest and most

[1] 1 Cor. xv. 3.   [2] Eph. vi. 24.

powerful corrective for the errors and follies of our time, whether they consist in a tendency to reject the Divine and supernatural elements of the faith, or in a desire to supplement and to overlay it by the pernicious machinery of unscriptural and unauthorised human additions.

STANLEY LEATHES.

89, ST. GEORGE'S SQUARE, S.W.
Sept. 24*th*, 1877.

CONTENTS.

	PAGE
I. I BELIEVE	1
II. IN GOD	13
III. THE FATHER	23
IV. ALMIGHTY	35
V. MAKER OF HEAVEN AND EARTH	47
VI. AND IN JESUS	59
VII. CHRIST	71
VIII. HIS ONLY SON	83
IX. OUR LORD	95
X. WHO WAS CONCEIVED BY THE HOLY GHOST, BORN OF THE VIRGIN MARY	107
XI. SUFFERED UNDER PONTIUS PILATE	119
XII. WAS CRUCIFIED	131
XIII. DEAD	143
XIV. AND BURIED	155
XV. HE DESCENDED INTO HELL	167
XVI. THE THIRD DAY HE ROSE AGAIN FROM THE DEAD	179

	PAGE
XVII. THE THIRD DAY HE ROSE AGAIN FROM THE DEAD (*Continued*)	191
XVIII. THE THIRD DAY HE ROSE AGAIN FROM THE DEAD (*Continued*)	205
XIX. HE ASCENDED INTO HEAVEN	217
XX. AND SITTETH ON THE RIGHT HAND OF GOD THE FATHER ALMIGHTY	229
XXI. FROM THENCE HE SHALL COME TO JUDGE THE QUICK AND THE DEAD	243
XXII. FROM THENCE HE SHALL COME TO JUDGE THE QUICK AND THE DEAD (*Continued*)	255
XXIII. FROM THENCE HE SHALL COME TO JUDGE THE QUICK AND THE DEAD (*Continued*)	267
XXIV. I BELIEVE IN THE HOLY GHOST	279
XXV. I BELIEVE IN THE HOLY GHOST (*Continued*)	293
XXVI. I BELIEVE IN THE HOLY GHOST (*Continued*)	305
XXVII. THE HOLY CATHOLIC CHURCH	317
XXVIII. THE HOLY CATHOLIC CHURCH (*Continued*)	329
XXIX. THE COMMUNION OF SAINTS	341
XXX. THE FORGIVENESS OF SINS	353
XXXI. THE RESURRECTION OF THE BODY	365
XXXII. AND THE LIFE EVERLASTING	377

I.

I BELIEVE.

Lord, I believe : help Thou mine unbelief.—ST. MARK ix. 24.

THE cry of the distracted father of the demoniac at his child's distressing condition and his own powerlessness to help him doubtless expresses the feelings of many persons in the present day. The complaint is often made, sometimes with sorrow, and not seldom with triumph, that the foundations of faith are being overthrown, and men's hold on Christianity is slackening. There is unquestionably something of truth in this, and something also to regret. But it is not without its better and brighter side also. Nothing can be worse than stagnation of thought. It was an unhealthy condition of things when all was taken for granted, when authority was invoked to stifle enquiry, and those who thought at all thought only as their fathers had thought before them; and when within the limits of the Church, at least, everything was supposed to have been settled once for all at the Reformation, or at the last revision of the Prayer-Book.

Now we are becoming familiar with a state of things totally different. Nothing is supposed to be settled ; authority, of whatever kind, is challenged ; prescription has a bad name ; Christianity itself is on its trial ; and novelty, whether in practice or in thought, is regarded as a recommendation.

There can be no question that to teach a man to think for himself is the ultimate object of education. Unless a man can think for himself his thoughts are not likely to be of much use to any one else. But if a man thinks for himself he is as likely to think wrong as to think right, or at least the privilege of being allowed to think right will not protect him from the liability to think wrong ; and if all men think for themselves it is perfectly certain that they will not all think alike.

Putting aside, however, the abstract merits and demerits of our present position, as not worth debating, it is obvious that our only practical course is to accept it. Alter it we cannot, act in it we must. We have not brought ourselves into this state of trial, but have been placed in it by the force of circumstances over which we had no control. Some would have done what they could to prevent or to retard its advent, but to no purpose, for come it must and would, and our only wisdom now is to adapt ourselves to circumstances, to make the most of our advantages, to be patient and to deal prudently with our drawbacks.

It is one of the features of our position that creeds and formularies are with many the special objects of aversion. The notion of a stereotyped expression of thought is conceived of as absurd on the face of it. Thought must either be fettered or be free: if it is to be expressed in creeds it must be fettered, if it is to be free it must dispense with them.

In the view, therefore, of all these considerations, it would seem that to discourse rationally and frankly on the articles of the Christian faith would not be otherwise than beneficial to many. To take the several topics, for example, which are implied and summarised in the Apostles' Creed, and treat them in a candid, intelligent, and at the same time reverential manner, will assuredly be found, we may trust, useful and likewise interesting to many. It may be presumed that all those at least who are in the habit of attending the public worship of the Church, and repeating on every occasion the significant formula, *I believe*, have as yet not broken with that time-honoured symbol of our faith, which is the cherished memorial of our baptism and of our confirmation, and is probably that profession in which we hope to die. On the other hand, it cannot be doubted that there are many of us who at times are sorely perplexed by various points concerning it; that thought and enquiry, in spite of ourselves, will arise and confront us, and refuse to be put aside, even if it were desirable to do so; and that consequently to have wholesome and substantial food for thought presented to us, would be an advantage not lightly to be esteemed. It is with this hope that we enter on the present course of lectures, trusting that by the Divine blessing they may be found helpful and salutary to many. We have neither the wish nor the intention to disturb the faith of any one. Our purpose is to establish, not to destroy; but since we can hardly imagine the case of a thinking person who is not also at times a perplexed or even a doubting person, we will endeavour to meet such perplexities and doubts, and yet, if it may be, not suggest them. Still, it must be borne in mind that to a certain extent it is impossible not to do this, and it may be questioned whether it is altogether desirable. The objection was brought against Bishop Butler's famous Analogy that it raised more questions than it solved. However this may be, there can be no doubt as to the value of that treatise, or the desirableness of its having been written, being, as it is, perhaps, the most precious heirloom of English theology. We must still believe that to think, and to be able to think, and to be allowed to think, with all its perilous responsibilities, is a greater privilege than to have no thought at all, or only such thought as we are on sufferance allowed to have.

Now it must be borne in mind that there are three periods in the history of human thought and of the human mind. The first is the period of childhood and youth, when every story is believed to be true, when faith is unwavering, when we accept what is told us, when we simply apprehend, or retain, or reflect the sentiments and the beliefs of others. Probably no one would be willing to affirm that this condition of mind is, in the abstract, a really desirable one; pleasing and enjoyable it may perhaps be, but hardly in itself a good, or at least not the greatest good.

But whether it is or not, it is certain that we outgrow it. We pass from it in spite of ourselves into the second stage, which is one of enquiry, discrimination, hesitation, and doubt. Whereas before we were happy in believing everything, now we scarcely think ourselves wise if we do not doubt everything. It is the result of a worldly-wise experience,—the maxim that the man is a fool who believes all he hears.

Now these two stages or conditions of thought which formerly applied for the most part to all subjects except the Christian faith, have been found in our own time to exempt not even that. It is this inherited possession of the Christian Creed which has now in its turn been dealt with as any other possession. Men treat it with no more deference than anything else which they have accepted on authority and believed traditionally. It is questioned, attacked, rejected.

This is true of our age. But it is true also of the individual. First there comes the period of implicit belief, secondly there comes the period of incipient doubt or explicit denial. But there is yet a third stage, which, though indeed it is not reached by all, is, at any rate, reserved for some. And this is the stage when, after having faith shaken to the very centre, or having actually surrendered it, we are enabled to emerge from a stage of perplexity, difficulty, doubt, or restlessness, to one of repose and assured belief. We are wiser for the experience we have undergone. Our views of truth are wider, our grasp firmer, our position is very different from what it was at first. We see things with other eyes; but the things we see are the same, though it may be we see more. Now there can be no doubt which, in the abstract, is the highest and most desirable of these three conditions, that of the unquestioning child, or that of the thoughtful and mature man. Neither can there be any doubt that the three stages represent a natural and consistently progressive series, in which as the third is higher than the second so also the second is higher than the first. It is indeed most undesirable to stop at the second, but so also is it to stop at the first. To carry into mature manhood the intellectual development of a child is not only undesirable but unnatural.

But may we not say that to find ourselves in declining years with nothing but the restlessness of youth or manhood for our portion is equally undesirable, if not unnatural? The spectacle of an old man who is still hampered and oppressed with the labour and anxiety of sturdier age is certainly painful. If rest and repose are to be obtained they must in themselves be good. Now it is precisely this second stage of thought which is characteristic of our own day. Everything is unstable, unsettled, anxious, restless. But the misapprehension which is only too common, is that this condition is other than transitional. That it is necessary, inevitable, and a symptom of progress, we do not deny; but it is a great mistake to suppose that it is in itself a final state, or that the very law of progress does not require it to be succeeded by another. Let us by all means avail ourselves to the very utmost of the experience we have gained; let us not reject any wider views that a longer toil, if it be circuitous, up the mountain of life, has perchance given us; by all means let us profit by the past and improve the present; but let us at least not stay where we are. The human soul cannot be sustained on doubt any more than the body can live on air; the mountain breezes may be very salutary, but they are not sufficing. To give up everything and arrive at nothing is indeed to pass from the first stage of thought to the second, but not to pass from the second to the third; and this we must do if we would be saved, for there is no salvation in resting where we are.

And our own age is not the only one which has illustrated the same truth. In the infancy of the world —that is to say, before Christ came—mankind were in the first stage of thought,—they rested contentedly in various absurd beliefs. When Jesus stood before Pilate, and Pilate asked Him, What is truth? then the second stage had been reached. Scepticism had eaten into the received religion. Men were growing weary of it. In many cases they had rejected it. Pilate's case was one. But there came a third stage. He before whom Pilate stood, by the silent but irresistible verdict of history, asserted Himself as the Truth of which Pilate despaired; and the throne of the Cæsars became, as a matter of fact, the possession of the Christ.

The third stage for a time was reached. But it was only for a time. The third stage again became the first,—the mature age of the Church relapsed into dotage. Everything was accepted with implicit credulity, till credulity gave place to scepticism; and when Innocent III. and Leo X. sat in the so-called chair of Peter, the second stage had been reached once more. Then came the glorious career of the noble and heroic Luther, whose preaching made the scepticism deeper than ever, and at the same time created earnest faith; and once more the second stage was succeeded by the third. How is it now? Judge for yourselves, my friends. We—that is, the majority of mankind (for some have not)—have passed out of the first stage into the second; but it is impossible that we can stop there, let the popular voice of admiration for the prevailing thought of the age be never so loud. The lessons of history cannot be lost, her teaching cannot be wrong. The destructive tendency must give place to one constructive, and the mind or the minds must arise that shall have the wisdom to erect out of the ruins of unbelief a solid and substantial edifice of faith.

It must be so, let physical and metaphysical science vaunt themselves as they please. We cannot rest in negatives, and any teaching of which the result is negative must give place to one whose results are positive and substantial.

Now the cry of those who feel the pain of this transition state, who feel that little by little everything is being taken from them, and nothing given in its place, is, or at least may be, this: *Lord, I believe: help Thou mine unbelief.* It is, at any rate, those, and only those, to whom I address myself,—those who believe that the Lord of the human spirit will hearken to the agonising cry of His perplexed and blindfold children,—those who believe that a prayer such as that of the distracted father of the demoniac cannot be proffered in vain, that there is One who can hear, and that He will hear. There may be those, who are strangers to such agony, who would call it infatuation or fanaticism; to such I do not speak, or at least, not now. Their condition of thought may be that of the first stage or of the third; if of the latter, they also will appreciate my words, for the effect of them will be to make their hold of truth more firm, their standing-ground more stable and secure; but even the others I would hope will be able to listen also, not without a certain degree of profit. It is one class only to whom the words spoken will be vain as wind,—those, namely, who are so well satisfied with their position of doubt and denial as not to desire to change it for any other; who are willing to ask with Pilate, What is truth? but are unwilling also like Pilate to wait for the answer, because they would rather believe there is none. There is only one way in which we can characterise such persons : they are not in earnest. The gospel which presents a secure resting-place for faith is not for them ; they prefer the so-called freedom of being tossed about on the billows of speculation, without a rudder or a compass, and with no prospect of a haven, to being steered across the ocean to the appointed shore of hope.

But if you ask me whether it is requisite that in every case the condition of childish belief should give place to one of doubt in order that it may be succeeded again by one of firmer faith, I should answer, I cannot tell. The Lord does not lead us all by the same road. I speak to those whom He is leading by this road, and who feel that they want a guide, or want to find in Him their guide. But I may say that the condition I describe is one of growth. It seems to me that no one can pass from childhood into youth, and from youth to manhood, and not have his thoughts strangely modified on many, and especially the most important, subjects. Such thoughts as God and Christ and heaven must surely have a vastly different meaning to the same person in childhood and in mature age, and if so there must be transition, and transition probably accompanied with very violent shocks,—a giving up of the old and a grasping of the new. We were all told something about God when we were children. That may have been true as it was told us then, but if we believe it now as we believed it then, it will not be true ; for if our minds grow, while the faith with which we supply them grows not, the result cannot be other than incongruous. Who, as a man, would wear swaddling clothes, or even be content to array himself in the garments of his childhood or his youth ? *When I was a child I thought as a child, I understood as a child; but when I became a man, I put away childish things,*[1] is true of belief as it is of other matters, and pre-eminently true of belief. And even St. Paul himself had of all men found it most true, for he had passed through the greatest possible transition when, having been exceedingly zealous of the traditions of his fathers, he found that Christ was the end of the law for righteousness to every one that believeth.

[1] 1 Cor. xiii. 11.

II.

IN GOD.

Without faith it is impossible to please Him, for he that cometh to God must believe that He is, and that He is a rewarder of them that diligently seek Him.—HEB. xi. 6.

IN speaking in the last lecture of the three progressive stages of thought which were evidenced in the history of the world, and sometimes of individuals, namely, the stages of belief, doubt, and faith, it must be borne in mind that this is specially true of the cycles of thought that may be observed in successive periods of long duration. It were absurd to suppose that every individual man or woman is to illustrate in personal history the vacillations of the centuries. Neither is doubt the indispensable prelude to belief, any more than it is invariably succeeded by belief. There are minds naturally constituted to believe, as there are minds naturally constituted to doubt. I question, however, whether any safe position of assured faith is attained without renouncing something we have already held. As Bishop Hall says, he that never changed any of his opinions never corrected any of his mistakes. The mature conviction of the whole man, which is what Christianity contemplates and demands, and with nothing short of which it can be satisfied, must differ materially and intrinsically from the unquestioning, unthinking, and unconscious faith of childhood. If the subject-matter of belief does not change, there must at any rate be a change in the manner of believing it. There must, therefore, be transition of some kind, showing itself in some way. This transition may or may not assume the form of doubt. In the present day it unquestionably often assumes this form; and I believe that a state of doubt is always a transition state, and that it will be seen to be so as the history of our time develops itself. And it is a transition state of this or a similar kind that is implied in the gospel idea of conversion. Our Lord told His own immediate followers that they must be converted. If in their case such conversion was needful, it is impossible to conceive of the case in which it would not be needful; and as a matter of fact we say that the heathen world in becoming Christian was converted to Christianity. Can we, however, say with equal truth that those brought up and instructed in the Christian faith, require to be converted to Christianity? I think we may, and I think it is this truth which it is needful to bring before men's minds in the present day. The relation of the Christian faith to the human soul is in no way altered because the world has nominally become Christian. That faith must still convert men to itself, or rather must convert them to Christ.

I believe it is impossible to make men Christians by simply instructing them in the facts and truths of Christianity. Such a course will not communicate to them the spiritual quickening without which they cannot become Christians. And this spiritual quickening alone, and by itself, will suffice to change all their previous conceptions concerning Christ, and will show them that whether they believed or whether they doubted, they had not attained to what the Scripture calls *faith*.

But *without faith it is impossible to please God.* Ponder these words, and then ask yourselves whether the mere childish assent to the articles of the Apostles' Creed makes it more possible for you, or can make it more possible for you, to please God; and I think the answer must be, No. If, then, we are to consider our relation to the articles of the Apostles' Creed, or their relation to us, we must first endeavour to understand what we mean by faith. " I believe in God the Father Almighty," if it means anything, certainly if it means what the text seems to say it ought to mean, must mean more than, " I have certain notions about God, more or less indefinite; certain opinions about Him, which I am able to express more or less philosophically and logically." God cannot concern Himself with what such poor creatures as we are think about Him, or are able to syllogise about Him. This is not to have faith in God. And strange to say, from first to last the Bible gives us little or no material for such exercise. It gives us no philosophical definition of God. It tells us, indeed, that God is a spirit, and that God is love, if you choose to regard these as definitions ; but these, I fancy, do not help us much, and these even are among the very latest declarations that are recorded. But the Bible assumes everywhere that we know and understand who and what God is, and yet it nowhere endorses any one's thoughts about Him, knowing that everyone's must be inadequate and vain. Thus we all probably have a different idea of God,—certainly should express it differently, and yet it speaks as though we all had the same idea, or at least had a common idea ; and so no doubt we have. If it were not so we should not have the witness that there is in human language; but the very fact that God is an idea which finds an equivalent expression in every human tongue, is a conclusive proof that the idea, whatever it is, is a primary idea, common to the human race, inherent in and indigenous to the human mind. When, therefore, the Bible speaks of God it speaks of that to which there is a witness in your heart and conscience that you cannot deny ; you may strive to analyse it and debate it with yourself, but you can do little or nothing with it. You can get no further, and you cannot get rid of it. And yet the Apostle says, *without faith it is impossible to please God,*— without telling us who or what this God is whom without faith it is impossible to please, or what this faith is without which it is impossible to please Him ;

for I apprehend that the definition in the first verse, that *faith is the substance of things hoped for, the evidence of things not seen*, does not help us much.

But in making this appeal to faith the Gospel shows its wonderful adaptation not only to the wants but to the character and constitution of man. It is faith upon which the whole intercourse of human life and human society is built. We cannot live for a single day, nor act for a single hour, without exercising that faculty to which the Gospel appeals when it appeals to faith. Where would commerce be without credit? Where would family affection be without confidence? Where would love be without trust? Where would our dealings one with another be without reliance on one another, and reliance on the unrealised? And, further, what is it that occasions so much disorder in human affairs, throwing out all our calculations, marring all our schemes, destroying our happiness, and bringing us to a standstill, but the want of faith, the abuse of trust, the failure of credit, the breach of confidence and the like—the absence, namely, of that very faculty 'or quality the necessity of which the actual constitution of our nature shows?

And here it is that light breaks in. Unless we feel and act towards God, whom we can never fully know, but whom we cannot help knowing of, with the same trust, confidence, faith, reliance that are so essential in our dealings with our fellow-creatures, we cannot please Him. Why, a moment's consideration will show us plainly that we cannot. How is it possible that we should please Him if we come to Him without that which we should require of any one who came to us, and the absence of which would be fatal to any intercourse between us? And if any one replies, Oh yes, but it is a great mistake to suppose that God is like ourselves, I answer, That may or may not be so, but the Bible proceeds on the assumption that there is sufficient analogy between our relation to one another and our relation to God, for the experience of the one to be a safe guide in our conduct of the other; and we cannot but see the reasonableness of this, and the absolute ignorance in which we are left if we reject such an analogy. For if it is not faith which is requisite for pleasing God, is it unbelief which is requisite for pleasing Him, or what is it which is requisite? We cannot tell. We can merely see, then, that without faith it must be impossible to please God.

Now the Apostle gives us two reasons which will serve to show yet further the nature of the faith which he declares to be so essential. *He that cometh to God must believe that He is, and that He is a rewarder of them that diligently seek Him.* The accurate language in which he spoke made this even more precise, for there is a difference between the *He is* and the *He is a rewarder.* It is this: He that cometh to God must believe that He is; that is to say, that He exists,—must believe in His existence;

which I should imagine is self-evident. How can a man come to God if he does not believe in His existence, or if he doubts or is not sure of His existence? The revelation of the Word enters at a point further advanced than that at which the preliminary question of God's existence is even possible; it accepts and assumes it. How can we predicate anything about God if He is non-existent?

But, further, the faith of which the writer speaks requires a man to believe that to those coming to Him by faith He becomes a rewarder if they seek Him such a way as to seek Him *out*, and so to find Him. And here is where the Gospel comes into collision with our modern philosophy. This latter will leave us our God as a bare existence, because there is considerable difficulty, philosophical and otherwise, in denying that; but it takes from us the *conditional* character of God, in which He *becomes* something to those with faith which without faith He is not. And here is the first point at which the Christian faith conflicts with reason, and is assailed by reason. We may as well confess it at once, and decide what we will do, for if we are staggered here at the very outset I do not see how we are to become Christians. Philosophy has sundry theories about nature being *God* —*becoming*, that is, God—in transition, and the like. If, therefore, philosophy can adopt such language for her own purposes, I do not see why philosophy should in the abstract object to the Apostle using such a phrase. At any rate, this is what he says, and in saying it he gives a definite truth for faith to believe. I come to God believing that He is. Do I come to Him believing any more than this, believing that if I seek Him out—that is, so as to find Him—He will become to me a rewarder; that He will stand to me in a different relation from that in which He would stand to me if I did *not* come to Him, or did not seek Him out so as to find Him; that He will become, and therefore be to me, what He does not become, and therefore is not, to others who do not seek Him? That is the question. Holding this faith, I can please Him. Holding it not, I cannot please Him. If I intend my profession *I believe* to be of any value, I must believe this. I must believe that upon faith, upon trust in God, I enter into a new world: I set my foot upon another sphere: I look up to another sky: I behold another landscape. That is the very reward. If God is not a rewarder, then He is to me nothing. My position is unaltered. Faith does nothing for me; it leaves me as it finds me. God is an abstraction, the contemplation of which can do neither good nor harm; certainly not good.

Now this is the kind of faith with which the world is very well satisfied; with which it is perfectly willing to make a compromise, whether in the way of ritual, or external acts of devotion, or sacrifice of substance, or anything else, because it is a faith which leaves us as it finds us, essentially unchanged, unrestored, secretly uninfluenced and unconverted. The shell of childish indifferent, unconscious faith has not been penetrated and broken by the germinant and vivifying seed within; whereas, on the other hand, it is impossible to believe that God becomes to us who seek Him out a rewarder, that is, one who modifies His conduct towards us, and acts towards us in a special manner, as a living and acting God, as a person dealing with us, controlling, guiding, moulding, influencing and blessing us, without being ourselves changed and influenced thereby. Such being the revealed character of God, we surrender and submit ourselves to Him by going to Him with that belief. We put ourselves in a position to receive of His influence, to be moulded by His spirit, and are moulded and influenced accordingly. For this is what is implied by God's being a rewarder; it matters not what the reward is,—in Abraham's case it was sheep and oxen, in David's it was victory in battle, in Elijah's it was national reform, in Paul's it was the conversion of many lands to the name of Christ. The reward is varied and various; the principle of the reward is one, and the principle involved in the reward is one; it is that of God acting in a special way, in which He would not otherwise act, in consequence of or on condition of a special character in those who come to Him. There is no thought that men repudiate more readily than that of God's action being conditional on man's belief or on man's action, and yet what else do the words imply, *He that cometh to God must believe that He is, and that He is a rewarder of them that diligently seek Him?*

It is possible, then, to believe this in a childish way, and yet, when we have learnt by experience its full meaning, to believe it very differently, and yet like a child. There must be a transition between the two conditions. It may or may not be one of doubt, but the sequel of the transition is none other than conversion. We are taught to believe in a living God who has affixed a special reward to special faith, which, in fact, is life. And without such a faith as this it is impossible to please God, because God can only take pleasure in what partakes of His own life and reflects His own work. He has no pleasure in anything short of this. He has no pleasure in the legs of a man, in his physical powers, or acquired skill, or mental endowments, or in the results of all combined, but in his faith, in the way in which he comes to Him, in the fulness with which he trusts Him, the readiness with which he serves Him, the willingness with which he accepts the dispositions and decrees of His providence and grace. Thus coming unto Him we shall have, as Enoch had, *this testimony, that we please God.*

III.

THE FATHER.

To us there is but one God, the Father, of whom are all things, and we in Him.—1 COR. viii. 6.

CHRISTIANITY, when it came upon earth, came not only as a positive but as a protestant religion. It was not only to an eminent degree constructive in its form, but also terribly destructive in its operation. It presented certain facts for man's acceptance, but waged likewise fatal war with the Pantheon of heathenism. Here we have an instance of this. *For though there be that are called gods, whether in heaven or in earth,* (*as there be gods many, and lords many,*) *yet to us,* says the writer, *there is but one God, the Father, of whom are all things, and we in Him.* The Gospel had come with destructive power against these gods many, and lords many, in heaven and in earth. If there was one only, there could not be many; the many must give place to the one.

It is to be observed also that the gods and the lords appear to be the same. Those who were gods were also lords, and those who were lords were also gods. This is important when we come to the one

God and the one Lord who are immediately afterwards proclaimed.

The Christian faith, therefore, believes in and declares one only God. "I believe in God the Father Almighty;" or, as the Nicene confession has it, "I believe in *one* God, the Father Almighty." This is the corner-stone of revelation as to the being of God. We must hold fast by the unity of God, or else we relapse again into the exploded errors of polytheism which Christianity denounced and did away with. Thus there is but one God. The Christian creed acknowledges one supreme object of worship, and only one. In this, indeed, it is not singular, for even polytheistic religions held that there was one god supreme over all the others; but the inferior powers and essences were exalted into gods. Now that we have learnt to study God through His revelation of nature, we find that all things point conclusively to the unity of God. There is but one will expressed and executed, from one end of the universe to the other. There is no trace of any opposite or conflicting power to divide with the one God the dominion of the universe. The Christian belief, therefore, so far, is in harmony with, and is confirmed by, the teachings of nature and the conclusions of reason.

And there is ground for much joy and comfort and consolation in this thought of the absolute unity of God. For if we have found out God, then have we reached the goal of all thought, and of all worship, and of all existence. We can get no further. The object that we have apprehended is indeed in itself infinite, but it is also one. There is none higher, none holier, none mightier. It is one and it is all. And thus being one, and being all, in relation to God time and space are altogether eliminated and taken out of the way. Thus the God who is near us in London is near us also in China, and in the uttermost parts of the earth, and is near our friends,· if we have them, there ; and thus God is a meeting-point between us and our friends who may be separated by vast tracts of space or by long distance of time. There is but One between us and them, and He is the same to us as He is to them, and the same to them as He is to us.

If the doctrine, therefore, of one God were a theory and nothing more, it would not be without a certain amount of attractiveness and moral influence, such as many opinions, which are opinions only, oftentimes possess ; but knowing, as we do, that it is a fact, and a fact of which we are assured by revelation, and which is confirmed to us by science and by reason, it cannot fail to be to us a source of strength. It is the ONE before whom we now stand who deals with us, and with whom we now deal; before whom the patriarchs, prophets, and apostles stood in the centuries that are past ; with whom Christ our Lord in His manhood had to deal, and Who dealt with Him. No wonder that the unity of God was found, in the seventh century, to be the mighty engine which Mohammedanism proved it, at a time when idolatry gross and multiform had usurped upon the life of the Christian Church, because it is a living truth, instinct with the life of Him whose truth it is, and whose nature it proclaims; and whenever it is apprehended in its truth it will come with power to the soul that grasps it. *To us there is but one God.*

But if this truth is mighty, how much more is the next, which is one of the cardinal truths of the Gospel, and, in some sense, its special and peculiar revelation. The one God is also named the Father. Our modern phraseology is very fond of speaking of God as a Father, and the Fatherhood of God, from the days of Edward Irving downwards, has been a very popular doctrine, and one calculated to awaken a hearty popular response. But I rather think that to speak of God as a Father, in the abstract, is something more, and at the same time something less, than is warranted by the teaching of the Gospel. As was shown in the last lecture, the Gospel reveals God as the conditioned and not as the unconditioned; it reveals God as He becomes to us upon accepting His offer. The Gospel speaks of God as *our* Father, as *your* Father, as *the* Father, but never simply as *a* father. That is to say, it pledges itself to no philosophical or merely abstract affirmation about the Fatherhood of God, or His independent character as a father, but simply assumes the relation in which He is willing to stand to us upon our coming to Him as He invites us. The language of the

Gospel is not, "I am a father, have a father's heart," and the like, however true in themselves these statements may be, but, *I will be a Father unto you;* which necessarily implies a condition to be fulfilled. And thus God is to us the Father whom He has proclaimed Himself.

But when we come to enquire how this is, we find that the earliest historical announcement of this truth was always, as a matter of fact, connected with the preaching of the Lord Jesus Christ. The original Gospel was not the Gospel of the Fatherhood of God, but the Gospel of Jesus Christ the Son of God, the Gospel of our Lord Jesus Christ. In treating, therefore, of this subject, it is difficult not to anticipate what must naturally, in the order of things, come later. God is *the* Father, because He is the Father of our Lord Jesus Christ, and because in Him, but only in Him, He is our Father. It may seem hard even to attempt to assign any limitation, or to appear to do so, to a truth so popular and so grateful as the Fatherhood of God; but I conceive by the whole tenor of the Gospel (which, pray remember, you can examine for yourselves, and so determine whether I am right or wrong) we are bound to do. Human language is inevitably deceptive and necessarily ambiguous. When men speak in a popular way of the Fatherhood of God, they not only state more, but they mean less, than the Gospel states or means. That God is a Father is a primary truth, not of revelation, but of instinct or of reason, however little reason or instinct may have been able unaided to discover it. In this sense, not only Christianity but also Judaism, not only Judaism but also heathenism, has conceived of God; and Father Zeus and Father Jove are terms familiar to us even in the heathen classics, as are likewise their equivalents in the Indian epic and dramatic poetry. And certainly the great Creator who has called into existence millions of immortal beings who hold an exalted and a supreme position in the scale of His creation, cannot be regarded otherwise than as their Father. His very creation has confirmed to Him that right, and established to them their claim to regard themselves as His children; but if the Gospel appellation " Father " has no deeper or further significance than this, then verily that Gospel cannot be a revelation. We are no further than we were, after the life and labours, the death and resurrection of the Lord Jesus, and the preaching and martyrdom of apostles and evangelists. But the Gospel teaches us plainly that to call God " Father " with the full depth and sweetness of the name is the result of the Holy Spirit's teaching, and consequently is neither ordinary nor natural, is something more than instinct, and higher than reason can pretend to be.

In fact, Scripture has itself furnished us with a standard whereby we may gauge the meaning and reality of this term " Father," as it is applied to God. In one of our Lord's conversations with the Jews, we find them asserting emphatically, *We have one Father, even God.* Whereupon our Lord rejoins, *If God were your Father, ye would love me, for I proceeded forth and came from God; neither came I of myself, but He sent me.* Now it cannot be doubted that the Jews, on this occasion, appealed to the Fatherhood of God very much in the popular sense, and something more, for their appeal was special and not merely general; but He disallowed it because they lacked the sure and infallible test of loving the Christ whom the Father had sent; so that there can be no true sense of the Fatherhood of God unless it is coupled with a personal love for Jesus Christ. Thus we are brought back by a different path to identically the same point as before—that God is only in the higher and the only worthy sense *a* Father according as He is acknowledged as *the* Father; if He is the Father of our Lord Jesus Christ, then is He indeed a Father to us; if He is acknowledged as the Father, then He becomes to us, in deed and in truth, a Father, and that is our reward.

And how shall we attempt to express, far less exhaust, the meaning of that word "Father"? I question if any one who is not himself a father can understand the fulness of its meaning. Who has not felt that when his own child has first called him father he has had opened out to him an avenue to the hallowed significance of that name which imagination was unable to depict before? There is always something about those consecrated relationships of life which experience alone can give us. There is no one who is ignorant of what fatherhood implies. We all know what it is to have had or to have lost a father; but those only who have children can know the additional elements of sacred love which are associated with the actual experience of fatherhood. There is a special fatherly joy which the father alone, and not the son, can know, and which is taught, not in idea, but by experience.

But with reference to God it is not only idea but experience also that fails to apprehend the full significance of the name. For what is the earthly relationship of father? Is it anything more than the reflex of the heavenly? God has stamped a relationship which is peculiarly His own, inasmuch as it is that in which He stands to His eternal Son, upon the very constitution of human society; but in so doing He has bestowed a copy and not the original, He has multiplied the stamp and not the die. He still remains, and must to all eternity remain, *the* Father, while each of us is nothing more according to the disposition of His providence than *a* father. We borrow our fatherhood from Him, as it is He alone who has lent us the application of the title " Father."

And what, then, is the upshot of all this? Why, brethren, that the Fatherhood of God, and that which is implied thereby, is something vastly more than even the most blessed experience of earthly fatherhood can enable us to apprehend. If we who are fathers know more of earthly fatherhood than those who are not, yet even we, the fondest and the tenderest of us, cannot rise to the full appreciation of that which His fatherhood involves. He loves us, if we belong to Him, as we who are fathers love our children, only with a love of which that is the shadow and not the substance, the reflection and not the image reflected. And when we say, as we often do, so thoughtlessly, "I believe in God the Father," this is what we ought to mean, if indeed we do believe in Him.

But this very fatherhood is itself a subject of belief. We cannot prove it. We can only believe it, and we can only experience it by believing it. Observe the difference. We do not create it by believing it, for then we should be the victims merely of delusion; it reveals itself to us, it has been revealed to us by Christ, it is revealed to us by the Spirit, and we apprehend it by believing it. But just as no exhibition of human love can produce the experience of that love if it is met with coldness or lukewarmness, or suspicion and distrust, so is it also with the Divine love,—the full experience of it is obviously and of necessity dependent upon faith; it cannot be otherwise, as faith worketh by love, and love is apprehended by faith, and cannot be apprehended without faith. If we do not believe that God loves us as a father, it is impossible that we can feel towards Him and love Him as children, and it is equally manifest that if He really does love us as a father, the practical evidence of that love us as a father, the practical evidence of that love must be sought in the reality of the love with which we requite it. *To us there is but one God the Father;* therefore, must we express, not the bare confession of an intellectual creed, but the heartfelt acknowledgment of a spiritual fact of which we have become experimentally conscious. This is further implied by the peculiar idiom which is commonly used in the New Testament, and is adopted by the language of the Creeds,—"I believe *into* God the Father Almighty." The faith is not something which we can regard as apart from ourselves, in which we have no vivid or vital interest; not something which we can talk about with indifference, as though it did not concern us; it is a belief by which we so to say project and cast ourselves on and lose ourselves in God. We find that the one God is He in whom we are, in whom we live and move and have our being; that, in the language of St. Paul, it is not only He, their Creator, from whom are all things as their origin and source, but also that we are not *in* but *into* Him. It may be fanciful, but it seems to me that there is something more implied here than that we are, as Alford has it, for him,— that is, His purposes, to serve His will; which is an obvious truth, if not a truism; as though the writer meant that the Father was indeed the source of all things, ourselves among them, but that we, moreover, in virtue of His paternal revelation and His fatherly love had been brought back again to Him, that we had returned like the rivers to the ocean from which they had been drawn by exhalation, that the very object of all God's dealing with us, whether in providence or in grace, was that we might return to and be lost in Him. This, at least, is the full force of the Apostle's language, whether or not we have expressed his thought.

What, then, is the conclusion of the whole matter? That there is one God and Father of all, who is above all and through all and in us all; that our relation to Him is not affected by time or space,— He is ever near to us and always with us,—but by the moral condition of the inner man. What is the index of the relation of the human parent to the child? is it not, in one word, the affections? When they are unmoved, or cold and torpid, is not the first principle of nature violated, her holiest law broken? It is so likewise with our relation to our Heavenly Father; there can be, if I may so say, no blood relationship between us, no vital bond of living union, unless our affections are kindled towards Him. We may boast of the Fatherhood of God, of the proclamation of that truth being the glory of our age, and the like, but unless we love Him, and the yearnings of our heart go forth to Him, we know Him not; for *we love Him because He first loved us*,[1] is St. John's assurance, and if we love Him not, we have no witness in ourselves that the love of the Father hath gone forth to us and embraced us as His children.

[1] 1 John iv. 19.

IV.

ALMIGHTY.

And when Abram was ninety years old and nine, the Lord appeared to Abram, and said unto him, I am the Almighty God ; walk before me, and be thou perfect.—GEN. xvii. 1.

THIS is the first time that the epithet *Almighty* appears in Scripture, and you will observe that it appears as a distinct revelation communicated by God Himself. It would be interesting to enquire whether the term was new, were it not clearly impossible to decide the question absolutely. Probably, however, most persons nowadays will be disposed to believe that it was not new ; that it sprang up naturally in the course of linguistic formation, and was adopted by God on this occasion. The passage in Exodus, *I appeared unto Abraham, unto Isaac, and unto Jacob by the name of God Almighty, but by my name Jehovah was I not known to them,*[1] may seem perhaps to militate against such a notion ; but whether it does or not, the statement of Genesis is that the Lord appeared to Abram and declared Himself as God Almighty. *That* was the revelation, the personal manifestation, and not merely the

[1] Exod. vi. 3.

invention or the adoption of the name. Let us try to remember that we know nothing of God Almighty unless we know Him; and this was the knowledge, or at least a step in it, which was now revealed to Abraham.

And it is interesting to observe the scriptural history of this word. It is found about half-a-dozen times in Genesis, once in Exodus as above, twice in Numbers, but not elsewhere in the Pentateuch. It is also found twice in Ruth, in the Psalms, and in Ezekiel, and once in Isaiah, and Joel, but more than thirty times in the book of Job. This is its use in the Old Testament, and we may perhaps gather that it is one of the oldest and simplest appellations attributed to God by the Semitic nations. When we turn to the New Testament we find it once used by St. Paul in his second epistle to Corinth, and eight times in the Revelation of St. John; but nowhere else. Thus, with the exception of the Book of Job, it is more common in the first and last books of the Bible than it is in any other. It is clear, then, that as in Genesis we find the Lord adopting this name, so in Revelation we find it still acknowledged and authorised as a Divine appellation. Among ourselves its usage is somewhat similar; it is an epithet pertaining to and characterising natural rather than revealed religion. When we speak of the Almighty we allude, I fancy, to the Divine Being in a somewhat distant and objective manner;

not as in immediate relation to ourselves, though on the other hand "Almighty and Everlasting God" is one of the most familiar and appropriate forms for the commencement of our prayers. And so I apprehend that Job, living, as he did, beyond the pale of direct revelation, although afterwards the subject of revelation, very commonly spoke of the Almighty as of a person known chiefly in the way of natural rather than of revealed religion; while the patriarchs were clearly more familiar with this ancient name than they were with Jehovah, the special name of revelation, though it was, as we have seen, a name readily adopted and sanctioned by God in His earliest, as subsequently in His latest, manifestations.

The apparent *meaning* of the name also, as we find it in the Old Testament, seems to differ slightly from its equivalent in the New; the one answering perhaps more nearly to our own term—Almighty—and suggesting the highest degree of power, and the other suggesting that rather of dominion.

So much, then, for the history and the signification of the name. What, then, does it tell us about God, and how does it affect our relation to Him? "I believe in God the Father Almighty" is one of the earliest announcements that we receive of God. Let us dwell upon it in the natural course of our subject at the present time, and take for our guide in doing so the words in which the Lord Himself first adopted the application of the name.

In continuation, then, of what was said in the last

lecture, if there is but one God and one supreme will, it is obvious that He must be almighty, otherwise He could not be one, or could not be supreme. Thus far, then, the declarations of the Creed are simply moving along a parallel line with those of instinctive and unrevealed religion, if indeed the lines be not identical. "The Almighty" is a name which spontaneously rises to our lips when we desire to express our innate conceptions of the Divine Being, so far as they refer to His power. The conception of a being who holds in his hand unlimited resources, who has absolute control of the affairs of men, and is Lord of all the powers of nature, is surely one that may be regarded as indigenous to the soil of the human mind. It is difficult to eradicate such a conception from the heart. Our own weakness and subjection to a variety of tyrannous and oppressive forces over which we have no control, and against which it is useless to contend, serves of itself to suggest to us the existence of a being whom, inasmuch as he is mightier than all, we term "All-mighty." Human language is itself a witness to the naturalness, not to say the inevitable rise, of such a thought.

And it is a very grand thought, for it implies that the Divine Being is on the one hand perfectly free, and on the other is absolutely independent of, and disengaged from, His works. It is a natural protest, therefore, against the old Greek notion of the Deity Himself being bound by fate; of there being some impersonal power mightier than the power of the Most High, some irrevocable decree of which He was not the author but the slave; and it is a protest also against that other idea, with which perhaps this is cognate, or to which it ultimately leads, that God is but another name for nature; that He is but the spirit of His works; that, in fact, His works are He. Those forms, then, of natural religion, which admit of our using the term "Almighty" and its equivalents, are opposed on the one hand to the doctrine of necessity, and on the other to that of God's being but the expression of His works, or at the best a sort of *anima mundi*. So far, therefore, as natural religion is what we may term orthodox, it goes along with the confession of the Creed. But if, on the contrary, natural religion approximates to an atheistic or a pantheistic belief, the Christian Creed is most distinctly opposed to it, and so also are the declarations of Scripture, of which the Christian Creed is professedly but the expression.

You will observe, therefore, that when the Lord appeared to Abram, as we are told in the text He did, and adopted, if He did not communicate, the word "almighty," He took no pains to refute either of the philosophical conceptions just alluded to, but assumed altogether their falsehood, and made a direct and positive enunciation of the truth,—" I am the Almighty God;" "I am God Almighty." The simple and unsophisticated mind of Abram had very possibly never been crossed with these double alternative philosophical conceptions; but whether it had or not—for we cannot affirm that it had not—the Lord concerned Himself only with the declaration of the truth ; and the other questions, as far as Abram was concerned, were for ever settled and disposed of.

And so they will be as far as we are concerned, if we are content to accept the revelation to Abram as a true revelation, and are willing to acknowledge that it marked a distinct and definite stage of advancement in man's knowledge of God. And I confess that I do not myself see how the abstract questions and claims of theism, atheism, and pantheism are to be finally set at rest on merely philosophical grounds if we do not admit the element of revelation to give the verdict of authority. The doctrine of necessity is one which has exercised its sway over many master-minds, and that is akin, if it is not equivalent, to atheism. The doctrine that nature and God are convertible terms, is one that is greatly in vogue at the present day, and numbers among its adherents minds of the highest power and most varied accomplishments ; but all these considerations are scattered to the winds and reduced to their just dimensions if we have adequate cause to believe that the actual voice of the Divine Being was ever heard to say, mercifully revealing that which His creatures could not finally and conclusively discover, "I am the Almighty God."

If, therefore, we are prepared to accept this announcement as in any sense Divine, and consequently authoritative and final, let us see what it brings us to. In the first place it assures us of the power of prayer. As soon as we are fully persuaded and sincerely convinced that the term "Almighty" is not a misnomer as applied to God,—that it is a term oftentimes rising involuntarily to our lips, which has had the direct sanction of the Lord Himself in His earliest and latest revelations, then there is an end altogether to any abstract theoretical difficulties about the possibility or the efficacy of prayer.

It is a very just remark, that though very few men are philosophers, yet an unconscious philosophy enters into and tinges all forms and phases of popular thought and speech. And so the mass of irrelevant and crude ideas on the subject of prayer that we frequently meet with are a true index of the philosophy that underlies them. Take, for example, the old stumbling-block of prayers for weather. If we are persuaded that there is a God, and that He is almighty—I say, if we are indeed persuaded of those primary truths, then what becomes of any theoretical difficulty about prayers for weather? Just this, that we who do not see the whole, but only see the smallest possible part, cannot regulate the whole, and cannot decide how the part is to be regulated without seriously disarranging the whole; that is to say, that we, who are not almighty, cannot conceive or determine how He, who is almighty, is to act under certain circumstances. I am at a loss to know what issue such difficulties come to, and I am sure that if we admit the theoretical cogency of these difficulties, it becomes very hard indeed to say at what point the difficulties cease, or to determine what particular thing it is we may pray for, or to decide whether any prayer at all is in the abstract possible, or, therefore, to affirm that the Son of Man did not deceive us when He who knew the Father said, *Ask, and it shall be given you*[1]; and, *All things whatsoever ye shall ask in prayer, believing, ye shall receive*.[2]

But, on the other hand, having settled that point once for all, and having accepted God's own endorsement of the term "almighty" as accurately appropriate when applied to Him, see what scope it gives to the exercise of prayer. I really do not know what it is that we may not pray for if only we are content to associate with our prayer the indispensable and the ever implied condition, if it be Thy will,—*Not my will, but Thine be done*.[3] When our blessed Lord said, *Let this cup pass from me*,[4] He was asking for that which, within all conceivable limits, could not be granted; He was certainly asking what was as theoretically difficult as any change in the weather; and yet that revelation did not prevent His asking it. Surely, then, His example, if He *is* an example for us, may be our guide in this matter.

My brethren, there is nothing more calculated to

---

[1] Matt. vii. 7.
[2] Matt. xxi. 22.
[3] Luke xxii. 42.
[4] Matt. xxvi. 39.

restrain prayer before God than any limitations which our carnal reason may choose to assign to the almighty power of Almighty God. That such limitations do exist is of course an obvious truth: for instance, God cannot recall the past, and God cannot tell a lie; God cannot make that which is in itself wrong to be in itself right. It is He who has established the eternal distinctions between right and wrong, and He cannot, because He will not, confound or abolish them. This also is the opposite side of that other truth which declares that God is almighty; but are our minds so exceedingly circumscribed that they cannot hold in their integrity and in their independence two distinct and opposite truths? All such truths are reconcilable because they are united by an invisible bond which we cannot discover, just as no man ever yet discovered the axis of the earth, on which, however, all men know that the earth revolves. But in the matter of prayer it is enough for us to know that there is absolutely no limit to the almighty power of God except the almighty will of God, coupled indeed with the knowledge of that which is for our absolute good. We that are fathers would gladly give anything that we can to our children if we believed it was for their good; and shall not He who is the Almighty Father give unto us, His children, out of His infinite resources, that which He knows is for our good?—and more than that we should not be wise in desiring.

The revelation of the name "Almighty" has, however, another and a very intimate relation to ourselves, with which it is joined in God's words to Abram, *Walk before me, and be thou perfect.* And it is here that we discover the evidence that the former announcement was a true revelation, because the truth which is now implied is precisely that which the natural mind cannot discover, and never has discovered, namely, that in the walking before God lies the secret and the power of human perfection. Now, man believes that so far as man approximates to perfection it must be by the development and integrity of his moral character. Humanly speaking, the perfect man is he who is perfect in his relations to his fellow-man, and human judgment can take cognisance of no other perfection. The just, the upright, the merciful, the pure, in human estimation, is the perfect man—at least it can exhibit and demand no higher perfection; and yet such perfection is but another name for imperfection, is in the highest degree imperfect, because it concerns itself only with one side of human nature, and that the smallest side. Now God says to Abram nothing about his moral character, that is, his conduct to his fellow-man, but only says, *Walk before me, and be thou perfect;* or, in other words, "Walk before me, and thou shalt be perfect. I will guarantee that thy perfection follows as a natural consequence upon thy walk before me." Perfection, therefore, is not a thing built up out of the materials of human life on the basis of conduct towards our fellows, but it is a thing which follows naturally and spontaneously from the just perception and true realisation of the position and relation in which we stand to God. That is to say, human perfection is to be found in God; not in human conduct, but in the Divine regulation of the life, in its disposition Godwards, which when it is as it should be carries with it and secures the right discharge of all duties relating to our fellow-man. And here we recognise very plainly the vital force of that blessed Gospel truth, that a man is not justified by his works, but by faith towards God. That which makes a man truly righteous is not any effort on his part to achieve in action a completeness and wholeness of character which may command, if it does not aim at securing, the admiration of his fellow-men, the commendation of himself, but the fact that, leaning on the invisible God, looking to the Father who is almighty, who can call those things which be not as though they were, he finds in Him a righteousness and perfection which he has utterly renounced in himself, but which having been found in Him has a necessary and inevitable tendency to dominate and sanctify all his human and mundane relations, and which is personally and inwardly the realisation of an idea which cannot otherwise be achieved, but is doomed to perpetual and recurring disappointment. And thus the old words are verified when we know the Almighty God, for we walk before Him and are perfect.

V.
MAKER OF HEAVEN AND EARTH.

Happy is he that hath the God of Jacob for his help, whose hope is in the Lord his God : which made heaven and earth, the sea, and all that therein is : which keepeth truth for ever.—PSALM cxlvi. 5, 6.

THE next truth which is brought before us in the Apostles' Creed is that God the Father Almighty is maker of heaven and earth. The Nicene Creed adds, "And of all things visible and invisible ; " thereby seeming to imply what the other does not explicitly state—the existence of an invisible, that is, an immaterial, world of spiritual essences. Hitherto the conception of God has been that of a supreme omnipotent fatherly Being, who stands in special relations to us His children, which He has made known to us by revelation. Now we have another aspect of His character, which is that of the Creator of this material universe, and of all the beings that inhabit it. This is a very important fact concerning our belief in God, and one by no means so simple as it may appear. For all difficulties about revelation easily resolve themselves into the question whether the God of the Bible is the God of nature ; and thus the very argument of Bishop Butler's Analogy was this, that objections to the Scriptural revelation were virtually groundless, because the same difficulties confronted us in our observation of nature which were thought to be fatal to the Divine origin of revelation. Now it is one of the most conspicuous glories of the old Hebrew Scriptures that they are distinct and unfaltering in their testimony on this point. There is no hesitation or ambiguity in their utterances about it. The very first words of them are, *In the beginning God created the heaven and the earth;* and here in this Psalm we have the clear assertion that the God of Jacob is He who *made heaven and earth, the sea, and all that therein is.* I would just point out by the way that the writer was manifestly conversant with, and is referring to, the Mosaic narrative of creation in the opening chapter of Genesis,—that must have been the foundation of his knowledge, even as it is the authority for ours,—and then proceed to develop the thought as it is here expressed, and deduce the consequences which follow from it.

When we say that God *made the heaven and the earth, and the sea, and all that therein is,* what do we mean? Is our assertion what may be called historic, or is it chiefly causal?—that is to say, does it refer principally to a moment in the past when these things did not exist, or does it speak rather of their existence in the present, and point us to what is behind them, out of sight, as their primal origin and cause? I think that commonly, from the ideas of sequence which are innate to our minds, we do associate with this statement one of time which does seem to carry us back to that distant past when there was no heaven or earth or sea. And at a period when the present existence of the world was commonly believed to date only from some six thousand years ago it was very easy not only to do so but to acquiesce in doing it. Vast as that space of time is, for it more than embraced the whole of known human history, it was as nothing to what was beyond it, for beyond it there was an eternity of nothing—chaos and old night. Now that science has taught us that the past of the existing universe is, humanly speaking, unlimited, that the human faculties are totally incompetent to measure or to grasp it, there arises at once a needless difficulty as to the conception of this particular point of past time in which God made the heaven and the earth, and the sea, and all that is therein. We not unnaturally find it impossible to conceive of such a moment or of such a condition of circumstances. It baffles our powers. Whereas then ignorance told us there was an eternity of emptiness preceding the existing order of things, which was, comparatively speaking, but of yesterday, science has taught us to extend the eternity to the existing order of things, and leave the previous eternity, which even science cannot get rid of entirely, alone, because our powers must fail somewhere, and they may as well fail there. The conception of an eternity of chaos, upon which there supervened six thousand years of order, may have been hard to conceive or realise; but it is not harder to accept what it is clear from science we must accept—an eternity of order supervening upon an eternity of what we know not and cannot designate. It may well be doubted how far the actual statements of the Bible are responsible for some of these conceptions which we know now to have been misconceptions. Certain it is that in Scripture no limit has been, as no limit can be, assigned to that beginning, in which we are told that God made the heaven and the earth. But now that from various causes our conceptions of past time have become so vastly increased, it may be as well to ask ourselves whether there is not another and more profitable way of understanding what is meant by God's making the heaven and the earth; because it is certain that the further we put backward the first original creative act the less practical bearing it has upon us. And therefore it is as well to inquire what this creative act of God implies.

Now although of course all attempts at investigating the first origin of things must necessarily be futile, because beyond our reach, yet it is as well to divest our minds of any erroneous notions which may serve to make the hard yet harder; and therefore I would say that it does seem to me that great light breaks in upon this profound and abstruse subject from our blessed Lord's words, *My Father worketh hitherto, and I work;* more particularly when His argument there seems to show that just as God's creative work ceases not on the Sabbath-day, so there is no necessity for His own redemptive work to cease then. For does not this show us that creation is not a completed but a continued work? that it is an act in progress, and not an act performed once for all? And I do think it is highly requisite that we should take this view of creation as being the really Scripture view, more especially when we are confronted with these inconceivable periods of past time which can only paralyse and astound the mind. There is no analogy between God's making the world and a man's making a watch or any other complex piece of machinery. For as soon as a man has made a watch his work is done, and it will continue to perform its functions, be they what they may, according to its capability and perfection; the work is made, and it goes on of itself; but this is not the case with God's piece of mechanism, the universe, for that when called into existence cannot go on of itself for a single moment without Him, nay more, it is even now in process of formation; the world of to-day is not the world of yesterday, nor is it the world which will be to-morrow. All things are in a condition of continual and constant change, and no two successive moments witness the existence of identically the same world. *My Father worketh hitherto,—* there is the creative energy now being put forth, now in operation. God is now making the world that now is, and to-morrow He will then be making the world that then will be. This is what creation implies; and this is how we are to look for the Creator, not as a being who six thousand years, or six hundred thousand millions of years, ago made the world, and left it as He made it, but as a being who now in every form of life is causing, upholding, creating, preserving, changing, and destroying what exists. It is a profound mystery; mind cannot fathom it, thought cannot follow it, tongue cannot define it, but of this sort it is. This is at least an aspect of the creative act upon which we must by no means suffer any bare, bald historic thought or conception of it fatally to usurp. What the relation is between the work created as we behold it and the Creator, or what the method of operation is which binds the two together, we cannot imagine; but this it is that the words *maker of heaven and earth* suggest to me; and when I am told that in the beginning God created the heaven and the earth, I understand that at some one inconceivably distant point or epoch of past time He caused to go forth that power which, however it may have operated at successive stages or periods, or on whatsoever graduated plan, we still see on every hand working the wonders that it worketh, whether in inanimate nature or in the complex machinery of our own changing bodies. And it is the Word alone which reveals or can reveal this God to us.

Has it ever occurred to you, as it often has to me, to ask yourselves what kind of a world this would be if there were no God in it? Let us put hypothetically the inconceivable and impossible hypothesis that the world as we see it existed, but that there was no God. Then, on the hypothesis, the trees would still be green, the flowers would be bright and fair and lovely, the breezes would still blow laden with the ravished scents of the gardens and the fields of May, the sun would still shine, the rainbow would still span the vault of heaven, the moon and the stars would still be bright and glorious, the sea would still smile with his many-twinkling radiant splendour, but there would be no God behind it all. Everything would be a cause to itself, and there an end. The greatest known brightness would be the brightness of the sun, the greatest known beauty would be the beauty of the earth, the greatest known strength would be the strength of nature, and there would be nothing more; there would be no past and no future, because all would be but the extension backwards and forwards of the same unvaried but ever-varying present; the life of the universe would proclaim no life, it would only proclaim itself; it would not say, " Look on me, and judge how fair, how glorious He must be," but only, " Rest content with me, for I am all, and there is none besides." The glories of heaven would not say,

> For ever singing as they shine,
> The hand that made us is Divine.

but "There is no hand that made us. We exist because we are, by some inscrutable, unaccountable necessity. We always have been, and we always shall be." Now I cannot venture to say what you would think and feel if this were so, but I can distinctly say for myself that fair as the trees and the flowers and the stars and the sky and the sea might be, they would have no beauty left for me. Their very loveliness would make me sick at heart, for I could not love them; they would fail to satisfy me, for they would be like the apples of Sodom, dust within; and this magnificent universe would be no longer the temple of the living God, but a pictured, painted charnel-house.

And then let me set over against this picture the simple, glorious words of the old Hebrew poet, *Blessed is he that hath the God of Jacob for his help, and whose hope is in the Lord his God: who made heaven and earth, and the sea, and all that therein is; who keepeth His promise for ever.* Or the words of the Christian Creed, " I believe in God the Father Almighty, Maker of heaven and earth."

And now let me show you wherein the difference lies. The one begins with what it cannot deny, with what it looks out upon and perceives with the natural eye and touches with the natural hand, and goes no further; it sees no more and feels no more. The other begins with what it does *not* see, with what it can *not* touch, and then comes down to behold the works that *He* has made, and because it comes with

Him, beholds them fair; it looks out upon them with the eyes of God; *and God saw everything that He had made, and, behold, it was very good.* And say what we will, this is the only true order: unless man will begin with God, he must end with nature; but ending with nature, he cannot even behold all the glory of nature. If we begin with nature, we cannot look up through nature unto nature's God; but if we begin with God, then we not only see Him before nature, but likewise in nature and beyond nature. Hence the Christian Creed and the words of the Psalmist alike show us the indispensable necessity of *faith.* We must begin, not with what we can prove, but with what we must take for granted. For we cannot prove the existence of God, or the love of the Father, or the being of the Creator; but if we accept these facts, they will explain all others; and if we reject them, all others will reject us as their interpreters; they will be and will remain unexplained and inexplicable enigmas.

If, then, the eyes of our mind are opened by faith so as to behold in nature the present and living God of nature, we shall know that though nature may and must be His handiwork, it can be no part of Him. It may proclaim Him, speak of Him, point to Him, be the echo of His voice or the shadow of His presence, but it will be other than He; and as He is apart from nature, utterly and entirely disengaged therefrom, choosing to reveal Himself in nature, but not obliged to do so, so likewise will He be before and after nature ; there will of necessity have been a beginning in which He was without nature, in which He called nature into being ; and certainly, as existing nature is ever changing and passing away, there will be a moment when He will at least be without nature as she now is ; when the first heaven and the first earth that were created in the beginning are passed away, and there shall be no more sea, whatever that may mean ; but we shall look out upon the new heavens and the new earth, even as He hath said, *Behold, I make all things new.* And thus the conception of the Psalmist will be verified, *Thou, Lord, in the beginning hast laid the foundation of the earth, and the heavens are the works of Thine hands : they shall perish, but Thou shalt endure ; and they shall all wax old like a garment, and as a vesture shalt Thou change them, and they shall be changed ; but Thou art the same, and Thy years shall not fail.*

Need we say, in conclusion, that unless a man can thus see in the Maker of heaven and earth, whom the external world, the sea, and the sky proclaim, the Lord *his* God ; unless he can recognise in the omnipotent Creator a Father, he will not, as the Psalmist says, be blessed? He may not only have an eye for the beautiful like the artist, a soul for the fair and lovely like the poet, but also the power of making these his own ; earth, out of the abundance of her stores, may pour into his lap of her treasures and her wealth ; but unless he has a part in the

Lord of all, her very riches and glory will leave him bankrupt and destitute : he will be like a sick man at a banquet, unable to taste the fatness of the pastures or the sweetness of the vineyard, for all will be dashed with bitterness and emptiness and poverty. It is he only who can say that his hope is in the Lord his God, who can claim Him for his own, and know that having given himself to God and his heart to Christ, God has given Himself in Christ to him, who has found, by the sure test of personal experience, that He keepeth His promise and His truth for ever,—yea, even to a thousand generations, —who can call himself blessed ; but he can, for the God of blessing is his portion here, and will be the fulness of his joy for ever.

VI.

AND IN JESUS.

Believe on the Lord Jesus Christ, and thou shalt be saved, and thy house.—ACTS xvi. 31.

HITHERTO we have been concerned with those articles of the Creed which receive light from the Christian revelation, but are not especially Christian,—the nature of God, the character of God, the relation of God to the world in which we live, and the like. Now we approach an entirely different stage, which is directly and exclusively Christian, inasmuch as it relates to the person of Jesus Christ. Let us observe, then, in the first place, that this comes before us in the Creed as a separate and additional article: "I believe in God the Father . . . AND in Jesus Christ." Now what do we mean when we say " I believe in Jesus Christ"? Clearly each person who joins in that confession of faith pledges himself to the acceptance of it. The prayers that are offered in this church are not offered as individual supplications. They are all couched in the language of number,—"Good Lord, deliver us;" "We humbly beseech Thee, O Lord," and the like. But with the Creed it is very different; there we seem to have no desire to lose our individuality, but to assert it. We do not attempt to merge ourselves and our own wants in the persons and the wants of others, but we try to come out of the multitude, we endeavour to individualise ourselves, and adopt the language of solitude and unity,—"*I* believe." Now this fact cannot be too carefully noticed, for it expresses and reflects a great truth. Faith is a personal matter; it concerns the soul in its solitude, in its individual responsibility before God. Our own faith is no concern of others, the faith of others is no concern of ours. Each unit is answerable for his or her faith to Almighty God, and to Him alone. But as Christians we all have a certain faith in common, the profession of which is a bond of union between the several units. If for any reason this common faith is not our own faith, then by that circumstance, independently of any other, we are cut off from the unity of the Christian body. It is obvious that this must be so. If Christians are people who believe in Christ, and we ourselves do not believe in Christ, then we are necessarily cut off from the unity of Christian people. This is surely self-evident. We may, of course, defend ourselves on the ground that we object, for example, to the formula of the Christian Creed ; we may deny its authority, or refuse to be bound by it; but so far as that Creed is the Creed of Christendom, so far as it expresses the faith of Christian people, we are excluded by our rejection of it. The test is applied to us, and we cannot stand the test. We are witnesses to ourselves, and the Creed is a witness against us. I do not propose now to examine the authority of the Christian creed, but to accept it as the recognised authority of all Christian men, and to enquire what it implies and involves, as it is propounded to us in the familiar apostolic symbol.

And it is manifest on the threshold of this subject that there are momentous issues involved. The Christian Creed is not a theory or a sentiment, or an opinion; it is a belief, it is that which is the subject-matter of conviction, the result of deliberate and entire persuasion; but it professes also to be the means and the condition of salvation. Among the ancient schools of philosophy, no one ever pretended that his own particular tenets were necessary to salvation. The disciples of the various schools were no doubt very eager and earnest for the maintenance of their personal doctrines, as men always have a tendency to become on any abstract question, but none ever went so far as to promise or deny salvation according as they were rejected or received. But this was notoriously and historically the case with the Christian Creed from the very first. It presented itself before men, alike in the teaching of our Lord and His apostles, as the one condition of salvation. The compendious assertion of the text was the answer given by Paul and Silas to the anxious jailer at Philippi, when he inquired with fear and trembling, "What must I do to be saved?"

He that believeth and is baptised shall be saved, were among the last words spoken by Christ upon earth. I do not see how it is possible to escape from this. If the Christian faith professes to do anything for a man, it professes to save him. It does not propose itself as an opinion he may hold or not as he pleases, but it assures him that in holding it— whatever may be implied by holding it—he is safe.

While, however, so much is absolutely certain, it must be borne in mind that in so doing the Christian Creed implies no reference to any who may happen to be beyond the reach of its influence. It tells us nothing about those who are ignorant of the name of Christ; it tells us nothing of those who lived before He came; it pronounces nothing as to the condition of Socrates, or of those ancient worthies for whom we hope so much, but of whom we know so little. It is absolutely silent with regard to all questions that may be asked on these and kindred subjects. All that it professes to do, is to put him who accepts it in a state of salvation, to assure him that his condition before and after acceptance is marked by the difference between being saved and lost. It reveals a great want in humanity, a deep gulf in the spiritual nature, from which it promises to rescue *us*, and which it offers to supply, but with respect to all others it asks, *Who art thou that judgest another man's servant? to his own master he standeth or falleth;*[1] and, *Shall not the*

[1] 1 Rom. xiv. 4.

Judge of all the earth do right?[1] Yea, we may go further. While the promises of the Christian faith are directly addressed to those who embrace them, and to those, therefore, whose consciousness readily and gladly responds to their truth, and while it cannot but withhold these promises from others who do not embrace them, it simply gives us no power to pronounce upon the case of those who from mental constitution or what not, are honest (but honest and truth-loving they must be) in their rejection of them, and are unable to embrace them; it distinctly declares that there is a special happiness and blessing reserved for those who do embrace them, into which no stranger can enter; but with reference to the rest it says, *The Father judgeth no man, but hath committed all judgment unto the Son.*

For be it observed that the Christian faith implies the consciousness of a great want; it does not enter the arena of public discussion for the sake of competing with the various systems of human invention, but it comes to a world which is awakened to its lost condition. It is only when the question, What must I do to be saved? has been asked, with all its attendant agony, that the reply is spoken, Believe on the Lord Jesus Christ, and thou shalt be saved. It is perfectly futile and hopeless, therefore, to advance the claims of the Christian faith, or to argue for them never so cogently, as long as there is no response within to the want which it offers to

[1] Gen. xviii. 25.

satisfy. *They that are whole have no need of the physician, but they that are sick.*[1] When we are in rude health and strength we may deem lightly of medical science and skill; but when those dear to us are in imminent danger, or we ourselves seem to catch a glimpse of the wings of the approaching angel of death, then, as drowning men who clutch at a straw, we are only too thankful for the advice and the presence of the physician, we anticipate his visits with eagerness, and take leave of him with reluctance. And so long as the spiritual state is whole-hearted and unconscious of something wrong within, it is vain to expect that the message of the Good Physician will be received with welcome. There are but too many obvious reasons why it should be unwelcome, and the only thing that man can do when his Maker has failed, is to stand afar off and watch. The hour has not come yet, and it is just possible. it may never come in this world; but this world is not all, and it is only when things visible have passed away, and things invisible have begun to be, that we can fully decide upon the actual merits of that which we reject.

And how is it, brethren, with ourselves? Have we hearts that are open to the message of the Gospel? Are we conscious of deep want within? Are we convinced that life itself, with all its beauties and bounties, has no power to satisfy; that pleasure can only fatigue and pall; that riches are inadequate

[1] Mark ii. 17.

to feed the cravings of the mind; that honour and fame and ambition are apt to lose their charm in proportion to the success with which they are pursued ? Does all this show us, or rather, does it not show us, that whatever our outward state, within we are not saved, we are not made whole and sound ? Putting aside for the time all questions as to the ultimate future, is it not sufficiently patent that now, at this present moment, there is something wanting, something wrong; that our position here, in the midst even of a prosperous life, is an eminently defective one, and that when death comes it is desperate, and after death—a blank ? In the contemplation of all this, can any man doubt that we are not saved; that there is, so to say, an open field for salvation, if only we could find it ? Setting aside, then, altogether, for the while, any fears and misgivings about the eternal future, about the just judgment of God, and the degree to which we may have incurred it, is it not plain that we want health and light and salvation, if so be we can get it ? Surely, on the most favourable estimate, our condition is not such that we need not gladly listen to the blessed announcement, *Believe on the Lord Jesus Christ, and thou shalt be saved.*

It is clear, then, that faith in Christ is propounded to us by the Christian Creed as the one condition of salvation. Now, what is implied by faith in Christ? For the present we may answer this question in a threefold manner, reserving the further consideration of it for future discourses. First, faith in Christ assumes and implies a basis of historic fact. It can never be sufficiently inculcated that the Christian Creed not only rests upon a series of historic facts, but concerns itself with facts rather than with doctrines. Taking the Apostles' Creed as an adequate and authentic definition of it, we see at once that it is concerned with doctrines less than facts. There are few doctrines, there are many facts. Christianity is an historic religion. The facts with which it is concerned are presented to us as of the highest importance in the history of the world; they have affected all other history. The life and death of Jesus was of infinitely more importance than the life and death of Alexander or of Julius Cæsar, though in a Christian aspect it is impossible not to see that the life and death of Cæsar and of Alexander, certainly their lives, had a very direct bearing upon the life of Jesus Christ, and the effects of His life. The conquest of Alexander, for instance, made Greek the language of the world, and so introduced to the knowledge of mankind the Greek version of the Jewish Scriptures; and the conquest of Cæsar opened this country to the preaching of the Gospel, and laid the foundation of its present position in Christendom. But the Christian Church cares more to teach her children the facts of the life of Jesus Christ than she does to teach them those of the life of Cæsar or of Alexander. We are baptised into a belief of the facts of the life of Jesus Christ, and when we are on our death-bed the profession which is required of us is not that of particular doctrines, but the profession of the articles of the Apostles' Creed. We cannot, therefore, over-estimate the importance of the historic basis to which the Christian Creed appeals. Though Jesus Christ was no conqueror, His place in history was of the utmost importance to mankind; and just as Lord Bacon or George Stephenson achieved a greater work in the world than Napoleon or Hannibal, so the historic importance of the life of Christ eclipses altogether that of the greatest names in history, and the entire mass of human history cannot but be affected by such significant historic facts as the life and death and resurrection and ascension of Jesus Christ.

For, secondly, the framework of fact on which the Christian Creed rests has reference to a particular man of whom these facts are related. It is manifest that whatever else faith in Jesus Christ may mean, it must mean that He truly existed, truly lived and died and rose again. Throw any doubt on the person of Christ, and there is an end at once and for ever to all belief in Jesus Christ. To believe in Jesus Christ manifestly implies that there was such a person. But, further, to believe in Him implies also that He was a *unique* person, because it implies an attitude towards Him which is demanded towards no one else,—it implies that we believe in Him as we believe in no one else. That is to say, it implies that we believe in Him as the Saviour, we believe in Him unto salvation. These two ideas are quite distinct. First, we believe in Him as a Saviour. This is the meaning of His name "Jesus;" this is why He was so named, that we might believe in Him as a Saviour, as one who could save us from our sins. That which we feel within, of want and guilt and uncleanness, and estrangement from God, and sin and wretchedness, is removed by Jesus; He is designed as the sufficient remedy for it, He was called "Jesus" that He might deliver us from it. This is as much His name, and a part of Him, as the name of Cæsar or Hannibal is inseparable from them. This man is only known in history as Jesus; it was the name by which He was called before He was born, it was the name which was written over Him when He was crucified; and in itself it speaks volumes, for it is a witness that He claimed to be, and is, a Saviour. For to believe in Jesus is manifestly to believe that He is what His name proclaimed Him to be, a Saviour.

In professing this belief, then, we profess that there is a man in whom we can find that salvation which we acknowledge that we feel we want. This belief implies, moreover, that the influence and power of this person is not over; that whereas a belief in any other historic character simply implies a belief that his character is historic, that he actually did exist, but implies no more, belief in this man shuts us up to belief in His present existence and His present power to save. I cannot believe in Jesus if I suppose that when He died there was an end to His influence and power, except so far as regards the moral influence produced by His life. If I believe in Jesus, I not only believe that His recorded words have a certain beneficial influence on me, but that He Himself is able to save me. I cannot believe in Him as Jesus unless I believe this, for His very name will otherwise give the lie to my belief.

This, then, is one thing to believe in Him as a Saviour; but it is quite another, and something vastly more, to believe in Him unto salvation, for that implies not only that He is able and willing to save me, but that He actually, and as a matter of fact, has saved me; it implies an experimental response in my spiritual being to the present influence and power which He is declared to possess; it implies that in Jesus I have found that salvation which I so much need, that my personal sin has met with its antidote in Him, that the yawning chasm in my nature which nothing in this life or this world can fill, though my cup were to overflow with sweetness, has been filled by Him, that the dread of death as an insuperable calamity which is incidental to me as a mortal man has at least been so far relieved and quieted that my heart can be glad and my tongue rejoice, and my flesh also can rest in hope; it implies, finally, that I have in myself the sure pledge and foretaste of eternal life and felicity, because the power of His resurrection worketh mightily in me.

This, brethren, is what it is to believe in Jesus. Suffer me, in conclusion, to ask you two questions: first, whether you have any anxiety like that which the jailer's words expressed, *What must I do to be saved?* and, secondly, whether, having earnestly asked that question, you have found, like him, to your intense joy, the blessed truth of the reply, *Believe on the Lord Jesus Christ, and thou shalt be saved.*

VII.

CHRIST.

*For he mightily convinced the Jews, and that publicly, showing by the scriptures that Jesus was Christ.—*ACTS xviii. 28.

THE subject of the last lecture was that portion of the Creed which is implied and expressed in the name of Jesus; to-day we shall have to consider the name of Christ and all that is involved in it. Now it is eminently characteristic of Scripture that a large amount of significance is assigned to the names of particular persons. We notice this from the very commencement. The name that was given to the first woman was a significant name—a name which was designed to express the character she was intended to fulfil. The name of Abram was changed to Abraham in order that it might express his future destiny. It is plain that in all simple terms and languages names must have a meaning, but it is commonly a meaning that has reference to the present or the past, rather than the future. In Scripture it is otherwise; and thus with the two names of our Lord one had reference to the work which He came to do, and the other to the office He was destined to fulfil. We must carefully distinguish between these names. To us they have very much the character of proper names or personal appellations. But they are not so. "Jesus" was our Lord's proper and personal name. When we say that we believe in Jesus, we say that we believe in the historic existence and reality of the man Jesus. We say at least so much ; we say indeed, more too; but, we undoubtedly do say no less. "Christ," on the other hand, is not a personal name, except so far as it has become such by appropriation. "Christ" is nothing more than the shorter form of *the Christ*, which is the designation of a particular office or function. It was an official not a personal name. We speak of Jesus Christ because we, being Christians, acknowledge Jesus to have been the Christ; but "Christ" was no part of His name which was assigned Him in its integrity by the angel before He was conceived in the womb. It was the object and mission of Jesus to show Himself to be the Christ, and this object was not accomplished till He had *ascended up on high and received gifts for men, yea, even for His enemies, that the Lord God might dwell among them*.[1] Trinity Sunday is the first Sunday when we are enabled, looking back upon the completed office and work of Jesus, to regard Him as the Christ.[2] In the full and complete survey which we are enabled now to take of all that Jesus did, we can, if believers, declare Him to have been the Christ; we can call

---

[1] Ps. lxviii. 18.   [2] Preached on Trinity Sunday.

Him "Jesus Christ;" we can say, "I believe in Jesus Christ," or, "I believe that Jesus is the Christ:"

And observe, there is very much more involved in this than many persons may at first imagine, and that which is involved is of the very highest importance. While God's purposes are in process of fulfilment, they are in the highest degree obscure and unintelligible; it is only when we can look back upon them as fulfilled, that light breaks through and their design is revealed. For example, that which makes our present career so dark is our inability to see the end. All things appear confused and perplexed, because at present we wait for the solution of them. When that is vouchsafed, then everything will become clear which is now so puzzling. And when in any case this position is arrived at, then it becomes absurd to doubt the reality of a solution which has thrown light on everything. Now apply this to the case of the New Testament. It is absolutely impossible to deny that everywhere in the New Testament —in each of the Gospels, in the Acts, and in all the Epistles—Jesus is spoken of as the Christ, that His being the Christ was to a large extent the very issue raised by the New Testament, that the name by which from the first His followers were known, and by which to the present day for a period of eighteen hundred years they have continued to be designated, is one which involves the acceptance of this issue; for they are called Christians, their home is termed Christendom, and their belief is known as Christianity. This implies, then, as a necessity that the rise of this society and the spread of this belief was inseparably connected with the recognition of Jesus as the Christ. There could have been no Christians, no Christendom, and no Christianity, but for the impression having been produced upon men's minds that Jesus was the Christ. If this had not been a prominent and distinguishing feature of the early disciples, they would have had no such name assigned them. This is quite apparent—it is obvious and irrefutable.

And, for a reason which will appear subsequently, I cannot but think that when we are told that the disciples were called Christians first in Antioch, there was a Divine provision in this, even if a Divine intention is not expressed in that passage by the remarkable and, so to say, oracular word which the historian there uses for *called* (χρηματίσαι). In laying the foundations of the Christian Church broad and deep, it was part of God's design that this name, however given—whether, as some have thought, in jest and levity, or else, as others suggest, in Divine earnest—should be permanently and inseparably affixed to it, so that by friends and foes alike the name of "Christian" should be distinctly understood, and perfectly unmistakable when applied to the disciples of Jesus.

For why? It is absolutely certain that the various centres of Christianity discovered to us in the New Testament are evidence of the extent to which this belief had spread, and of the main features by which it was characterised. All these persons, whatever their number, in Rome, in Corinth, in Galatia, in Ephesus, in Philippi, in Colosse, in Thessalonica, in Crete, in Jerusalem, in Antioch and elsewhere, believed in Jesus as the Christ. Of that there can be no shadow of doubt, for otherwise they would not have been called Christians. And it must be borne in mind that though many of them had been Jews, they were not all Jews; that various nationalities were represented by them. But, in all cases alike, the very foundation upon which their belief as Christians was built was the conviction that Jesus was the Christ; was the truth, that is, with which Jesus fulfilled the office of the Christ; was therefore the existence of such an office for Him to fulfil. Now observe this carefully, because it is extremely important. You cannot account for the special phenomena which we know were presented by the early spread of Christianity, without acknowledging that somehow or other—rightly or wrongly, for it matters not now—there was such an impression in men's minds of the ideal character of a Christ,—such a belief in the imaginary functions, if you will, of the Christ,—as would admit of the superstructure being reared thereon, that Jesus was the Christ. No man could have become a Christian, that is, who did not believe in the reality of that particular function of the Christ which Jesus claimed to discharge. Somehow or other, then, wherever

Christianity spread, and that among the Gentiles no less than the Jews, there must have existed so much preparation of the mental soil as was implied in the conception of that office and function of the Messiahship without which the Christian confession and the Christian name was an impossibility. That this conception should have existed among the Jews is the less remarkable because we know that a belief in the advent of a Messiah was fostered by their sacred writings. It was part of their national inheritance that they believed in the existence of such a person, and looked forward to His coming. But it is surely not a little strange that those Gentiles —and they were many who became Christians— should have passed through, as it were, a preliminary phase of Judaism in becoming so; and yet this is neither more nor less than they must have done. For they must have accepted mentally the entire framework and foundation of the Jewish belief about the Christ before they could have acknowledged Jesus as the Christ. The one belief obviously involved and implied the other.

It is manifest, therefore, that this widespread fundamental conviction about the person and office of the Christ could not have existed but for the Jewish Scriptures. It was mainly and directly attributable to them; if it was not actually and exclusively created by them, it was at least developed and kept alive by them. And thus we know, both from the text and many other passages, that the great storehouse of argument upon which the early preachers of Christianity drew in their discussions with the Jews, was the Old Testament scriptures. To them they were never weary of appealing. In them they had ready to their hand a large amount of material, which was acknowledged as of unquestionable authority and of the highest value. There they found a certain portrait depicted, a certain character delineated, a certain office described, a certain hope excited, and promise given ; and if in every case they could show the correspondence between the written ideal and the actual person and work of Jesus, all that they desired was accomplished. The Jew was rationally persuaded into becoming a Christian. He had no need to be persuaded into a belief in the Christ ; he only had to be persuaded that Jesus was the Christ. Sometimes this was done successfully, sometimes the evidence was resisted, but never, be it observed, on the unsoundness of the premises, only upon the alleged incompleteness of the conclusions.

We are not fully informed as to the process adopted in the case of the Gentiles ; it seems probable that the dissemination of the Jewish Scriptures through the Alexandrian Greek version had been the means of infusing generally into men's minds anticipations of the advent of some great personage, so that these anticipations furnished a sufficient basis for an appeal in favour of Jesus ; but if not, it is pretty certain that the early preachers would point to the obvious correspondence between the sacred record and the historic character of the Saviour, and on that ground demand a verdict in His favour; and it is perfectly clear that in a vast number of instances the appeal was not made in vain. The premises were invariably admitted, because the conclusion was accepted. We know, moreover, the several passages that were alleged by the early preachers to refer to the Christ, and we know yet further that these were the passages which for a thousand years after Christ were still applied by the Jews to their Messiah. In the face, therefore, of the undeniable results which were brought about, and of the special conditions without which they could not have been produced, we are, comparatively speaking, independent of those questions which have been raised in the present day as to the propriety of interpreting the Old Testament as the Jews and early Christians interpreted it. Had it not been for this interpretation, the Christian Church could not have been founded, as a matter of fact it was founded; therefore, this interpretation was sufficiently satisfactory in its time to be the direct and immediate cause of a vast revolution in thought and history, with which no other can bear comparison. Even if the means employed are declared defective, that cannot touch the reality of the results produced; rather, the greatness of those results becomes the more remarkable if the means were feeble or inadequate; but as a matter of fact the accomplishment of the results by the means is no slight confirmation of the adequacy and reality of the means employed. When Apollos *mightily convinced the Jews, and that publicly, showing by the Scriptures that Jesus was Christ,* the greatness and solidity of the work done was sufficient proof of the soundness of the means resorted to. The Scriptures as we have them, being written ages before Christ came, and corresponding as they do with the life and character of Christ, are clear and unfaltering in their testimony to Him.

And it is a testimony which nothing can ever silence. Wherever there is a prepared heart, the testimony will be accepted, and will do its work; and wherever Jesus is believingly acknowledged as the Christ, there it will not be possible to impugn the testimony of the Scriptures. The testimony, therefore, is one which will work in a twofold manner; either branch of it taken alone is incomplete, both taken together are conclusive. The Scriptures without Christ are unintelligible: Christ without the Scriptures is an impossibility. We may seek to estimate the character of Jesus, but we cannot separate it from His claim to be the Christ; we cannot recognise His claim to be the Christ and yet demur to the Divine authority of the Scriptures.

And thus, brethren, we see what is involved in that name Christ which we all confess in that name Christian which we all bear. It has been designed in the providence of God that that word Christ should contain in itself an abiding testimony to the person of His Son. To be a Christian is now what it was in the days when Corinth rang with the eloquence of Apollos. We cannot be Christians unless we acknowledge Jesus as the Christ; we cannot acknowledge Jesus as the Christ and not confess that ages before He came God gave the promise of His coming, and endued with supernatural light and knowledge through the inspiration of the Holy Spirit those who spake of Him. We cannot be Christians unless we confess to a Divine portrait in the Old Testament which has been fully realised in the New. These are the two halves, then, which being put together make up a perfect whole. When the Spirit of God moves upon the face of that mighty deep of Holy Scripture, then one part answers to the other part, as face answers unto face in water. The Psalms, the Prophets, and the other writings are full of the coming Christ, if we read them aright; and the Gospels and Epistles tell us of a Jesus who is the Christ come.

But what is the import of the name? It is "The Anointed One." He is our anointed Prophet, Priest, and King. Anointed with what? With the Holy Spirit. To Him the Spirit was given without measure, in order that He might be our Prophet, Priest, and King. Our Prophet, because He who stands between us and God, and comes, in the name of God, with a message from Him, with the truth of God upon His lips. We cannot accept Christ, then, as our Prophet if we reject His testimony regarding

Himself, which is clear, unfaltering, and unmistakable. He announced Himself as our Saviour, as our Judge, as the Son of God, as He who is to heal, redeem, forgive, and sanctify us, as He through whom alone we can come to the Father. Is this our testimony concerning Him, as it is His testimony concerning Himself? Do we gladly recognise the anointing which rests on Him? Does He touch our hearts with love, and make us ready to do that will which He proclaims? But He is our Priest, also; because He has offered a full, perfect, and sufficient sacrifice for sin, He has procured remission and bestowed it in His blood-shedding, He is consecrated as our High Priest for evermore; by Him we have boldness and access with confidence by the faith of Him; and accepting His priesthood, we are enabled to become priests ourselves, and to offer up spiritual sacrifices acceptable to God by Him; and having boldness to enter into the holiness through His blood by a new and living way which He hath consecrated for us through the veil, that is to say, His flesh, we are able to draw near with a true heart in full assurance of faith, having our hearts sprinkled from an evil conscience. And thus He becomes our King, to whom we owe allegiance and fealty, who is fairer than the children of men, with grace poured upon His lips, because God hath blessed Him for ever. And so being in this threefold capacity our Messiah, that is, our Anointed One, He is able to bestow upon us those precious priceless gifts with which He is endowed Himself; He is ordained and qualified to pour out upon us the gift of the Holy Spirit, that blessed, sanctifying, purifying, strengthening, hallowing, consoling grace, which can alone make us one with Him, as He is one with the Father in the unity of the Holy Spirit. The sole condition of receiving that blessed endowment is the confession of Jesus as the Christ; for when we acknowledge Him as the Anointed One of God, then the Spirit of God is shed abroad in our hearts by the Holy Ghost which is given to us, and we are enabled to say "Abba, Father" with the voice of the regenerate, who, being re-created in Christ Jesus, are made partakers of His sonship, to the glory of God through Him.

VIII.

HIS ONLY SON.

God so loved the world that He gave His only-begotten Son, that whosoever believeth in Him should not perish, but have everlasting life.—JOHN iii. 16.

HAVING endeavoured to unfold the significance of the double name of our blessed Lord, we must pass on now to consider His person and character more fully,—what He is in Himself, and the relation in which He stands to us. In the simplest Christian Creed He is called "His only Son" which in the Nicene form is expanded into "the only-begotten Son of God, begotten of His Father before all worlds; God of God, light of light, very God of very God; begotten, not made, being of one substance with the Father, by whom all things were made." This latter language has a very much more elaborate cast about it, and rings of polemical theology; but I do not know that it is really stronger than the other, or that it suggests any truth that the other does not imply. The one word which is central and essential in the Nicene confession is that mysterious word preserved to us by St. John in the text—" only-begotten ;" a word which is not indeed expressed in the Apostles' Creed, though it is most undoubtedly not rejected.

With regard, then, to this word St. John gives us to understand that it was adopted by our Lord Himself. It is quite useless going into the question of showing this. If we are not willing to accept the authority of St. John, we are not much more likely to accept any other authority. For those who desire to be guided and to abide by the teaching of Scripture, it is enough to know that this term is four times used in the Gospel of St. John, and once in his first Epistle, with reference to Jesus Christ, and on two occasions is spoken by our Lord of Himself. To dispute further as to the possible conditions with which it may be understood, or the possible limitations with which it may be used, is vain and idle cavilling. Here is a most exalted epithet ascribed to Jesus Christ, and if we are staggered by it, we are clearly out of harmony with the teaching of the beloved disciple touching the nature of his Master. But in point of fact, though it is true this particular term is peculiar to St. John just as it is peculiar to the Nicene Creed, yet the truth which it expresses is that to which the teaching of all the rest of Scripture leads up. It is not possible to examine carefully any one of the Gospels and observe attentively what our Lord tells us of Himself, and not see that the inference we are intended to draw is identical with that which St. John has explicitly commended to us. The direct assertions of the Gospels—not of one Gospel, but of all—are inconsistent with the notion that Jesus Christ was merely man, however high the position we may

be willing to assign Him in the scale of humanity.
These assertions are no less inconsistent with the
notion that Jesus Christ was not man but some
higher and intermediate kind of being between God
and man, but neither the one nor the other. Logically, therefore, the only conclusion at which we
can arrive is the conclusion of the whole of orthodox
Christendom, that He was both God and man. I
am sorry to have to use this word "orthodox," but
it is difficult to avoid the use of it. There are those,
of course, to whom it will mean nothing and to whom
it will carry no weight, as of course it will prove
nothing; but sooner or later we shall find ourselves
driven to decide who and what Jesus Christ was,
in what sense He was the Son of God, and in what
sense He was His only Son. It seems to me there
are but two courses open to us—we must either determine that He was some intermediate kind of being,
neither God nor man ; or we must acknowledge that
He was truly God and truly man. This, of course, is
dogmatic theology ; but how are we to escape from
it? We cannot escape from it. Until this dogmatic
issue is decided there are the most momentous
questions in abeyance. For example, shall we pray
to Jesus Christ or not? If we pray to Him and He
is anything less than God—that is, an intermediate
being it matters not how exalted—then we are
guilty of idolatry; for to pray to any one who is not
God, angel or archangel or mediator, is idolatry,
and can be nothing else than idolatry. If we pray to

Him and it is right to do so, it can only be because in one aspect of His being He is God. I say "in one aspect of His being" because we must never forget there is another. Jesus Christ is truly and completely man—in one aspect of His being He is only man; but He is also truly and completely God—in one aspect of His being He is only God. And thus it is that there is room for so many statements about Jesus Christ which shall carry with them the conviction that they are true, and yet shall seem to contradict other statements that are true likewise. Neither by itself is the whole truth—both are true and go to make up the integrity of the whole truth.

Essential, however, and important as I believe this dogmatic aspect of the matter to be, it is itself but one aspect of the truth, and that an aspect on which it is not right or healthy to dwell exclusively or to excess. Jesus Christ has told us something about Himself; He has told us that He is the only-begotten Son of God. If He has told us this, He must intend and desire us to believe it; He cannot regard it otherwise than with displeasure if we do not believe it; but still, after all, He does not wish us only to believe something about Him—He wishes us to *believe in* Him. If we *believe in* something about Him it is pretty clear that we have confounded believing something about Him with *believing in* Him. To believe in Him, as it seems to me, involves believing something, and, in fact, a great deal, about Him, even all that He has told us of Himself. In fact, I do not see how we can in any sense believe in Him and not believe a great deal about Him; but I am sure we may believe a great deal about Him, may take a delight in repeating the strong expressions of the Nicene and Athanasian Creeds, perfectly accurate in themselves, and yet not believe in Him.

For why? Belief expresses that attitude of the mind which it can hold only with reference to the Infinite. It has nothing to do with the understanding or the reason, except so far as the sphere of its operation includes them as the greater includes the less; but it is distinct from them, and expresses the exercise of a separate and independent faculty. If, then, this is what belief is, the position or attitude of my mind with reference to the Infinite, it is clear that I cannot exercise belief in, or faith towards, Jesus Christ, unless He is Himself the Infinite, or unless I can find in Him an avenue to the Infinite. Now this is what He has told us over and over again about Himself implicitly in a thousand ways and explicitly when He has taken into His lips such a word as this— μονογενής (only-begotten). It is, therefore, mere subterfuge and cavilling when men say, as they sometimes do, that St. John's language is very different from that of the other Evangelists, that he claims more for Jesus Christ than they do, that it does not appear from them that Jesus claimed to be Divine, and the like, in order to avoid what they regard as the objectionable conclusions of theological language and ecclesiastical tradition about our blessed Lord. The real question is, Does He demand from us allegiance and fealty that we cannot give to man? Does He assign to Himself positions and offices that no man can hold? Does He use language which we cannot regard as other than ambiguous, if we may not be excused for understanding it in the way which the express declarations of St. John undeniably lead us to understand it? And I believe that to these questions there is and can be but one answer, if we are honest with ourselves, and deal honestly with the record.

But in order that we may the better see the bearing of this marvellous and mysterious epithet, let us observe what it is that our Lord tells us besides in the text. He says, *God so loved the world that He gave His only-begotten Son, that whosoever believeth in Him should not perish, but have everlasting life.* I do not know how other persons feel, but I can only say for myself that, after being wearied with the conflicting theories, arguments, speculations, and doctrines of men, there is the greatest possible relief, sweetness, and repose in the simple, childlike acceptance of such words as these. Here is a definite, explicit statement, perfectly intelligible and easy to be understood,—difficult to mistake or to misunderstand. Shall we accept it in its length and breadth, its simplicity and integrity, or shall we dispute about it and reject it?

God so loved the world. How was our Lord in

a position to make so distinct a statement unless
He had been one with the Father before all worlds
and was the only-begotten Son of God? Can we
trust the fulness of the statement if it is not authoritative? How can it be authoritative if Christ
had not authority to utter it? How could He have
authority to utter it if He was not what He said He
was? If He was not what He said He was, is not
that absolutely fatal to the truth of the statement
which He affirmed? For this, you observe, is not
one of those truths of which the evidence lies in
my sense of its being true. For I may have no
sense at all of its being true. I may be unable to
determine with myself whether or not God does love
the world. Sometimes I may fancy I can see that
He does; at other times, in the sight of appalling
calamities which are continually occurring when the
movement of His little finger might prevent them, I
may have serious doubts, and extremely painful
doubts, whether He cares at all about it; but at all
events, there can be nothing in me capable of de-
ciding whether or not God *did* love the world as it
is here said He did, except the acknowledgment that
that love is proved by the particular act referred
to, the acknowledgment of which act, on the same
principles, must itself depend upon my sense of its
being true, which, if adequate in my own particular
case, is certainly far from being adequate in all other
cases. Certainly we can know nothing about the
love of God unless we have cause to believe what

Jesus Christ told us about it, and we can have no such cause unless He had more ground for knowing than that very sense of truth in Himself which in us is shown to be inadequate to judge of Him. That is to say, unless He had a definite and distinct mission, which depended on something else than His conviction about it, we are literally and actually none the better for all that He has told us about God, because it may after all not be true, and on these principles can only be proved to be true by our sense of its truth.

Then how was this love shown? By God sending His only-begotten Son. Then clearly He was His only-begotten Son when He sent Him: He did not become His only-begotten Son by being sent, for that would be absurd, and a contradiction in terms. He who was naturally the Son of man would thus become the Son of God by being made the Son of man,—which is manifestly absurd; therefore He was the only-begotten Son when given and sent. Ponder this, I beseech you, and you will find yourselves, inevitably, in spite of yourselves, led upwards, through the avenue of Christ's humanity, to the boundless regions of God's infinity. Paradoxical as the language is—because all finite language on such matters must be inadequate—we are on the confines of the infinite when we come into contact with Christ.

Again, the love of God, we are told, was altogether without reference to the way in which it would be met. As a matter of fact we know how it was met.

But God loved that very world which was in darkness and misery, in sin and enmity, which required Christ to be sent, and was lost without Him. Thus we see that in no case was there anything to move this love. Had there been desert in the object of the love there would have been no need for the manner in which it was manifested. In every case, even in that of the beloved disciple, the love of God preceded the love of man. *We love Him because He first loved us.*[1] And as the love was without reference to the worthiness of the objects, so was it universal in its extent,—it embraced the whole world, for Christ was a gift to the whole world. And yet the whole world did not accept Christ, but where He was accepted there the love took effect, and evoked love in return, the love of which it was worthy. Only, in saying that the love took effect we must question our own language,—Was it accidental that it took effect, or was it intentional? None of the actions of God, least of all such actions as these, are accidental; it must therefore have been intentional. Wherever the love took effect there was the result of intention; but intention on the part of whom? If intention on our part, then our intention had the power of controlling the exercise of God's love. Impossible! *Are we stronger than He?*[2] Or is there anything, can there be anything, in us to make Him love us? Impossible again; for otherwise it could not be true that *we love Him because He first loved us.*

[1] 1 John iv. 19.   [2] 1 Cor. x. 22.

And here, verily, we approach a profound mystery—the operation and movement of the love of God ; a mystery into which we must not gaze too intently, or we shall be lost in perplexity and hopeless confusion. God loves the world. He loves especially those of the world who accept His Son. Does He love them because they accept Him, or do they accept Him because He loves them ? Certainly the latter ; but I think we may also say that He loves them because they accept Him, for that is the condition on which He virtually promises that they shall become recipients of His further love. *He so loved the world that He gave His only-begotten Son, that whosoever believed His love might not perish*—not believing the love wherewith he loved him—*but might have everlasting life;* that is, the living reception in himself of the Father's love, issuing in the interchange of love towards God, and of yet further love of God towards him.

To perish, then, we observe, it is only too obvious, is to be without love towards God, to be without any feeling of God's love towards us. Observe very carefully, not any general love towards us, but the particular and special love which was declared to be manifested in Christ. Unless, then, we believe that Jesus is the only-begotten Son, it is impossible that we can feel God's love in giving Him, for we shall not believe in the reality of the gift ; but our Lord declares that in this belief there consists the possession of everlasting life. Everlasting life is the response in the heart to the love of God which was manifested in giving Christ, which therefore is contingent upon belief in the Christ given. I do not see how we can escape from these conclusions. A certain definite belief about Christ is involved in that belief in Him which is the condition of eternal life. It cannot possibly be a matter of indifference what our particular personal opinions about Christ may be, certainly not if we literally accept the declarations of His own language. He is to be the means through which we apprehend the Infinite. We can, it is most true, apprehend the Infinite without Him, but then, it is only too evident we shall not be Christians, for to be Christians we must apprehend the Infinite through Christ. *No man cometh unto the Father but by Me.*[1] I am quite aware that there is, and always has been, and always must be, a vast amount of popular thought in direct defiance of this statement; but the question for us to determine is, whether the statement is to correct our thought, or whether our thought is to modify or to set aside the statement. If God is a Father in Christ, then it is perfectly evident that He is a Father in a totally different sense to any other; and if He is a Father in Christ, then it is plain that we can only appprehend this His fatherhood, in which His love is infinite, by seeking Him in and through the Son.

May it evermore be ours thus to seek Him, that

[1] John xiv. 6.

believing in Christ we may find Him more and more to be the sweetness of Divine love, and the centre of Divine life, and the fulness of Divine truth ; so that, bowing our hearts and minds before Him as the only-begotten Son, we may dwell with Him in the presence of the Father, and rejoice in the sunshine of His light and love.

IX.
OUR LORD.

*To them that are sanctified in Christ Jesus, called to be saints, with all that in every place call upon the name of Jesus Christ our Lord, both theirs and ours."—*1 COR. i. 2.

WE come now to the consideration of those words in the Creed, familiar and of universal occurrence as they are, which speak of Jesus Christ as *our Lord*. They are actually employed by St. Paul in this place, and he couples with them others which may either be taken as expanding them or as referring to the "every place" just before mentioned. That is to say, his words mean, "Jesus Christ is our Lord, and theirs too as well as ours;" or else, "The Epistle is addressed to all that call upon the name of Jesus Christ our Lord, whether in their country or in ours." The statement in the Creed really comes to the same thing whichever way we take the literal meaning of the words.

Jesus Christ belongs to others as well as ourselves, whether we are in this place or another, whether we are in this country or another, whether we are in this quarter of the globe another, whether we are in this hemisphere or another, whether we are in this world or another. The great thought, then, which is here brought before us is our unity and union in Jesus Christ. To us there is but one Lord, and because there is but one Lord we are one body in Christ.

This, then, is a very apposite truth for us to be reminded of upon St. Peter's Day,[1] when we commemorate the gifts and calling of an apostle whose name more than any other has been constituted a false centre of unity. The true and the only centre of unity is *our Lord*.

Let us see, then, what this implies.

Jesus Christ founded a Church. The Church consisted of believers in Him. Their belief in Him made them members of His Church. Their being members of His Church did not make them believers in Him, for it was only by believing in Him that they became members of His Church. This was perfectly true when the whole area of the Church was confined to the four or five disciples who were first called. And the truth of it did not alter when the area became of an indefinite extent. It is not altered now. The Church that Jesus Christ is now building up is the vast body of believers. According as we belong to that body, we belong to His Church; but no formal or outward membership with what is called His Church can constitute us members of that body, the only means of entrance is the moral act of faith.

For, let us clearly understand it, Jesus Christ did

[1] Preached on June 29, 1873.

not come to form a guild or corporation which was to be united by certain Masonic tokens of membership. Any one could have done that; I could have done it, you could have done it, hundreds have done it. Every city in this empire has such a guild or corporation. Jesus Christ came to do much more than this; He came to infuse into humanity a new, an original, an extraneous, a peculiar and unique moral influence; which He did by attaching men to Himself, by constituting Himself a new centre of unity. Before He came there existed various centres of unity. A monarch, a lawgiver, a statesman, a city or a country, constituted such a centre, and for a time men realised a certain unity in allegiance thereto. When Christ came He acted on the same principle, but He fulfilled it in a totally different way. He made infinite faith in His own person to be the bond of unity. It was thus that Peter became one with Christ. When he uttered his noble confession, *Thou art the Christ, the Son of the living God*, he passed out of himself and his old nature, and apprehended the new nature in Christ. Peter then became a saved man, and he continued a saved man by continuing to retain his hold on Christ. But he had nothing in himself which he found in Christ. He could not be to others what he had need for Christ to be to him. He could not give to others what he could only obtain by giving himself to Christ. He needed life, neither more nor less than life, and this he found only in Christ, for he said himself, *Lord, to whom* shall we go?[1] Thou hast the words of eternal life. That confession shows Peter destitute—himself hungering and thirsting; it shows him likewise apprehending all that he wanted in Christ, dependent upon Christ for it. And what we see to be true of Peter is obviously true also of the Church. The Church—that is, the aggregate of believers like Peter—is in need like him, and dependent like him for the supply of that life which is only to be found in Christ.

It is sufficiently clear, therefore, that to seek for that in the Church which the Church itself cannot have except as she finds it in Christ, must be a fatal error. And yet this is the error which the entire Church of Rome notoriously commits, and of which multitudes among ourselves are but dimly conscious. People seem to think that Christ has delegated certain functions and privileges to the body of believers which He has bestowed upon no individual member of the body manifestly and confessedly, not upon Peter himself. But if no one member of the body taken separately can be conceived of having that in himself which he must either go to Christ for or else not stand in need of a Saviour, how is it possible that we can find in a multitude that which is seen to exist in no unit of the multitude? If every unit of the multitude is devoid of life, how can the multitude itself possess life, or how can we find life in union with a multitude every member of which stands as

[1] John vi. 68.

much in need of it as we ourselves? We can have no union with Christ by ourself having an apparent, visible union with those who belong to Him. We can have no union with Christ by being in union with Peter, unless that union with Peter is the result of union with Christ. Union with Peter may or may not lead to union with Christ. Unless it does, it is absolutely worthless in itself. Least of all may it be substituted for union with Christ. As Peter is not Christ, so neither can the office of Peter be confounded with that of Christ, nor the office of the Church which Peter represents. Christ proposes Himself as the one centre of unity and source of life, and we can invent no other.

This, however, is so sublime and ethereal a truth that the ordinary mind cannot grasp it. We want successive chains and gradations, steps and links, leading from the lowest to the highest; we cannot soar all at once into the pure ether of heaven; and if we do, we find it difficult to breathe there, and consequently we take refuge in the facile thought that accommodation must have been provided for the weak and halting on their way to Christ. But all this is but a confirmation of the great truths, *Except a man be born again he cannot see the kingdom of God;*[1] and, *The natural man receiveth not the things of the Spirit of God, for they are foolishness unto him, neither can he know them, because they are spiritually discerned.*[2] We want that very faculty

[1] John iii. 3.   [2] 1 Cor. ii. 14.

of sight which Christ alone can give, that very gift of life which Christ alone can bestow.

But, then, ample provision is made for all that we want in Jesus Christ Himself; He is the sufficient as well as the only Saviour. For example, the truth that He is our Lord, in which this is implied, is developed out of and flows from the truth we last considered, that He is the only-begotten Son of God. That truth enthrones Him on the summit of the universe; it constitutes Him supreme over all, God blessed for ever. In that capacity He is the exalted One who is equal with the highest, and is Lord of all. But, then, from His very exaltation He is unapproachable, like the sun, whose glory we behold, but dare not gaze upon.

Besides all this, He stands in a relation to us— He is our Lord; that is, the head or lord of our humanity, for this is a title expressly relating to our human nature; He is its natural—or shall I say supernatural?—head, for in Him the natural and the supernatural are one and at one; they are blended in Him and reconciled in Him. Mark that. We feel and know that He was naturally man, like ourselves; He was not a phantom, He was a real man, eating and drinking, wearying, sorrowing, suffering, toiling, weeping, bleeding, dying, like ourselves. But we have gazed upon Him to little purpose if we have not seen in Him something more than all this, if we have not seen through every action of His natural life the supernatural betraying and revealing itself. Is it possible that we can gaze on Him and not believe in Him? is it possible that we can survey Him with cold, critical, lack-lustre eyes, and calculate with supercilious indifference the probabilities of the claims He put forward being valid,—of His being what He said He was? Oh, surely not! And yet we cannot in any sense believe in him unless we see and confess that He is the very incarnation of the supernatural, that there is no character in all history at once so natural and yet so supernatural as His. Then assuredly He is our Lord, for we can nowhere find any one so truly lordly as He is. He virtually had every one at His command when on earth, whether it was the moneychangers whom He put to flight in the Temple; or the Scribes and Pharisees who brought to Him the woman taken in adultery, but whom He made to feel that they were none of them without sin; or the band of men and officers who, when they came to apprehend Him, started backward and fell to the ground at the simple question, Whom seek ye? or Pilate, the representative of Imperial Rome, with her legions and her lictors, when upon being reminded that he could have no power at all against Him except it were given him from above, forthwith sought to release Him, notwithstanding the clamour of the people. On these and a hundred other occasions He manifested the existence in Himself of that fountain of authority which compels an involuntary recognition and is the inalienable birthright of those who are born to rule. Who is the more lordly character,

Christ suffering on the cross, with the twelve legions of angels standing by with their hands upon their sword hilts, but bidden not to draw ; or Napoleon inditing despatches on the bloody but victorious field, with thousands of the dying and the dead around him, unheeded and uncared for ? The character of the lordly conqueror, whose source of irresistible might is his victorious sword, is nowhere in history more conspicuous than in the great Napoleon ; but it pales for grandeur and for dignity, for simple absolute lordliness, before the character of the Son of Man, whether you behold Him at the grave of Lazarus or see Him dying on the cross. Search through the annals of the world and the records of many nations, and you shall find nowhere any man of whom you can say so unhesitatingly, so incontestably, " This man is the first-begotten of our race, this is our natural lord, this is the rightful heir to the throne of humanity, this is our legitimate Head and King." For there is no one so truly man, and there is no one because so truly man who is so undeniably Divine.

And thus it is that because of the genuine Lordship of Christ we all have an equal right in Him: He is the natural and unique Head of our race, the crown of our common humanity ; and therefore, because He is our Lord, no one has a greater share in Him than another, because that humanity of which He is the Head is not a thing that admits of degrees, it is the common attribute of all, and none can monopolise a larger share of it than another. We do indeed say that such and such a one is more or less of a man, but this is merely because he exhibits more or less of the ideal attributes of a man, not because his human nature differs from that of others, because if it did it would not be human. And, therefore, the queen upon her throne, or the nobles in her court, can have no larger share in, no nearer interest in, or access to Christ our Lord than the meanest beggar in our streets, or pauper in our workhouses. The only difference of share is that which can be measured by the difference of faith. If you have more faith in Christ, no matter what your outward circumstances are or inward state may be, then you have a larger interest in Him, a larger share in Him; but not otherwise. And it is because He is thus our Lord that we can each go to Him with our several wants, with our varied sins, and claim our share in Him; it is here that we can lay our hand upon the unapproachable and touch the inaccessible. We want no Church, no organised society, no intermediate agencies of any kind to enable us to do this; the more we let the mind rest upon these things, the more likely we are to let them come between us and Christ. The only right we have to go to Him, is the right of that humanity of ours of which He is the Head, and the only encouragement we need, and the only claim we can advance is the fact that He has called us to come to Him. There is one simple solitary link which unites us to Him, one only means by which we possess ourselves of Him and pass into the actual personal enjoyment of all the privileges and blessings of His humanity; and that is, faith. Peter himself was no nearer to Christ, was not more truly one with Christ, than you and I may be if we like Peter believe in Jesus; and the Church, of all times and countries, was never, is not, and never can be more near to Christ or more truly one with Him than you and I may be if we, by believing in Jesus, pass into the innermost circle of His invisible Church. Only, let us beware of the fatal error of interposing the Church between ourselves and Christ. The Church is not a mediator, cannot become a mediator. The Church without Christ is an aggregate of lifeless units, and the Church with Christ is but an aggregate of the same units, each of which lives according as it receives life, not from the Church, but from Christ. Receiving life from Christ, it becomes a living member of the Church; but not by being a member of the Church, howsoever defined, does it receive life from Christ; for this life is a moral and not a mechanical gift, and the Church has no power to give that which it is Christ's alone to bestow, in virtue of His being the revealed Head of our humanity.

Now sundry important truths are deduced like corollaries from all this. First, as the head is one so the body is one. The unity is a fact; we cannot bring it about, we can only realise it. Men are trying in the present day to effect and bring about a formal unity; sundry associations exist for that purpose, which attempt upon this or that basis of general agreement and sympathy to create a unity. The intention is laudable but the principle is mistaken. We cannot create unity. Christ has done it. He has revealed Himself as the Centre of unity, the solitary Head of our nature. We become one with each other by becoming one with Him and realising our union with Him. If we are built upon Him, then we must partake of His unity, whether or not our angles fit closely into the angles of our brethren. That stone which is built into the one foundation at the east, is virtually one with those at the west and the north and the south, though they are all alike separated in position and will never be brought together. Diverse as their functions, their forms, their positions may be, they are one in the unity of the building; which is an essential unity, that nothing short of total destruction can destroy. So, then, those who believe in Christ are inevitably one with each other, because one in Him, though their nations and languages, their times and countries, their modes of thought and sentiments may widely differ. He Himself becomes responsible for their unity, which is constituted indestructibly in him. But if they are not personally united to him no efforts of theirs can create their unity.

Lastly, the very object and idea for which we are thus associated with Christ our Lord is that we may become partakers of His holiness. There is indeed no true life in Christ without a holiness correspondent. This is the family likeness by which all the children of the King are characterised and known ; this is the title of royalty by which Christ as the King of humanity will be always acknowledged among men, because He is declared to be the Son of God with power according to the spirit of holiness. Let us seek to realise our union with Christ our Lord by faith in Him, and our union with each other by our union with Him, and then strive to exhibit to our fellow-men that likeness to our Master which consists in being holy as He is holy.

X.

WHO WAS CONCEIVED BY THE HOLY GHOST.

The Holy Ghost shall come upon thee, and the power of the Highest shall overshadow thee: therefore also that holy thing which shall be born of thee shall be called the Son of God.—LUKE i. 35.

THIS is the Scriptural statement of that which the Creed expresses in the words, " Who was conceived by the Holy Ghost, born of the Virgin Mary." St. Luke tells us that it was a statement made by the angel Gabriel. If there are such beings as angels—which the materialistic philosophy of the present day may perhaps hesitate to admit—and if they have ever taken part in the affairs of men, we can readily believe that they would do so at the birth of Him who is the Lord of angels and of men, and on such an occasion as the one which is here referred to. It is, then, we must at once see, perfectly hopeless to get rid of the supernatural in dealing with the life of our blessed Lord. Rather, He is Himself our escape from the perplexities attending the definition of the natural and the supernatural, by combining in Himself the characteristics of both. In Him we see the two, not in collision, but in, so to say, natural harmony. If our Lord's birth was after the manner of men, destruction is laid at the root of all that He ever did and said; if it was not, the door is forthwith opened to the admission of the supernatural, which prepares us for its presence elsewhere, and we may then thankfully confess that we have known the incarnation of the Son of God by the message of an angel. It is no doubt perfectly true that nearly every one in our assemblies may reverently and devoutly hold the Christian faith on this and similar points, and never care to contemplate the alternative; but forasmuch as we know there are at times, at any rate, those present in them with whom it is otherwise, and because it is not seldom laid as a reproach against us clergymen that we go along in the rut and take a one-sided view of things, it may be as well to show that we can contemplate the position of faith and *no*-faith, and that we are not blind to the difficulties to which faith exposes us, and from which it can leave no one free.

Now the birth of Jesus Christ introduced into the family of man a new and a divine principle. This is too much lost sight of. The philosopher estimates Jesus Christ by what He did. Philosophy takes the measure of Him according to the wisdom of His recorded teaching and the greatness of the movement which He originated. But Holy Scripture attaches an importance to two perfectly natural incidents in our Lord's career, which in fact the Creed places in juxtaposition, of which philosophy takes no account; and these are, His birth and His death. As Christians, we are bound to believe that the mere fact of our Lord's birth was, in some sense at least, the salvation of man,—not as containing in itself the pledge and promise of the life which was to follow, with all its saving consequences, but as being by its own virtue the commencement of salvation. And what do I mean by this? I mean that which I shall try to work out in the present lecture. The Scriptural account of our physiological and ethnological constitution is that all nations of men are made of one blood. Science has not, at present, disproved that, nor is it likely to disprove it, for even allowing—which is the utmost that science can ask us to allow—that the human race instead of springing from one centre sprang from many, what have we granted then? Certainly not that the human race of which we speak and cannot help speaking as one is after all not one. Does any one doubt that any two units of this nation, taken where you please, of the best blood and the basest, are not essentially one now, though it is impossible to conceive the actual case in which the blood of both flowed in the veins of the same individual man. Is not this unity something altogether independent of the real genealogical origin? So that it was not virtually greater at the distance of two generations from the actual common origin than at the distance of five hundred, that it will not be less in the descendants of both a thousand years hence than it is at the present moment. It is something more than community of descent to which we owe our common humanity. Our great poet teaches us this when he says, " Hath not a Jew eyes, hath not a Jew hands, organs, dimensions, senses, affections, passions, fed with the same food, hurt with the same weapons, subject to the same diseases, healed by the same means, warmed and cooled by the same winter and summer, as a Christian is?" Our common humanity consists, not in the continuity of origin, proved or disproved, but in the continuity of all which makes up man ; and this we share with the Maori and the Hottentot as much as we do with the Saxon and the Celt. The blood which flows in the veins of all, whether or not it was originally one, is after all human blood, can be physically identified as human blood, and is so far an evidence of union, whether or not it is historically the basis of unity. And of this blood the commonest and the most universal characteristic is its transmission from sire to son. Science has given us no instance, professes not to give us any instance, disdains to give us any instance, in which this transmission has been broken. Revelation, historical revelation, has given us one instance, and only one. So that even granting that the theory of evolution held good as regards the historic origin of man, revelation, historic revelation, would propose to our faith one solitary instance in which the links of evolution were sundered, and that instance the person and the birth of Christ.

Now this is proposed to our faith; it is utterly and

hopelessly beyond the reach of reason alike to prove and to comprehend it. But yet, at the same time, no one can say that it is unreasonable; on the other hand, it appeals in the highest degree to reason by the very magnitude of the results which, if true, it would accomplish. For then you would have introduced into humanity—what we cannot but acknowledge is our common humanity—an entirely new element which had never been imparted before ; you would have communicated not only the human but the *Divine* element.

And now see the necessity for this. There is something common to us besides blood, and something for which evolution cannot account whether or not it accounts for community of blood, and something which is strangely connected with this community of blood, something which, if not seated in the blood, is mysteriously associated therewith. For example, we know that the blood is the seat of life, that, in the words of Scripture, *the life is the blood ;*[1] and in the life is bound up the very germ of personality, so far as our personality is dependent on and expressed by our living, sentient humanity ; so that all the marvellous complexities of the will, and the reason, and the affections are wrapped up in that word "life," which is intimately and inseparably associated with that word "blood," so that if you shed the blood you shed the life,—you dissolve the connexion with humanity of the will, and the reason, and the affec-

[1] Gen. x. 4 ; Lev. xvii. 11.

tions, because you dissolve the integrity of the man. What is there, then, which is generally, universally associated with us all in this life, and therefore in this blood, which is common to us all? It is, in one word, sin, Sin pervades our life, is seated in our blood. None will deny that sin pervades our life, or, if any deny it, sin itself will testify against them. But, more than this, sin infects our nature; it corrupts and taints our very blood. We cannot wash our hands clean from sin, as Pilate sought in vain to do. No moral lustrations will purify us from sin. Fasting will not eradicate it. Penance will not destroy the tendency thereto. Prayers and sacraments will not abolish the natural proclivity. Confession, which some imagine to be a panacea, will but develop it. We cannot get rid of it, because we possess a sinful nature; and the nature which I have my father had before me, my son will have after me, and so on even to the years of countless generations. We do not say that the nature develops itself, that it progresses or recedes,—we do not undertake to pronounce upon that; but we say, and we appeal to the testimony of facts, that the nature has been, and is, and will remain, essentially sinful and corrupt, that the sin is rooted in the will, which is immediately connected with the life, which is intimately associated with the blood. And it is obvious that if this nature is the nature of all,—for though many may differ in the degrees of sin, yet there is none who is not sinful,—

then no one who shares the nature can redeem or deliver or purify the nature which he shares. He is incompetent to redeem himself, and how can he redeem his brother? I use the word "redeem" in no technical sense, but simply as expressing that riddance of the nature from sin which the sinful nature is obviously incompetent to effect. But given the admission into our nature of a new element, given the admixture with our blood of a sinless because a Divine principle, and you have, at any rate, a conceivable passage opened out for the deliverance of the nature from sin. For in one particular case the entail of sin is cut off, the connecting links are sundered. Here isolation is at last effected. At this point sin could not enter, did not enter into our nature. Man felt that if he could only begin afresh much might be done towards redemption; but he never could achieve this beginning—the power of old association was too mighty. This has been felt and exemplified time after time in the individual, and it was virtually the consciousness of the race. But One was revealed to us who had another consciousness, and in whom every individual could find his own consciousness renewed and regenerated; and this was He whose birth was announced by the angel Gabriel, even He who was conceived by the Holy Ghost and born of the Virgin Mary.

Thus far, then, you see that the Christian faith proposes to our apprehension a distinct and definite fact which took place in human history, namely, the communication to the race of a new element or principle, in the person of Christ, who should henceforth be the unit of attraction, cohesion, centralisation, the foundation of a new society, the head of a new family. Not, however, as heretofore, to be perpetuated by the ever-recurring relation of sire and son, but by the ever-recurring repetition of the moral act of regeneration, through contact by faith with the sinless person of the Son of Man. It is in the highest degree essential to understand this. If we have not a sinless Christ to believe in, we have no one to believe in. If we have not a Christ to believe in, in whom there was not the taint of a sinful nature, then the death-blow is struck at all our hopes. There was in Him perfect humanity, but humanity sinless because perfect, humanity that was in its origin without the taint of sin, and which in its immediate contact with sin had asserted and proved its freedom from it and power over it.

But then the great question arises, How do we become partakers of this humanity? how can it be communicated to us and become ours? In answer to this question two theories have been advanced, which should be clearly distinguished. The one theory is this, that the sacraments ordained by Christ were ordained by Him for the purpose of communicating and extending the effects of His participation in our nature; that so the baptised man is metaphorically grafted into the body of Christ, and in the Holy Eucharist partakes of that spiritual body into which he was in baptism grafted; that thus there is, through the sacraments, a direct communication of the renewed nature of Christ. The objection to this theory is that in it metaphor appears to be substituted for reality. In baptism there is nothing that answers to the metaphor grafting, unless it be spiritual union, and in the Eucharist there is nothing that answers to participation unless it be spiritual communication. But we cannot have spiritual communication except by spiritual means. Now the water and the bread and the wine, whatever else they are, certainly are not spirit, even though they be the channels, or the tokens, of spiritual communication. We have the highest authority for saying that *it is the spirit that quickeneth; the flesh*— that is, all that is short of or other than the spirit— *profiteth nothing*.[1] And I think we must acknowledge that it is alien to the entire teaching of Christ to understand that to be done by a succession of sensible means, by the setting in motion of a visible machinery which must after all in its method of operation and its effects be of the nature of a moral influence. And therefore we are bound to say that even admitting this theory to be defensible—and it depends for its truth rather upon subtlety of argument, and upon a particular interpretation of the word "spiritual," which appears to assign it an intermediate position, between the moral and material, that namely of an inappreciable *tertium quid*, than upon the simplicity

[1] John vi. 63.

of scriptural demonstration; but accepting it as theoretically correct, it must certainly derive all its real virtue from the other theory, which, in professing to supplement, it too often supplants. And this theory is very simple ; no less simple than the direct statements of Scripture itself, namely that we become partakers of the benefits of Christ's humanity, and the virtue of that humanity is actually communicated to us, by faith in Him.

Now as it is admitted on all hands that the sacraments without faith are ineffectual, we can only say that that which alone can give efficacy to the sacraments must be more potent as a means than they. The man who communicates without faith, communicates to no purpose—he does not become a partaker of Christ's humanity. Throw into his communion the indispensable element of faith, and he becomes a partaker of Christ by faith, not by his participation in the visible elements which are intended to assure him of that union which he already enjoys through faith. Believe me, brethren, that so far from deprecating the sacraments by any such notions, we cannot truly appreciate them till we become experimentally acquainted with what is implied by communion with Christ by faith. We enter into direct personal union with the Sinless One, into actual participation in the blessings of His renewed humanity, and into conscious oneness with Him, when by faith we can say, "Thou, Lord, art mine." If we can come to Him and say, " There is,

Lord, nothing in me but sin, and death the wages of sin : I come to Thee to be rid of sin, and to have life, even abundant and eternal life in Thee. Thou art my perfected and restored humanity, for Thou art that Son of Man, who is the Son of God. In Thee I find that which I can find nowhere else, least of all in myself. In Thee there is righteousness and peace and joy in the Holy Ghost, for in Thee I am one with the Father, even as Thou in Thyself hast made the Father one with me," then we shall find, as thousands have found before us, that our faith hath made us whole. This will be our blessing and our reward ; we shall know that we do indeed live because He lives and we are partakers of His life.

But this mighty change is a moral and not a mechanical change ; it cannot be brought about by participation in any ordinances, by clinging to any means which come between us and the end they signify; it is a change that can alone be produced, as the first entrance of the Divine element into our corrupt human nature was effected, by the overshadowing of the Holy Ghost. Spirit alone can act on spirit. The only way in which prayers, or communions, or anything else can be made effectual to our salvation is by our being united to the Saviour, which union is effected by the Holy Ghost through faith. The person of Jesus Christ is the depositary of the Holy Spirit, if we may so say; through union with Christ we have union with the Spirit, and through the guidance of the Spirit we have union with Christ. There is an appearance here of circular motion, but it is of a kind analogous to that by which the earth moves round the sun. Jesus Christ is our Sun of Righteousness; and if we believe in Him and give ourselves to Him for life or for death, and serve Him in truth, we shall find the harmony of all the varied and opposite points upon the circumference in the unity of the centre, and in our union therewith.

XI.

SUFFERED UNDER PONTIUS PILATE.

Pilate therefore took Jesus, and scourged Him.—JOHN xix. 1.

THE ancient confession of faith known as the Apostles' Creed has this advantage over every formula of a similar kind,—that it is a summary of facts and not of doctrines. There is little or nothing in it, strictly speaking, of a dogmatic character. It is for the most part a simple record of historic events. And more particularly is this the case with what it affirms of our Lord Himself. We are not taught some special theological tenets about Him, but merely the bare incidents of His human life. No doubt in many quarters this is regarded as a great defect in the Creed. For myself, I believe it to be the highest merit, and the principal cause that the Creed has lasted for so long a time. It would long ago have passed away had it not been for the wisdom and tenacity with which it had seized upon the more prominent facts of our Lord's existence, and presented them as the all-important matters of belief.

And thus, for instance, after having, in no ambiguous terms, stated the Christian conviction as to who Jesus'

Christ was, it proceeds immediately to say that He suffered under Pontius Pilate. It is this brief but pregnant truth that we are to consider to-day. You must observe, therefore, that the Creed does not tell us *why* our Lord suffered; it presents no theory for our acceptance to explain the necessity of His suffering; it propounds no scheme setting forth the consequences, actual or supposed, of His having suffered, —it is content merely to enunciate the cold, frigid, jejune and barren fact that He did suffer. Many probably would have wished it had been more explicit. But so it is.

You will, however, upon a moment's consideration, at once see that whatever may have been the reasons for our Lord's suffering, or the consequences of His having suffered, all these must gather round and centre in the fact itself that He suffered. Let the reasons be never so valid which made it needful for Him to suffer, these would all come to nothing if the suffering was unreal or unhistoric. Let the consequences which were supposed to follow be what they might, these also would fade away completely if the act or event of suffering had not happened. And, therefore on every ground the truth to be set in the foremost place was not some theory about the suffering, but the fact itself that suffering was undergone.

Pilate therefore took Jesus and scourged Him. That was an incident in our Lord's suffering,— which suffering, be it remembered, the Creed distinguishes from the crucifixion which followed. Let us try, then, to concentrate our minds upon this one point—Jesus Christ suffered: He suffered under Pontius Pilate.

It is not a little remarkable that all the sweetness which is associated in our Lord's name is centred, not in the divinity which was veiled in human flesh, not in the majesty which He ascended into the heavens to share, not in the throne which He forsook in order that He might resume it, not in the miracles of power which He wrought when on earth, but in this single fact that He suffered. And it is no less true that the sufferings of other men, though they may elicit our sympathy and call forth our compassion, are yet not regarded in themselves as elements of attractiveness. People who are continually obtruding their own misfortunes or sufferings, are certainly not those who are most eagerly sought after. The world at large shrinks from contact with adversity, and finds no sweetness in sorrow. But it is quite otherwise with the sufferings of Jesus Christ. There is in them an undefinable element of attractiveness and sweetness—so marvellously true are His own marvellous words, *And I, if I be lifted up, will draw all men unto me.*[1] Though there may be many who pass the suffering Jesus by unheeded, yet where He is cared for, there it is the sufferings He endured for which men care.

There are certain characters in history which claim our affection because of their misfortunes.

[1] John xii. 32.

For example, I suppose most persons in the present day, whatever may be their political bias, feel a certain degree of affection for Charles I., when they regard him on the side of his suffering rather than his policy. "Pity melts the mind to love," and the human heart, when mindful of its own liability to sorrow, is apt to be drawn out in sympathy towards those who suffer, and to feel a tenderness for the unfortunate which is not felt for others; and yet in all these cases it is not the sorrows but the sorrowful that we feel for. We love the sufferers on account of their sorrows; the mere contemplation of the suffering itself gives no pleasure. Now it is quite otherwise with Jesus, and the sufferings of Jesus. For example, we dare not say that we are moved with compassion for our blessed Lord. We dare not presume to approach Him with anything like the sentiment of pity. In His human lifetime we never find Him asking for anything like sympathy, and certainly His historical character is one to which we cannot venture to offer the tribute of condolence. It is so sublime that it says to us, *Draw not nigh hither: put off thy shoes from off thy feet, for the place whereon thou standest is holy ground.* And yet, withal, His sufferings have an attractiveness in themselves. They never repel us; they never produce in the mind anything which answers to satiety. We may turn away from them we may come like the Levite and look at them and pass by on the other side, but the more we contemplate them the more they fill our mind with sweetness. It is undeniable that in this respect the sorrows of Jesus differ from those of all others, as does the effect also which the contemplation of them produces on the mind. In the history of the human sensibilities the sufferings of Jesus Christ have produced an entirely new and original phenomenon, which has no parallel elsewhere. And when we attempt to analyse this sentiment, or enquire into its nature and its meaning, we find that it arises not on account of the person who endured the sufferings, but on their relation to ourselves. We feel that we cannot approach Jesus Christ with anything like condolence, partly because He does not stand in need of our pity, and partly because of His intense exaltation of character.

At the time when the beloved sovereign of this nation was smitten with that terrible stroke which left her desolate and a widow, it was often remarked that there was an element in her grief which was lacking in that of all others, who might be smitten as she was, in that the eminence of her position left her in unapproachable solitude. Where could the friend be found, who, as an equal, could draw near with the message of consolation? If this was in any degree true of her, how much more true must it be of Jesus. And, yet again, here also was the strongest possible contrast, because she was in sore need of sympathy, but was debarred from the access of it in consequence of her exalted rank; whereas He, although pre-eminent in suffering, no less than in exaltation, had, strictly speaking, no need of that which His creatures were utterly unable to bestow, while at the same time He was literally in the very extremest need. And thus, we are told that while the chosen partners of His sufferings, and witnesses of His agony were asleep, or heavy with sleep, *there appeared an angel unto Him from heaven strengthening Him.*[1] Surely it was this very element of solitude in our Lord's sufferings which rendered them transcendent in their intensity.

We were led, then, on Sunday last, to see that there was that in His origin which necessarily separated Him from all those whose nature He assumed. Needful, however, as it is to lay fast hold of this truth, it is no less needful to grasp its correlative and opposite truth. And the declaration of the Creed that He suffered under Pontius Pilate, is calculated to help us in doing this.

For what is there that at once and in a moment reduces all men to a common level like suffering? Suffering is the demonstration of equality. The wise man dieth as the fool. The rich man quails before the agony of pain like the poor. Death, said the poet of the Augustan age, smites with his undiscriminating footstep the hovels of paupers and the towers of kings. If there is one thing which gives the lie to our selfish isolation and proud exclusiveness and makes us one, it is community of suffering. But community of suffering does more than this; it

[1] Luke xxii. 43.

not only makes us one, it not only compels us, as it were, at the point of the bayonet, to surrender at discretion, and forego our claim to a fictitious and delusive superiority, but it also shows that we are one. Whence this aching of the heart, this racking of the brain, this writhing of the limbs, this troubling of the soul, which we all feel and shrink from, but because we are all made of one dust, to which, being heirs of the same mortality, we shall all return? We suffer alike because we are made alike, we die alike because we have sinned alike. There is not only community of origin but community of end; and the community of end shows the community of need, and the community of need shows the unity of nature.

Now apply all this to the sufferings of Christ. If Christ suffered, He was one with those who suffer. He was scourged, crowned with thorns, pierced with nails, rent with a spear. Was there no suffering in all this? He was mocked, jeered at, spat upon, reviled: He *endured such contradiction of sinners against Himself.* Was there no suffering in all this? The more delicate the organism, the more acute the suffering. It could not be but that His organism, being most refined and delicate, was most acutely sensitive. It could not be, therefore, but that He suffered. But further being what He was, shall we say that there was no suffering in the all but universal rejection which He met with among men? Was

[1] Heb. xii. 3.

there no suffering in the agony and bloody sweat, which was His night-long preparation for the dreadful morning of torture and death with which His earthly career was closed? Was there no suffering in the bitter cry, *Eli, Eli, lama sabachthani,* with which, having witnessed the flight of those nearest and dearest to Him, He endured as a true man, and the Son of Man, the desertion of His Father on account of sin? Yes, verily, here in the person of Jesus Christ you find the perfection of suffering intensified and sublimated, without one redeeming element of mitigation, the fulness of a bitter cup without dilution or diminution anywhere. In all our sufferings there is generally some bypath along which we can approach to the goal which is fixed unalterably in our just deserts; but here it is otherwise, and we can but confess with the dying thief, *We indeed justly, for we receive the due reward of our deeds; but this man hath done nothing amiss.*[1]

Here, then, there is suffering in the perfection of its refinement and purity, and the perfection of the suffering showed the unity of nature in the sufferer with those who suffer. He showed conclusively that He felt with us. He was one with us in suffering, for had He not been one with us He could not have suffered. But because His sufferings are so refined and purified, because there is discernible in them no trace of sin or self-reproach, none of the smitings or rebukes of conscience, therefore it is that they are

[1] Luke xxiii. 41.

endued with an inexpressible sweetness. We cannot presume to pity Him, but we can love His sorrows. We dare not think of compassionating Him, but we can adore His sufferings. We may seek to find our fellowship in them, and finding our fellowship in them we can adore Him.

For it is through the relation that His sufferings have to us that we taste their sweetness. As long as the sorrows and sufferings of Christ are regarded with indifference, as things at a distance, they have no effect upon us ; it is only when we find in them a true link of connection with ourselves that they become potent and effectual. And their potency consists in this, that they take away sin. *Christ*, we are told, *hath once suffered for sins;*[1] *He died for our sins according to the Scriptures.*[2] The Creed has not embodied this truth, because it is mainly careful of the fact. The more we contemplate the fact, the more we shall find ourselves at a loss to account for it, the more we shall find ourselves face to face with a profound mystery. Why did Christ suffer? Suffering is inexplicable except on the supposition of guilt. Suffering must either imply guilt or else it cannot be suffering. Pain implies the presence of a disturbing element, or else it is only another form of pleasure. But intense pain is practically, if not philosophically, the antithesis of pleasure ; and so suffering, if it be suffering, can only be traced home to a source which flows from guilt. But in the sufferings of

[1] 1 Peter iii. 18.   [2] 1 Cor. xv. 4.

Christ we lose ourselves in the search for a source of guilt. We must either say that in Him was no sin, or we must say that He justly suffered. Then if we cannot trace suffering in Him to a cause of sin, we must explain it as the remedy of sin.

And this is where we discover its great sweetness. As we taste the sufferings of Christ and feel their sweetness, we lose the sense and the taste of sin, we find therein the antidote of the bane. We find that they have an unexplained and inexplicable moral connection with human sin, and the connection is that of the remedy for it. Given the fact of Christ's sufferings, which the Creed proclaims, we must either acknowledge that they are like all other sufferings, or else are unlike them. If they are like them, then there is personal sin directly connected with them, and they were the consequence of personal sin in Christ, which God forbid; if they are unlike them, they are unlike only in this, that whereas all other sufferings more or less directly flow from sin, these sufferings flow against sin, to counteract, redeem, and cancel it. And this is what they do,—though that they do it is a matter of faith, and not of demonstration. We may believe that Jesus Christ suffered under Pontius Pilate, but that bare fact will be barren in ourselves unless we know and believe that He suffered for *us*. This is the way in which the belief of the fact affects us unto life and salvation, but it cannot do so unless it is a fact. And therefore we say that He suffered under Pontius Pilate, because that is the point by which the fact is fixed in the history of the world. We know when Pontius Pilate lived, and who he was, and whence he came, and whither he went, and as every fact in human history is in order of time, and sequence of events fixed by its relation to other events and facts, so with the fact of Christ's suffering. That took place during the time when Pontius Pilate was the governor who represented Tiberius Cæsar at Jerusalem. He was the imperial viceroy or lord-lieutenant, and under his viceroyalty Jesus Christ suffered. It is a simple matter of history, attested by a variety of independent witnesses and events, that cannot be gainsaid. In those days the man Jesus Christ as a man suffered. Those were the days of His suffering. He then had taken our humanity, and was sharing our sufferings.

From that commonplace visible fact which takes its place among the other commonplace facts of this very commonplace, and every day world flows the unseen fact of our redemption. Destroy the one fact and the other is destroyed ; but you cannot destroy the one fact, and therefore the other is indestructible. Christianity is a religion, the roots of which are planted deep in the soil of this sinstricken earth, but the effects of it are felt in heaven. It is like a tower, of which the foundation is laid deep down in the solid rock, but the top of it reaches to heaven. Of old men tried to rear such a tower, but they could not rear it, and even now from time to time they try and try again, but they cannot succeed, for God hath reared the only tower, which He hath ordained as a refuge for the sons of men, and that tower is the person of His Son, who having His roots in the natural soil of our humanity, and His foundation in the solid rock of human history, hath nevertheless ascended into the heavens as our representative and redeemer. We have the abiding witness of His being and having been one with us in the record of His sufferings, which He suffered under Pontius Pilate, when He was scourged, and pierced, blasphemed, and spit upon, reviled, rejected, and set at nought. And in the assurance that we have, that these sufferings were on our behalf and for our sins, we have the proof established and confirmed that our sins have been forgiven, and that through His sufferings we have been redeemed. And thus, in all our sufferings for a brief space here on earth, we have the confident hope, if we belong to Him and have Him with us in them, that we through them shall be raised eventually to triumph and rejoice with Him in heaven.

XII.

WAS CRUCIFIED.

And it was the third hour, and they crucified Him.—MARK xv. 25.

THE Apostles' Creed is very full and circumstantial in its reference to the termination of our Lord's earthly career, which is the subject of no less than five separate statements : " He suffered under Pontius Pilate, was crucified, dead, and buried ; He descended into hell." Each of these incidents is worthy of separate and independent consideration. To-day, we have to consider the statement, "Was Crucified." Here, again, we are dealing with the simple fact, which must of necessity be the essence and kernel of any doctrine that may be based upon it. And of this fact there is the fullest possible proof from the concise words of the historian Tacitus, *supplicio affectus erat*,[1] to the elaborate and detailed narratives of the four evangelists. The statement of the text, however, *And it was the third hour, and they crucified Him*, has the appearance of being in collision with the corresponding statement of St.

[1] Ann. xv. 44.

John, "*And it was the preparation of the Passover, and about the sixth hour, and he saith unto the Jews, Behold your king.*[1] *But they cried out, Away with Him, crucify Him,*" which seems to point to the inference that the crucifixion did not take place till the sixth hour, that is twelve o'clock at noon, instead of the third hour, that is nine o'clock in the morning. Of this apparent divergence the utmost has of course been made by the opponents of the Christian faith. On this point, however, we may in passing just make two observations. First, that even allowing the actual divergence to be as great as it appears to be, and to involve the whole difference of three hours as to the time of crucifixion, yet even then the credibility of the fact is in no degree affected thereby. In ordinary life, if there were four witnesses to a particular fact, about which they all agreed, though one of the four differed from the rest as to the time at which it occurred, no man would for a moment doubt the reality of the occurrence by reason of this minor discrepance. And secondly, the best explanation of the difficulty that I have seen is the supposition that St. John alludes not to the sixth hour of the day, but to the sixth hour of the preparation he has just before mentioned, and that this hour is counted not from the commencement, but after the Jewish manner, from the close of the preparation. As the preparation ended about three o'clock on Friday, six hours before it would be about nine

---

[1] John xix. 14.

o'clock on the same day, which is the time, when according to St. Mark, our Lord was crucified.

Now as to the particular death He died, crucifixion was not a Jewish but a Roman mode of punishment. Had our Lord died by the Jewish law, He would have been stoned, but the Jews in their subject condition had not the legal right to stone a prisoner for blasphemy. When Pilate, therefore, had reluctantly given his consent to the execution of Jesus, it was as a Roman citizen and not as a Jewish subject that He died. And this was the second occasion on which we find our Lord outstripping the narrow bounds of Jewish nationality, and asserting His identity with the Gentile world that, as well as the Jewish world, He came to save. The first time was when He went down into Egypt, to take refuge from Herod ; the second was when He was led forth without the holy city, to be crucified as a Roman malefactor on the hill of Calvary. Thus it was that He broke down the middle wall of partition, between the Jew and the Gentile, and in His death united those who in their lifetime had been irreconcilably divided. It is one of the most remarkable features of our blessed Lord's character, that it is entirely devoid of nationality. Whereas we have no difficulty now in recognising the Frenchman, the German, the American, the Englishman, as a member of the particular nation to which he belongs, and we none of us can divest ourselves of our own peculiar national characteristics—in the character of Jesus Christ we find not the special features of the Jew, the Roman, or the Greek, but that genuine breadth and simplicity of character which we should expect to mark the life of one who was emphatically the Son of Man ; and in the particular kind of death He chose to die, we see Him breaking loose from the trammels of Judaism, and condescending to assert His oneness with the heathen nation under whose authority and jurisdiction He was content to suffer.

Now, this fact of our Lord's crucifixion, has, it is needless to say, stamped itself on the mind of the nations of Christendom. The cross is the most conspicuous feature of our material and artistic life, from the dome of the magnificent cathedral that looks down on this vast metropolis, to the ornaments of personal attire, that are cherished and worn by men and women alike. In the foreign countries of Christendom this is of course even more obvious than among ourselves. But if the figure of the cross has in certain cases been turned to a superstitious purpose, there is no reason why it should be proscribed by us. In itself, it has manifestly and can have no virtue or intrinsic merit, any more than the actual wooden framework to which our Lord was nailed could have ; but as the memorial and token of the extremest and most transcendant act of love that was ever witnessed or performed, it can never cease to be dear to the imaginations and the eyes of Christians, and may justly be regarded as a token full of the most significant meaning, and consecrated by the most blessed associations. In St. Paul's epistles, moreover, we find that the cross of Christ has become so familiar to the minds of His followers, that it has passed altogether out of the realm of mere historic occurrence into that of ideal association and significance, as for example, when He says, *God forbid that I should glory, save in the cross,*[1] or, *We preach Christ crucified, to the Jews a stumbling-block, and to the Greeks foolishness.*[2] There can be no question that in such cases, what the writer means is the ethical and spiritual doctrine connected with the fact of Christ's crucifixion, and not that fact alone apart from the doctrine, but still we must always bear in mind that the doctrine depends upon the fact, and not the fact upon the doctrine. It was the fact that originated the doctrine, and gave the impulse to the doctrine, and not the doctrine that originated the fact.

Let us then attempt to apprehend some of the many and solemn lessons that are involved in and inculcated by the fact of the crucifixion of Jesus. First, by His crucifixion our Lord set the seal to all that He had before taught and done. It was not, humanly speaking, inevitable that He should be taken and crucified. More than once we read of His escaping from the hands of His enemies when they were on the point of taking Him. More than once we read of His deliberately avoiding such places and persons as would naturally compass Him about with peril. More than once we find Him

[1] Gal. vi. 14.   [2] 1 Cor. i. 23.

saying that His hour was not yet come, and acting accordingly. The natural inference from all this is that He who could and did at times protect and deliver Himself, could have done so at the last, had He seen fit. We must either believe that He was finally circumvented by His enemies, of which there is no evidence, or we must allow that when the fulness of the time was come, He shrank not from allowing His enemies to accomplish their malice upon Him. We cannot but feel that the terrible end to which He submitted, was, in effect, the confirmation of the truth which He had before inculcated. We have but to compare the difference of feeling that would have been produced in our minds if our Lord had shrunk from the last crisis, instead of facing it, if He had preserved His life, instead of consenting to lose it. There would have been an end to our love for Him, His name would *not* have been regarded any longer as a blessing to mankind. And yet it was clearly in His power to avoid the final catastrophe, if, when He was adjured by the high priest, He had been willing to retract His former teaching, and forego His claim to be the Son of God. That was the very point in the indictment upon which He was convicted. By that, therefore, He must be judged; and so His death must be acknowledged as the very proof and establishment of His doctrine, unless, we, like the high priest, are prepared to rend our clothes and exclaim, *He hath spoken blasphemy, what need we any further witness?*[1]

[1] Matt. xxvi. 65.

But again, the crucifixion of Jesus was not only the seal of His own teaching, it was likewise the fulfilment of prophesy. Ages before, there had been dark utterances of no ambiguous import, which, when the events foreshadowed had come to pass, were found clear as day. *Awake, O, sword, against my shepherd, and against the man that is my fellow, saith the Lord of Hosts: smite the Shepherd, and the sheep shall be scattered, and I will turn my hand upon the little ones.*[1] *They shall look on me whom they have pierced, and they shall mourn for Him as one mourneth for his only son, and shall be in bitterness for him as one that is in bitterness for his firstborn.*[2] *As for Thee also by the blood of Thy covenant, I have sent forth Thy prisoners out of the pit wherein is no water.*[3] *They parted my garments among them, and upon my vesture did they cast lots. I may tell all my bones, they stand staring and looking upon me.*[4] Of these and many other passages we may truly say that in the light of the crucifixion of Jesus they receive a depth and fulness of meaning, which, on any other supposition, they wholly lack ; and I believe it is simply impossible to read the scriptures of the prophets as a whole, and not feel convinced that there is in the combination of them a marvellous anticipation and foreshadowing of events to come, which was either baffled or thwarted altogether, or else was most remarkably verified in Jesus Christ. If you take passage by passage singly,

[1] Zech. xiii. 7. [2] Zech. xii. 10. [3] Zech. ix. 11. [4] Ps. xxii. 18, 17.

and are determined to destroy the expectation of the Saviour, you can do so, just as if you take a bundle of sticks, you may break them singly, but the combined result is one of conclusive strength, which it is impossible to resist or to deny. The cross of Jesus Christ has shewn in a manner altogether unique and unparalleled, that the mission of the ancient prophets was Divine, and that in their varied utterances was expressed the mind of One who most wonderfully spake by them, and who intended us to understand that it was He by whose Spirit they spake.

But again, in the cross of Jesus Christ we have the whole mystery of redemption, as the apostle says, *The preaching of the cross is to them that perish foolishness, but unto us which are saved it is the power of God.*[1] With this double aspect of the cross let us bring our present meditations to an end. To some it is a stumbling-block, and it is foolishness. In the Jewish mind, and in the Greek mind it encountered and offended national and inveterate pride. The Jew wanted an exhibition of national power, of external and material glory. In the cross of Jesus, and in Jesus he found one who had blasphemed the law, who had died in disgrace, and had quenched for ever his inherited hopes of power. The cross was the exact opposite of all that he had longed for. It seemed to ruin his fondest day-dreams, it was to him a stumbling-block, a scandal. To the Greek, whose highly-disci-

[1] 1 Cor. i. 18.

plined intellect found pleasure only in the problems of the mind, the speculations of the fancy, the dialectics of the reason, the cross of Christ was simple folly. There was nothing to satisfy the intellectual taste. The cross dealt with no theoretical questions, though practically it answered all; but the Greek mind was not practical, and the blood of Jesus Christ was too sober and commonplace a fact to possess any interest for the mere theorist. Besides, it spoke to a sense of sin, and struck at the root of vice. It trampled upon moral pride, and therefore it was accounted folly.

But notwithstanding the imputation of foolishness under which it laboured in the estimation of the Greeks; notwithstanding the scandal and the stumbling-block which it cast in the path of the Jews, the cross of Christ was the power of God unto salvation; and we can appeal to the testimony of eighteen centuries in proof of the assertion. The schools of Athens have brought all their glory and intellectual wealth into the church of Christ. The dreams of Plato have been more than realised in the perfect constitution of the kingdom of heaven. The wisdom of Aristotle has exercised no influence to be compared with that of the cross of Christ: for while the wisdom of Aristotle has enlightened only cultivated minds, the cross of Christ has illuminated the darkest spots of human existence, and penetrated the mass of society from the highest to the lowest. The dominion of the gospel has long ago been acknowledged by a territory far wider than that first promised to Abraham or afterwards ruled by Solomon ; vastly more extensive than the empires of Cyrus or Alexander, the Pharaohs or the Cæsars ; and the conquests it has achieved in the past, and is yet achieving in the present, are but the earnest and the pledge of that universal empire to which it is surely destined in the future. Is not this the power of God ? A power which beyond all question has never been exhibited by man or by the sons of men, and compared with which any power recognised on earth is but very weakness, because it is the power of Divine love. The cross of Christ comes to the heart of each separate individual as the revelation to it of God's love ; as the personal exhibition on the part of Christ of the value He sets on each individual soul. The crucifixion of Jesus as an actual historic fact, which cannot be gainsaid, is the distinct message of Jesus to each one of you declaring His love for you. He hath loved you unto the death. He hath given His life for you. His cross is the power of God unto salvation. For it is the destruction of sin in the individual—*the blood of Jesus Christ cleanseth from all sin.*[1] We are not told how it does this, but we are told it does it. When the blood of Christ comes into contact with sin it eliminates, abolishes sin. And the fact that it does this, a fact which is over and over again witnessed in the conscience of the

[1] John i. 7.

believer, is the evidence that the cross of Christ is the power of God unto salvation. There is nothing else which can deal with sin : nothing devised or invented by man is competent to deal with it, because sin is violence done to God, disorder introduced into God's world, and therefore only a special act on God's part is competent to deal with it. But such an act we have in the cross of Christ, *for God commendeth his love towards us in that, while we were yet sinners, Christ died for us.*[1] The act of Christ is claimed as God's act. He proceeds on the assumption that it is His own act. He presents and recommends it to us as the all-conclusive proof of His love ; and when it is so accepted it becomes the power of God unto salvation ; it is mighty through God to the pulling down of strongholds ; it overthrows carnal pride, it subdues prejudice, it rebukes and expels sin, it brings in peace, and so it saves us ; it makes us whole where we were before sick, it heals us where before we had need of healing. And yet it is only too evident that there are many on whom it fails to produce any such results. Those who were spectators of the death of Christ were only moved by it as by a spectacle of sorrow. It was the *moral* consequence of the death of Christ that made those whom it influenced new men ; and this result can only be produced where the death of Christ is received by faith. When we severally and personally find in that death the union of our mor-

[1] Rom. v. 8.

tality with God, the extinction of our sin through His righteousness, the destruction of the old man in the resurrection of the new,—then His death becomes to us the power of God unto salvation. It asserts its power in us; it fulfils in us the Divine will, and makes us strong to bear what He shall lay upon us. In the broken body of the Lord we find our own death unto sin, our own life unto righteousness, and the fulness of ultimate redemption in the assurance of present redemption from sin. Thus "He was crucified" becomes the indelible mark in human history of God's forgiveness of mankind: a forgiveness which becomes individualised and personal according as it is personally apprehended; and the token also of that perpetual covenant whereof He sware and will not repent, who said, *Thou art a priest for ever after the order of Melchizedec.*[1]

[1] Ps. cx. 4.

XIII.

DEAD.

And Jesus cried with a loud voice, and gave up the ghost; and the vail of the temple was rent in twain from the top to the bottom.—
MARK xv. 37, 38.

WE come now to the consideration of that one solemn word in the Apostles' Creed, namely "dead," which marks the close of our Lord's human and natural career. And little did I think, my brethren, when I last addressed you, of the solemn and mournful illustration which our next meditation would receive in the lamentable accident which deprived this nation of one of its brightest ornaments, and this church of her greatest prelate.[1] To be sure the blow had already fallen on us, but for the most part we knew it not. It came upon me like a thunderclap, upon returning home after the evening service; but in such a form that I scarcely knew whether to believe it, just as when the sun is bright and warm, and the birds are singing, and the flowers are gay, there is a sudden murmur heard, and we pause and ask, Was that thunder? For myself, I believe enough has not been said, and it is hardly possible

[1] Samuel Wilberforce, Bishop of Winchester, killed by a fall from his horse, July 19th, 1873.

to say enough of him whom we have lost. Just ten days before his death I had the great privilege of hearing him preach, in King's College Chapel, what must have been almost, if not absolutely, his last sermon. Very beautiful and touching it was, and now never to be forgotten. In words almost prophetic, he turned to his younger hearers and said, "You who are coming forward into the life from which I am fast retiring, let this thought, the thought of my text, be your stay, *He knoweth the way that I take; when He hath tried me I shall come forth as gold.*"[1] Little, however, could he have thought that his own time was so near. Little did I know, when I grasped his hand, and gazed on his beaming and brilliant countenance, and listened to his silvery voice, that it was a privilege granted for the last time. We need grieve, indeed, only for ourselves; for, as the Primate truly said in Parliament, we cannot call it a calamity for a man to be summoned away in the midst of his vigour, and in obedience to a voice which he had long expected, not unprepared but ready for the summons. It would be out of place in me to attempt to offer anything like a eulogium on Bishop Wilberforce; but I could not bring myself to pass by his death in silence, and it seemed that the incident I have mentioned had now a special and peculiar interest from its being connected with probably the last occasion of a public and general kind on which *he* was seen among us, of whom it is

[1] Job xxiii. 10.

not too much to say that "we shall not look upon his like again."

And now, brethren, we pass from the death of the great, the illustrious, the eloquent, the brilliant, the polished, the sparkling, the pure-minded, the beloved, to another death without which the contemplation, or the possession of any, or of all these qualities combined could give us no pleasure, from the death of the servant who did his work nobly and well, to the death of the Master whom he served, and by whose death, we trust, he lived and yet lives. Jesus Christ died: He was crucified, *dead*, and buried. I have taken for the motto of my subject those words of St. Mark which express the simple fact and its immediate results. We have to contemplate the spectacle of death never unfamiliar, now, alas, become so painfully familiar, in Him whose death was the redemption of mankind. We have to gaze upon that favourite subject of the old masters, the dead Christ. The ninth hour has come, the sixth of the crucifixion, the third of the supernatural darkness spread over all the earth, the great cry has been uttered, and Christ has made His soul an offering for sin. We must not forget His own words, *Therefore doth my Father love me, because I lay down my life that I might take it again. No man taketh it from me, but I lay it down of myself: I have power to lay it down, and I have power to take it again. This commandment have I received of my Father.*[1] Our

[1] John x. 17, 18.

Lord did not die from the effects of crucifixion,—at least, it does not appear that He did. Crucifixion did not kill the thieves who were put to death with Him. To pierce the hands and feet is not mortal; to place a crown of thorns upon the brow is not mortal. When the side was pierced with the spear, which would have been a mortal act, Jesus was already dead. But besides this, we are told that in the very article of death He cried with a loud voice, that heaven and earth might hear, *Father, into Thy hands I commend my spirit. It is finished.*[1] There was no exhaustion there, there was not even the gathering together of the powers of the system for one last convulsive effort; but there was, as indicated, the deliberate resignation of the life into the hands of Him that gave it, when the hour was come. This was the sacrifice of Christ—the crowning act of self-sacrifice, not the self-immolation of one who rushes madly on to death; but the calm, conscious, devoted surrender of the life that was dear to its possessor, to Him who claimed it as His own. Into the question of the physical causes of our Lord's death I do not propose to enter. We are not concerned with the verdict that a jury in a coroner's inquest would have returned. To us there remains the undoubted fact that our Lord was dead. *Pilate marvelled if he were already dead:*[2] he did not suppose that the sufferings inflicted had been sufficient to extinguish life; of the other sufferings undergone,

---

[1] Luke xxiii. 46; John xix. 30.   [2] Mark xv. 44.

and the mental agony of the sleepless night which had sorely taxed a delicate and sensitive frame he knew nothing ; but *calling unto him the centurion, he asked him whether he had been any while dead, and when he knew it of the centurion,* who was responsible for the fact, *he gave the* lifeless *body to Joseph.*[1] There was the perfected sacrifice. The teacher at the early age of three and thirty was summoned away, and his body became a corpse.

The sect of the Docetæ in the first ages of the Church denied the fact of our Lord's death—they could not bear to think that He had actually succumbed to the conditions of mortality. They would rather contemplate His departure as a solemn and sublime spectacle, very affecting and tragic, but like a tragedy, unreal. To us there is no temptation of this kind ; we cling to the blessed assurance that Jesus Christ expired, breathed out His life, gave up the ghost, as much as we do to the assurance that *Jesus wept*—each is a proof to us of His complete humanity, that He was very man.[2] He died as we all die: as we watch our friends one by one fall asleep, whether suddenly and in a moment without any warning, as he whose loss is uppermost in our minds, or in lingering hours of slowly advancing disease, and ever increasing feebleness and pain. That fatal state which comes alike, and in time to all, came also to Jesus, in identity of results, though not as in our case, without any concurrent will, because He was

[1] Mark xv. 44, 45. [2] John xi. 35.

not only the Sacrifice who died, but also the self-sacrificing Priest who offered up Himself.

And I want to bring you near, brethren, to the dead body of the Lord, I want you to feel that Jesus Christ was dead, that in His human body life was vanished, obliterate, quenched. The chills of death came over Him—His body became cold, rigid, passive, unresisting, motionless. Look upon the picture by Rubens of the descent from the cross, see how truly Christ is dead, the light is darkened in the pallid face, the eyes are closed, the limbs hang down, the pulse has ceased. The body is dead, and dead because of sin. What He was we all shall be, none knows how soon, and none knows in what form, or under what circumstances death shall come. But this we know, that the death of Christ has taken away the sting of death for us. We can now say, *O death, where is thy sting?* And why is this? because of the momentous issues which the death of Christ involved. These issues were, properly speaking, not consequences such as every important death involves, whether it be the death of a prelate or the death of a king, but issues gathered up and concentrated in the death itself. Christ was the high priest of humanity, the representative man. When He breathed out His Spirit, the human spirit was redeemed, it was delivered from the burden of the flesh, it was surrendered to God, and safe in the hands of God. That is a fact, therefore, which requires to be apprehended, to be grasped and laid hold of, retained and clung to. There is redemption for you and for me in the death of Christ. The death of Christ is our hope and our stay. We die unto sin with Him. We lay our sins on Him, and lose them in His death. Let us believe this truth with all the heart, and live by it.

We see then in the death of Christ, God's method of dealing with the evils of our position. There can be no doubt that our constant liability to death is a terrible drawback. What a frightful shock to the immediate companions of the late bishop must his fatal accident have been—what a cruel and bitter mockery of the golden and sunny hours of relaxation they had hoped to spend; but this is the condition of of our existence here, we walk in the midst of pitfalls, and know not which is to engulf us. Now, how does God deal with such a condition, how does He redeem us from the misery of it? By submitting to it Himself—not by avoiding but by yielding to that very stroke of death which we so much dread and shrink from. He bows His own neck to the yoke, and in doing so takes it off our neck. This being once for all done, becomes evermore the sure remedy for death and the liability to death. We have but to accept it as this, and we find it to be so. The circumstances are not altered, they are rendered innocuous; the bitter waters are healed when the cross of Christ is thrown into them. To know that in death, whether the death of our friends or our own death, we have Christ with us, as one who has passed through it Himself, is to have the burden of death lightened, and the venom of its sting counteracted. For the issues of the death of Christ are illustrated to us by the immediate incident which followed it, *The veil of the temple was rent in twain, from the top to the bottom.* We have this fact on the authority of three evangelists,[1] it shews us very clearly the Divine significance of the Jewish ritual, and the completion of the Jewish system. It shewed that the great High Priest had passed through into the holy of holies. It shewed that he was never more to be excluded, that all mankind might enter in where He had passed. It shewed that this was a work done by God Himself, because the veil was rent from the top to the bottom, not from the bottom to the top. It shewed that there was an end to the unholy and profane, that nothing could be called common because God had cleansed it—that in the death of Christ the mysteries of God were all revealed, that there was nothing to shroud off, nothing to conceal, nothing to hide that man could or might know. Christ was Himself the revealer and the revelation; the death of the living Redeemer is the climax of revelation, because it shows us the union of all opposites, the highest and the lowest, the eternal and the transient, the holiest and the sinful. And then in the death of Christ, we have access to the presence of God. We have boldness to enter into the holiest, by the blood of Jesus through the

[1] Matt. xxvii. 51; Mark xv. 38; Luke xxiii. 45.

new and living way, which He has consecrated for us, through the veil, that is to say His flesh.[1] We have no further need of any priest, or any altar, or any sacrifice. The price is paid, the sacrifice is offered, the atonement is completed. We may pass through the veil into the holiest of all. We need not stay, we must not wait till we are worthy or even worthier, but we must draw nigh as we are, and press through the rent veil to the sacred presence of the Most High, and so passing we shall find that Christ hath made us worthy. Oh, blessed issue and result of the death of Christ, which follows after it as soon as it becomes an accomplished fact. When the great High Priest enters in, the veil of the temple which conceals the mysteries of God is rent in twain from the top to the bottom. Oh my brethren and fellow-sinners, have you felt the significance of this fact? There is but one thing which can keep you back from the presence of God, and that is sin, but sin cannot now keep you back, because it is done away in the death of Christ. When you kneel upon your knees in secret you may know that there is nothing to hide God from you, nothing to destroy your communion with Him, nothing to mar the fulness of access and approach to His mercy-seat, because Christ hath died and rent asunder the veil of the tabernacle which concealed the mercy-seat. It is very sad to think how many there are even of those who profess and call themselves Chris-

[1] Heb. x. 19, 20.

tians, who are practically ignorant of the effects of Christ's death, and who are totally unable to realise the privilege of assured access to God by reason of the perfected work of Him who was dead and is alive again, and now liveth for evermore. And yet this is the privilege which has been purchased for us by the Captain of our salvation. He claims to have done that on our behalf, which we could not do for ourselves, and it follows that because He has done it, we should thankfully avail ourselves of what He has done. For the death of Christ which is the pledge of God's love for us, and the assurance of the forgiveness of sins is also the foundation of our hope towards God. We hide ourselves under the shadow of the cross of Christ, and the darts of the evil one cannot reach us, they fall short of their object, and glide off blunted and pointless. There is no condemnation to them that are in Christ Jesus, for He is their Vindicator and Redeemer. There is this mysterious virtue about the death of Christ, that it becomes the object of grateful contemplation. It gives us no pain but only pleasure to contemplate His death. In no human instance can we fail to have our thankfulness mingled with regret, beautiful as the death may be. But here in the death of Christ regret is unknown, we are not affected with grief but only with humble and heartfelt joy. Surely this is very wonderful, but nevertheless it is the special characteristic of the death of Christ. But strange to say, though this characteristic is peculiar to the death of Christ, yet His death has also the power of imparting it to the death of every Christian. We are bidden not to sorrow as men without hope, for them that sleep in Jesus. His death is the one atoning, reconciling, expiatory death, and in that respect it must stand alone; but it throws a halo of glory over every Christian death, for we know of those who sleep in Jesus, that them will God bring with Him. Christ's death therefore is not only the death of sin, and consequently the foundation of our hope, but it is also the death of death. The swollen waters of destruction reached their highest point when they overwhelmed the Lord of Life, and thenceforward they began to recede. He who holds in His hands the issues of life and death, said to them, " Thus far shall ye come, but no farther; and here shall your proud waves be stayed."[1] They are destined still to accomplish a great work, for they shall not finally assuage till they have overwhelmed the whole family of man, and have swallowed up the generations yet unborn, like the generations that are past, but it is a work as far as believers are concerned, which is limited to the present life and the yet visible world. Our friends vanish from our sight here, they fall like soldiers in battle, who one by one drop out of the ranks, and forthwith another and yet another takes their place, but we shall surely meet again in that far-off mysterious land of which we know so little, for which we long so much, but which

[1] Job xxxviii. 11.

though it seems to be far off is in reality very near, as the continual warnings of God evermore remind us. Be it ours, beloved, so to live by the power of Christ's death,

> "That so, before the judgment seat,
> Though changed and glorified each face,
> Not unremembered we may meet
> For endless ages to embrace."[1]

[1] *Christian Year;* St. Andrew's Day.

XIV.

BURIED.

And that He was buried.—1 COR. xv. 4.

THESE words are remarkable as being found in the very brief summary of Christian truth given by St. Paul in the fifteenth chapter of his first epistle to Corinth. He mentions the burial of Jesus Christ as one of the facts which he had *received.* Subordinate, therefore, and unimportant as it may probably seem to us to declare among the articles of the creed that Jesus Christ "was crucified, dead, *and buried,*" we may nevertheless be sure that it was not without its meaning in the providence of God, nor without its essential place in that foundation of fact upon which the edifice of Christianity is reared, and without which it would be nothing better than a cunningly devised fable.

And it is plain that such a statement as this by St. Paul points to a small nucleus of incidents connected with it which were alike present to his own mind and to those of his correspondents at Corinth. In other words, the casual mention of this incident is no slight confirmation of the various narratives which are extant in the four gospels.

St. Matthew tells us that Joseph of Arimathea, having obtained from Pilate the body of Jesus, *wrapped it in a clean linen cloth and laid it in his own new tomb, which he had hewn out in the rock, and rolled a great stone to the door of the sepulchre, and departed.*[1] St. Mark adds nothing but that Joseph had *bought fine linen, and taken him down and wrapped him in the linen.*[2] St. Luke merely states of the sepulchre that it was one *wherein never man before was laid;* that the day was *the preparation,* and that *the sabbath drew on.*[3] St. John, with the particularity characteristic of himself, tells us that Joseph was not alone in his kind offices to the dead, that Nicodemus also had *brought a mixture of myrrh and aloes, about a hundred pound weight,* a circumstance which is rendered the more probable, though the other gospels have not mentioned it, from the obvious difficulty that Joseph would have had in disposing of the body by himself: *then took they,* continues St. John, *the body of Jesus, and bound it in linen clothes with the spices, as the manner of the Jews is to bury. Now in the place where he was crucified there was a garden, and in the garden a new sepulchre, wherein was never man yet laid, there laid they Jesus, therefore, because of the Jews' preparation day, for the sepulchre was nigh at hand.*[4] The single assertion of St. Paul at Antioch that *when they*

[1] Math. xxvii. 59, 60.
[2] Mark, xv. 46.
[3] Luke xxii. 53, 54.
[4] John, xix. 39–42.

had fulfilled all that was written of Him they took Him down from the tree and laid Him in a sepulchre,[1] completes the entire bulk of that which sacred tradition has preserved to us concerning the matter of our Lord's *burial.* It is very brief; but brief as it is, allusion has been made to it in the briefest and most ancient Christian creed which remains thus embedded in one of the Pauline epistles. One other reference to the same event is found, and that, strange to say, in the words of our Lord Himself. When His feet were anointed by Mary, in the house of Simon the leper, he said of her, *For in that she hath poured this ointment on my body she did it for my burial: Against the day of my burying hath she kept this.*[2] He therefore regarded His burial as having a special significance, and spoke of it with a touch of mournful anticipation. Once also in the Epistle to the Romans, and once in that to the Colossians, St. Paul uses the burial of our Lord in a mystical and figurative way, and speaks of our being *buried with Him by baptism into death,*[3] and *buried with him in baptism.*[4] And these I believe, from first to last, are the only occasions on which mention is made of our Lord's burial. If, then, the burial of Jesus Christ has been thus recorded and referred to, but only thus recorded and referred to, what is it designed to show? First we may reply that it has its place as a sub-

---
[1] Acts xiii. 29.
[2] Matt. xxvi. 12; Mark xiv. 8; John xii. 7.
[3] Rom. vi. 4.
[4] Col. ii. 12.

stantial and permanent stone in the substructure of Christian evidence : that our Lord died is the very central point of Christian faith, the pivot upon which everything else turns. And the manifest concurrent testimony which we possess to the fact of His being buried, with the attendant circumstances that have been specified, is at all events a strong collateral proof of His death. Even supposing that life had not been actually extinct at the moment when the body was taken down from the cross, as it clearly was believed to be both by Pilate and the soldiers who forbore to break the legs of Jesus, yet after the wound inflicted by the spear which pierced His side, and the exhaustion consequent upon the long torture of the cross, it is obvious that burial in Joseph's sepulchre would have been not only most unfavourable to anything like the restoration of vitality, but would have effectually quenched every remaining spark of life ; to have been immured for many hours under such circumstances would have been nothing short of death itself: and consequently the burial of Jesus Christ is virtually a confirmation of His death, an evidence of its reality. And being so, it becomes an additional basis or pillar for the resurrection itself to rest upon. It is not only the apparent death of Jesus, but the attendant circumstances of His burial that we have to account for before we can explain away the evidence for His resurrection. And unquestionably in the providence of God it was so designed.

This, however, is an aspect of the matter which may be more or less forced upon us by the peculiar necessities of our own day. But it is by no means the only one. We must not forget that the gospels were not only written by Jews, but that those who took part in the transactions they record were Jews. And we have only to run our eye through the narrative of the Old Testament, to see how prominent a feature the rites and associations of burial formed in Jewish life. The first commercial transaction of which we have any account in history is that of Abraham purchasing a burial place of the children of Heth for the interment of Sarah ; and the field so purchased became actually the only pledge which for many generations his seed possessed of their inheritance in the land which was promised to his posterity.[1] The earliest associations, therefore, of Israel with the land of hope and promise were those of burial. The bones of her who was the first mother of them all were laid there.[2] Abraham, Isaac and Jacob were buried there, and during the long captivity in Egypt this link with the eastern land no doubt kept alive in the recollections of the people the promise which had been made to their fathers, and the interest they themselves had in its fulfilment. Frequently, also, we are told the circumstances which attended the burial of such and such a personage. The bones of Joseph were to be taken up out of Egypt that they might rest in the

[1] Gen. xxiii.   [2] Gen. xlix. 29—31; l. 13.

soil of the ancestral grave.[1] The very expression "to be laid with his fathers," indicated that burial among the royal tombs which was the common lot of the descendants of David in Jerusalem. And though in this respect of burying the dead, the Jews were not singular among the nations of antiquity; nowhere is there so sweet a fragrance arising from the garlands cast upon the tomb, as in the narratives of sepulture which grace the scripture record. If, therefore, Jesus Christ was to take His place in the family of man as its prince and head; if He was to be the hope of the kings and patriarchs of Israel and the promised Seed, it was surely fitting that the record of His interment should find its place in the brief narrative of His personal history, And so it does. Nor is there anywhere among all the annals of sepulture a more exquisite and lovely picture than that which has been given us of the burial of the Lord. Nowhere is death so beautiful, and the very tomb so chaste and lovely as it is at the cross of Jesus, and in the sepulchre hewn out in the rock in Joseph's garden, wherein never man before was laid.

And there was surely special and abundant room for the kind of glorification which the burial of Jesus was designed to bestow. Death is an event sufficiently terrible and appalling in itself. But surely it is not only the *loss* which is involved in death that constitutes its chiefest terror, but much rather all that follows death. The bitterest draught

[1] Gen. l. 25; Josh. xxiv. 32.

of that very bitter cup is the sad necessity which
hides for ever features that perhaps were only beautiful, and at least were only loved ; the thought
that we who love so dearly, would not for the whole
world gaze on that once angelic form of childhood,
or of youth, or it may be of old age; the busy,
ruthless touch and step of perfunctory and inevitable
service, which tries to be sympathetic but can
scarcely be less than hateful ; the wicked paraphernalia of woe that attend the departure from
the home, and the passage to the grave, and all
the long etceteras of grief and pain that are remembered but cannot be expressed ; it is these that
make death itself more painful and the grave to be
fraught with horror. Yes, it is not the act of dying,
or of seeing our loved ones die, that concentrates the
bitterness of death, but much more the untold and
unexplored awfulness of the grave. To be buried
at sea with the wave for our winding-sheet, and the
howling of the tempest for our dirge, or to be buried
in haste as we fall upon the battle-field, that is a
thought endurable; but to be carried by hired mourn-
ers to the crowded cemetery, and to be laid to our
dust with a parade of misery is indeed a thought most
miserable. We can face the thought of dying, for
die we must, and we hope that to die will be to fall
asleep ; but oh ! to be buried with all which that
by the exigences and conventionalities of an odious
civilisation is made to imply, *that* is something
which we dare not contemplate.

But with the recollection of Christ's burial there is a marvellous alleviation even of the horrors of the tomb. For not only is the story of Christ's burial, as I have said, most pure and lovely, without one element of painful association; not only is the story beautiful, but how exquisite also is the memory of the fact,—He was buried. His dead body was laid in the tomb in the cerements of death; it was wrapped in fine linen with myrrh and aloes; the fragrance of the spices filled the sepulchre; and there His body rested in silence and in darkness, keeping its Sabbath amid the sweetness of the spices within, and surrounded by the fragrance of the vernal flowers without, awaiting the resurrection morn. Was there ever any grave like that? Most certainly not. No peaceful nook in the sweetest and most lovely of English churchyards, themselves the loveliest resting-places of the dead that anywhere exist, can compare with that, the new sepulchre hewn out in the virgin rock in the deepest recesses of Joseph's garden. Verily here, at any rate, the grave itself is despoiled of all its terror. If He was buried, we need not shrink from going down into that tomb where He has kindled once for all the light of the resurrection. Behold then the simple dignity which attaches to these solemn words we rehearse in the Creed, "And buried." Well might the great apostle not omit from his short and rapid summary of Christian fact the statement which he also had *received*, and add that He *was buried*.

For, take away this blessed assurance and what have we left? The darkness and horror of the tomb unmitigated, unenlightened, unsoftened, and therefore unendurable. Take away even the story, and you have robbed universal literature of one of its purest and brightest jewels; but take away the fact which the story perpetuates, and you have robbed humanity of the one only thought which can lend courage to the heart in the prospect of our own descent into the pit of corruption, which can give those who mourn the loss of their nearest and dearest and strew flowers on their grave, the vestige even of a hope.

For just as the sting of all horror connected with death is centred in the thought of corruption, so is there the spring of all hope in the memory of the ancient words which were fulfilled in Chrst, *Thou wilt not suffer thine Holy One to see corruption*.[1] Jesus Christ tasted death for every man; He went down into the tomb that He might once and for all take out of it that association with corruption which is so unutterably painful. He has strewed the fragrance of myrrh and spices over the chill and dark recesses of the grave; He has put into it what did not exist before, and now there is peace where there once was terror, and sweetness where there once was only the memory of corruption.

The circumstances of Christ's burial have not seldom been made the vehicle of a mystical interpre-

[1] Ps. xvi. 10; Acts ii. 27; xiii. 35.

tation; for instance, the body of the Lord is to be laid up in a pure and virgin heart and surrounded with the fragrant associations of hallowed thoughts, and the fine white linen of saintly action and the like. But I am averse from this kind of treatment, because to my mind it savours of unreality, and there is a danger when we begin to allegorise lest we break down the stonework of solid and substantial fact which must after all be found to be sooner or later our only hope. The burial of Jesus Christ was an historic fact, if it was not this it was nothing; but being an historic fact it was only one incident out of many in His human career, and, like other incidents, it was necessarily transient and of a limited duration. Jesus Christ did die and He was buried, but He is not dead now nor does He still rest in the grave. The body of the Lord is the centre and fountain of eternal life. We do not worship a dead Christ, but one who is alive for evermore: let us beware then how far we allegorise the story of our Lord's burial, whether with reference to the sacrament of His death or otherwise. Though in the communion of His body and His blood we do show the Lord's death till He come, yet that sacrament is emphatically the pledge and evidence and memorial of the resurrection. We are only partakers of Jesus Christ in proportion as we are partakers of His life. The dead Christ would profit us nothing, even though we could grasp Him in our hands or clasp Him in our arms, and carry Him with Joseph and Nicodemus to the sepulchre in the garden. What we want is the present evidence and power of Christ's eternal life, and that is only to be had by faith in His life. No allegories or minute directions of devout behaviour or imaginary repetitions of the scenic accidents of Christ's death can avail to give us life—that is only to be had by the quickening influence of the Spirit of life.

There is, however, another mode of allegorising the burial of Jesus Christ, which has the authority of St. Paul, and it is a healthier one. He compares the one momentary fact of our baptism to the transient and historic fact of Christ's burial. He tells us that we have been buried with Christ by baptism into death. That which corresponds in our history to the burial of Jesus Christ, once for all never to be repeated, a whole in itself and the completion of all that went before it, is our baptism. We were buried, figuratively at all events by immersion, virtually by the analogous act of sprinkling, which blotted out all the past and originated all the future and the new, with Christ in our baptism. When the body of Jesus was immured in the tomb, that was the last that was seen of His natural body, for it was raised a spiritual body, a change indescribable and inconceivable passed over it. There was an end to all the past of royal, prophetic, patriarchal hope and longing. There was the commencement given of all the future, incorruptible, undefiled and that fadeth not away, the inauguration of all life, and progress, and eternity, and rejuvenescence, and deathlessness. So is it in the fact that is symbolised in Christian baptism, which is itself a symbol of Christ's burial—it is a single act of which the consequences are unalterable and permanent, if only the significance of it which abides in Christ Himself and not in the rite He has ordained is apprehended. We look to Christ and we find that our sins are buried in His burial, there is no more condemnation as there is no more death—ransomed, pardoned, healed, restored, we have cast off once and for ever the old, we have put on once and for ever the new. We are among those who have been washed, and having been once washed to the purifying of the heart and conscience by the bloodshedding of Christ which can never be repeated, we have no need, save from time to time, to wash our feet from the dust and mire of occasion and convention, but are clean every whit, and with the help and reliance of a sinless and ever-living Christ we may go from strength to strength, until we appear, each one of us, before the God of gods in the heavenly and eternal Zion.

XV.

HE DESCENDED INTO HELL.

Therefore being a prophet, and knowing that God had sworn with an oath to him, that of the fruit of his loins, according to the flesh, He would raise up Christ to sit on his throne; He seeing this before spake of the resurrection of Christ, that his soul was not left in hell, neither his flesh did see corruption.—ACTS ii. 30, 31.

THE descent of our Lord into hell is the subject of a distinct article of the Church of England. "As Christ died for us and was buried, so also it is to be believed that He went down into hell:"[1] to which, in the prayer-book of 1552, there was added, " For His body lay in the sepulchre until the resurrection, but His Spirit, which He gave up, was with the spirits which were detained in prison, or in hell, and preached to them as the place in St. Peter testifieth." The passage referred to is 1 Peter iii. 18-20, *being put to death in the flesh, but quickened in the Spirit, by which also He went and preached unto the spirits in prison; which sometime were disobedient, when once the longsuffering of God waited in the days of Noah, while the ark was preparing, wherein few, that is, eight souls were saved by water.* And in illustration of this passage, we must add that other in the following

[1] Art. iii.

chapter. *For for this cause was the gospel preached also to them that are dead, that they might be judged according to men in the flesh, but live according to God in the Spirit;*[1] and possibly also the words of St. Paul, Eph. iv. 9, *Now that He ascended, what is it but that He also descended first into the lower parts of the earth.* These several passages, together with that from the Psalms, which is quoted in the text, make up all, or nearly all, that is told us in Holy Scripture of that which we profess when we say He descended into hell. It is to be observed that in the ten years which followed the promulgation of the earlier article, a considerable change had taken place in men's minds, as is indicated by the omission of the second clause referring to the passage in St. Peter. That omission can only be explained by a growing dislike to retain anything which, whether rightly or wrongly, was thought to give any possible countenance to the doctrine of Purgatory. Since that memorable year, 1562, men have gone on reciting the article in the Apostles' Creed, and subscribing to that in the Prayer-book, as though no modification in their belief had taken place in the three hundred and ten years, although a modification so important had been registered in the previous ten years. Some persons, also, I believe, are staggered by the assertion in the Apostles' Creed that Christ descended into hell, and have been for generations past. And although it seems to me that this,

[1] 1 Pet. iv. 6.

among many others, is a very trivial ground on which to separate from the outward oneness of Christ's body in this land, it may be as well to give our attention for a brief space to the article of belief in question, since it comes under our notice in the natural order of these discourses.

The first point then, to be resolutely maintained here, is the meaning of the word Hell. St. Peter's statement in the Acts of the Apostles, which is very important, and must be allowed to interpret, or at least to throw light upon his words in the Epistle, is based entirely upon the declaration of David in the sixteenth Psalm. It must, therefore, be limited in its meaning by the necessary limitation of David's own words. Now David's own words about his soul not being left in hell cannot possibly contain any reference to a condition or place of torment, from the simple fact that there is no word in the language of the Old Testament which bears that meaning. People go on reciting the verse in the Psalms, *The wicked shall be turned into hell, and all the people that forget God,*[1] and think that they are, or at least the Psalmist is, denouncing a terrible doom upon such persons, and fancy, moreover, that if it is not so, a very powerful restraint will be withdrawn from evil action, and that sinners will be encouraged in their wickedness. It is sad in these days of enlightenment, first, that so much ignorance of the real meaning of the Psalmist's language should prevail; and secondly, that people

[1] Ps. ix. 17.

should be apprehensive as to the possible consequences of a knowledge of the truth, and should acquiesce in the perpetuation of ignorance, rather than recognise a truth for fear it should act as an encouragement to sin. Surely, we may say that this is nothing less than unworthy cowardice—let us at all hazards seek to know the truth, believing heartily that we can know nothing better, and believing also that it is abundantly capable of taking care of itself, for that the truth is great, yea, greater than all, and that it will prevail. The meaning, then, of the Hebrew word Sheol, which is necessarily used in both these passages, is sufficiently declared by the patriarch Jacob, when he says, *I will go down into the grave unto my son mourning*,[1] and *then shall ye bring down my grey hairs with sorrow to the grave.*[2] It is this, and nothing more than this, that David expresses when he says, *The wicked shall be turned into hell, and all the people that forget God. For Thou wilt not leave my soul in hell, neither wilt Thou suffer Thine Holy One to see corruption.* If we choose to infer from such language that in the Psalmist's mind there was no difference between the death of the righteous and the death of the wicked, that inference is one for which we alone are responsible, and not the language he has used, an inference, also, which is directly negatived by the prayer of Balaam centuries before, *Let me die the death of the righteous, and let my last end be like his*, to say nothing of the irrepressible dictates of

[1] Gen. xxxvii. 35.   [2] Gen. xlii. 38.

the universal conscience of mankind. We may rest assured that we greatly err when we suppose that we can place any other more effectual or salutary restraints to vice than those which are placed in the eternal instincts of the human conscience. It was no part of the revelation of the gospel to chain fetters on the conscience, but rather to give it perfect freedom, in order that it might serve God acceptably, with reverence and godly fear. It is no part then of the teaching of Scripture that after death the soul of our blessed Lord was the subject of torment, nor does the Creed teach us to believe this when it tells us that He descended into hell. On the other hand, those who quarrel with the teaching of the Church must quarrel also with the teaching of Scripture, because if it was true of Christ that His soul was not *left* in hell, it is obvious that it must first have gone down into hell.

Again, some ground for the preposterous notion that Jesus Christ endured a foretaste of the torments of hell is found in the equally erroneous conception which prevails as to the nature of His atonement. It is conceived that God, by the requirements of His infinite justice, was pledged to the eternal punishment of all the saved, unless Christ, as an infinite substitute, had been found willing to endure an equivalent amount of torment in their place ; but as the torment of hell can only be endured in hell, and as the torture of the body can never be an equivalent for the torment of the soul, therefore, if He was to redeem His people from hell, He must Himself go down into hell, and then the infinite value of His soul would add an infinite value to His sufferings, even though in duration they were limited. I need not say how contradictory any such awful notion is to the narrative which we considered on Sunday last of our Lord's burial, as well as to the universal silence of Scripture on the subject, and to the notion which, at least, was countenanced by the appointment of the fourth chapter of the Epistle to the Hebrews as one of the lessons for Easter eve, that the rest of the Mosaic Sabbath was typical of the rest of Christ in the grave.

Rejecting, then, all such notions of our blessed Lord's work as no part of the authentic teaching of Scripture, let us pass on to enquire what is meant by the article in question. I believe the key to the true understanding of our Lord's redemptive work is to be found in those words from the epistle just mentioned, *Forasmuch then as the children are partakers of flesh and blood, He also Himself likewise took part of the same; that through death He might destroy him that had the power of death, that is, the devil.*[1] In other words, the basis of our Lord's redemptive work was laid, not in vicariousness of suffering, but in identity of nature. In Him there was to be a revelation of humanity; He, in fact, was to be the one pattern and type man to whom

[1] Heb. ii. 14.

the creation of Adam looked forward. *Wherefore in all things it behoved Him to be made like unto His brethren;*[1] and, *It became Him, for whom are all things, and by whom are all things, in bringing many sons unto glory, to make the Captain of their salvation perfect through sufferings.*[2] As, therefore, identity of nature was the basis of His work, so also was that work to be carried out by complete identity of condition with man. Man dies as a sinner; Christ died as the chief of sinners, for *He was numbered with the transgressors.*[3] Man is laid in the grave and turns again to his dust; Christ also was laid in the grave, but the Scripture had said that He should not see corruption, and should triumph over death. As, however, the turning to corruption is not an essential part of death, although a necessary and universal consequence of death, and as corruption is that from which we yearn to be delivered, so Christ, as the redeemer, brought back His body from the grave, and did not see corruption. But it is not all of death to die and see the grave, for that is the accident or condition of the body alone. Where is the vital spark of immortality when the body gives up its animal life? We know not, for Scripture has not told us; the language of the Old Testament calls its place or state *sheōl*, that is to say, the condition in which we *ask* after our lost ones, Where are they? or, according to others, the all-craving

[1] Heb. ii. 17. [3] Isa. liii. 12; Mark xv. 28.
[2] Heb. ii. 10.

and devouring abyss which insatiably demands the whole of the human race. It seems better then to conceive of this, which is called in our Scripture language *the grave* or *the pit*, as a state rather than a place, inasmuch as it appears more consonant with the nature of spiritual existence to predicate condition of it than place. The spirit even in the body is not bound by the limitations of space or place, much less when disenchained and disentangled from the body; but the spirit, when so enfranchised, is in an unknown state, and that state may be one of incipient weal or woe. We simply know nothing about it, for Scripture has told us nothing, and science with all its boasted acumen and knowledge of the secrets of nature can discover nothing, for the mystery lies hid deep in that impenetrable land,

> "That undiscovered country, from whose bourne
> No traveller returns."

But we know thus much, that Christ died exclaiming, *Father, into thy hands I commend my spirit;*[1] and we are certainly led to believe that the condition of our Lord was different at His death from what it was at His resurrection; and different at and after His resurrection from what it was on His ascension, and from what it has been ever since and is now. There remains, therefore, the mysterious interval between His death and His resurrection to account for. Where was His human soul then? or more accurately, what was the con-

[1] Luke xxiii. 46.

dition of His human soul then ? It was in hell, for He descended into hell; there where Jacob said he should go down to his favourite son; there where David said he should meet his infant child;[1] there where the dead are gone, and there where we shall go.

And I cannot speak of this, my friends, without a few brief words of tribute to the memory of those two eminent Christians of Switzerland and Spain, Pronier and Carrasco, who were called to a watery grave but a few days back, in that ill-fated Atlantic steamship.[2] They were noble servants of Christ among the very noblest who met in those happy meetings in New York in October last. Carrasco was the head of the evangelical movement in Spain, and had suffered persecution for his attachment and loyalty to the Word of God. Pronier was a young man of ardent and simple faith. They are gone to their rest, for their work was done; but I, who crossed the same ocean but a month before, on my return from the same mission as theirs, have been mercifully preserved and snatched from peril in which one was taken and another left. Why? Because my work is not yet done. I have yet work to do for God and for Christ, and may the life which has thus been spared be evermore consecrated to the energetic doing of His work; *for whether we live we live unto the Lord, and whether we die we die unto the Lord; whether we live, therefore, or die, we are the Lord's.*[3]

[1] 2 Sam. xii. 23.
[2] The *Ville du Havre* sunk Nov. 22, 1873.
[3] Rom. xiv. 8.

But while we linger here we cannot forbear to ask, Where are our loved ones gone—where do they go ? And the only answer we can give is derived from our Lord's own words to the dying thief, *To-day shalt thou be with Me in paradise*.[1] That is where Christ went, He tells us Himself; that is where the penitent thief went; it was where Christ was. The whole subject is impenetrably dark, and human language cannot enlighten it, because human thought cannot pierce it ; but we know that when we say He descended into hell, we confess that Christ our Lord, as the perfect and true man, submitted to fulfil all the conditions of deceased humanity. His body was in the grave, His soul was in paradise, that is, in hell, in a state of incipient bliss ; not such as He in His manhood was to enjoy subsequently, but one which was antecedent and preliminary to it.

This is what we mean when we say that Christ descended into hell. The term is indeed, unfortunately a most ambiguous one, and the American Prayer-book has prefixed to the Apostles' Creed this rubric : " Any churches may omit the words 'He descended into Hell,' and may instead of them use the words, ' He went into the place of departed spirits,' which are considered as words of the same meaning in the Creed." Notwithstanding, however, this permission, I never heard any American congregation avail themselves of the option given, although the tendency of that prayer-book is to

[1] Luke xxiii. 43.

remove as far as possible every supposed blemish arising from archaic or antiquated language. It seems to me that to speak of the *place* of departed *spirits* is, for another reason already specified, no less objectionable than to speak of hell in this acceptation.

What Christ did when His soul had descended into hell it is idle to speculate. St. Peter's language certainly seems to intimate that our Lord's mission, as the first and great preacher of the Gospel, was not accomplished when He died. There were those waiting for His mercy in Paradise who were eager to receive it. The patriarchs, prophets, and psalmists, who like Abraham and David had seen His day before He came, and who were in Sheol, Hades, or Hell, would be the first to hail the glad message of salvation accomplished and wrought out which He thus was the first to bring them. This was to Him the rest of the holy sabbath, that antitypical period of rest which His body was keeping in the grave, and to which every sabbath had looked forward since *the morning stars sang together, and all the sons of God shouted for joy.*[1] This may be so—we know not and cannot tell, and it is useless to enquire; and we need not desire to know. Before very long the mystery will be revealed to each of us. It is one of the surest tokens of the Divine Gospel, that it has not ministered to a vain spirit of speculation. It gratifies no idle hunger of curiosity. It

[1] Job xxxviii. 7.

deals with facts, with facts which contain in themselves the resolution of all mysteries, which are the incipient germ of future and complete knowledge.

And the great facts which it reveals are these, that Christ, as the Divine Son of the eternal Father, has entered into all the conditions of our mortal or fallen humanity, saving only that of personal guilt, on account of sin committed, but not excepting that of personal consciousness of sin in consequence of intense sympathy and complete identification with the sinner. He has suffered hunger, thirst, weariness, weakness, pain, loneliness, desolation, desertion by God, the hiding of His face, which is the very bitterness of death. He has gone through the conditions of this low estate in which we are dwelling now, and He has encountered death and explored all the mysteries of the undiscoverable state, the darkness and solitude of the tomb, the shadowy visions of the shadowy world where the spirits rest, as it were, in prison; in a state of inchoate and incipient joy, waiting for the dawning of the resurrection morn, when they shall come forth in glorious array, a mighty and triumphant army, glistening like the dew-drops of returning day, and reflecting each the likeness of the Sun of Righteousness, the undying and victorious Captain of their salvation.

XVI.

THE THIRD DAY HE ROSE AGAIN FROM THE DEAD.

And that He rose again the third day according to the Scriptures.
—1 COR. xv. 4.

THIS statement, which also forms part of the early creed preserved to us by St. Paul, agrees in word as well as in substance with that in the Nicene Confession, while it differs from the article in the Apostles' Creed by the addition of the words "according to the Scriptures." That addition is a very important one, and it is not a little significant that it is found in the apostle's letter to Corinth.

We come, then, at last, to the fundamental and characteristic fact of the Christian faith. For a long time we have been dealing with events which were not only transacted in the sphere of ordinary life, but which did not transcend the limits of ordinary experience. This was the case when we said that "Jesus Christ suffered under Pontius Pilate," that "He was crucified, dead, and buried." Nor was it essentially otherwise, when we confessed that "He descended into hell," for the significance of His descent into hell was His conformity with the conditions of ordinary mortal existence. But now we take leave of the ordinary, the human, the experimental. Now we approach, enter into, and deal with the extraordinary, the supernatural, the Divine. It is, then, with the Christian faith, as it was with the ladder that Jacob saw in vision, which was established on the earth, while the top of it reached to heaven. The foundation of Christianity is laid in the earth in the natural, the human, the temporal : but having established and planted itself there, it does something more, it rises into heaven, and takes us with it. Unlike the ancient tower which was built on the plains of Shinar, by which men sought to reach the heavens but failed hopelessly, as they always must, this was a tower raised by God, having its foundation deep in the earth, but with its summit penetrating the heavens. It is, therefore, what from the first mankind felt the want of. It gives exactly that which is confessedly desirable and desired, and which is continually being sought after in one way or another, even when its own way is rejected. If the headstone of the corner is refused, it is only refused that another stone may be taken in its place. Men cannot do without stones to build with ; it is only a question as to the choice of the fittest and the best.

We must, therefore, by no means hide from ourselves the nature of the territory which we are now entering. It is not of this world, it is not of the earth earthy, and therefore not of the perishing perishable. We must resist, as the most unfair and insidious of all endeavours, the attempt to represent the cardinal truth we·are now to contemplate, as a mere distortion of the natural and the ordinary, a mere accommodation to the thirst for the supernatural and the marvellous. We start therefore with this question, Can any rational being think it probable for one moment that the writers of the New Testament did not themselves believe, and intend their readers to believe, that Jesus Christ, their master, having been dead was raised to life again, that His body having been extinct of vitality was restored to animation? If any one can suppose that probable there is an end to all argument. But as it is absolutely impossible that we can have misunderstood the disciples in this respect, it is the more incumbent upon us to look the matter simply in the face, and to resolve that we will not be the victims of any deception or special pleading or word-juggling on the subject. What we have to concern ourselves with is the obvious belief that, the body of Jesus Christ, having been actually dead, and, in popular language, severed from His soul, which was "in hell," was as actually by His own Divine power raised to life again, how of course we do not presume to say; it is a supernatural fact that we have to treat, a *bonâ fide* miracle, and nothing less than the greatest of all miracles, though at the same time, if a fact, a miracle which sheds a flood light over history, and nature, and life, and science, and the whole world of the miraculous.

And, brethren, terrible as it is, we must regard the subject in this light, because there are sentiments propounded by so-called Christians in the present day which deliberately endeavour to explain away the Lord's resurrection, to represent that which is a miracle—or it is nothing—as no miracle at all.

I wish, then, to guard myself most carefully against all possible misinterpretation, and to state plainly what I desire to be understood as plainly —that in the creed of Christianity we confess that the human body of the Lord of life was actually raised to life again after having been dead; that it was not merely that the disciples thought they saw the Lord, and thought they talked with Him, and thought they ate and drank with Him after He rose from the dead; that it was not merely their senses that were imposed upon, but that a truth answering accurately to those impressions of their senses had really taken place in the word of fact and nature.

So, brethren, let us clearly understand each other. This is what you profess to believe, this is what I have to enlarge upon and to maintain; and it is, with all its stupendous difficulties and contradictions, what I deliberately believe when I deliberately repeat those words of the Apostles' Creed, " the third day He rose again from the dead."

You see, then, that though the character of the facts which the Creed asserts is altogether changed, yet they are not changed in regard to their being facts. Christianity requires us to believe that it is as much a *fact* that Jesus Christ rose again from the dead, as it is that He was born, or died, or was buried: these are what we may call natural facts, that is a supernatural fact; both took place in the world of nature; but this fact, though it took place in the world of nature, altogether transcended the limits of that world: it not merely seemed to transcend them, but it actually did so. In the resurrection, then, of the Lord of glory, there was, just as there had been at His birth, a new exceptional fact introduced into the category of historic occurrences; a fact which, had it been possible for science to be cognizant of it, science itself would have been bound to register, so that, in the report of the transactions of such and such a society, we should have had it recorded that on such a day, at such an hour, and in such a place, a particular man who had been dead was acknowledged on sufficient and satisfactory evidence to have been raised again, or to have raised himself again, to life. Let there be no mistake about it. This, and nothing less than this, is the direct statement of the Scriptures; this, and nothing less than this, is the professed belief of Christendom. If, therefore, on this count the Scriptures are not reliable, they are a dead letter; if here they are worthy of credit, then, in this respect alone, waiving all others, they are different from the reports and blue-books of all scientific and statistical bodies, inasmuch as they do record a fact which confessedly no scientific body has ever had to record, and which, in fact, we know, as the Scriptures themselves give us to understand, that no scientific body will ever have to record.

It is, brethren, verily a stupendous statement. But I do not see that there is any getting out of it. This, and nothing less than this, it was which gave the impulse to the spread of Christianity in the first age of the Church, and caused the desert of the Roman world and of Roman civilisation to rejoice and blossom as the rose.

Nor must we let our expressions of belief in this cardinal fact take the form of self-revenge, which is not seldom discernible in the case, for example, of bigoted Romanists, who will maintain a belief in the most monstrous statements simply because they trample upon soul and sense, and because there is a kind of self-gratification in so triumphing over self. Doubtless we must confront miracle somewhere, and, if anywhere, we must confront it in the resurrection of our Lord; but it is not merely for the sake of confronting it that we do so. A miracle merely as a miracle is a worthless thing to contemplate, nay, it is even a pernicious thing. And therefore it was that our Lord was always so careful to place even His own miracles in their proper position and aspect; to represent them only as parts of a whole, as elements, ingredients, and items that had their use in confirmation of moral and spiritual truth, but which were by no means to be confounded with that truth. It is so with His own resurrection : let us by all means allow that it transcends the earthly, and exceeds the natural, and belies the ordinary ; but let us not turn it into an idol of the cave, a kind of mental fetish, and worship it for its own sake, or for the sake of worshipping it. Let us remember that the resurrection of Christ was the highest and most expressive symbol of the life which was in Him, and that it is in and by that life, expressed as His resurrection expresses it, that we must live, and not by the mere confession of an outward fact which may after all leave us lifeless and dead. It is in Christ the Life who Himself rose from the dead that we are to believe, and, it may be, *because* He rose from the dead ; but not in our own bare and barren belief that He so rose.

And surely, brethren, you will at once see that this makes a vast difference, if we start with the moral and spiritual conviction that there is a life which is stronger than death, absolutely separate from death, and into which death cannot enter, which conviction may itself serve as an index of our own spiritual constitution to show whether we are, so to say, physically capable of becoming Christians ; if, I say, we start with this conviction,—and I believe there are some who have it not,—and start also with the further conviction that such a life can be personally embodied in a man, then it becomes not only easy, but we may even say natural, that the life so embodied should surrender itself to death for the express purpose of utterly throwing off death. And this is what we believe Christ did. He was not a mere unit out of the innumerable units of humanity, who alone of all of them did the unnatural and impossible thing, rise again from the dead, but being in His personality as a true man the One man who was fore-ordained to bring life into this dying world, He Himself was found willing to die in order that He might cast out death from them who were willing to accept His life. Looked at in this light, approached, if we may so say, from this direction, and from this quarter, the resurrection of the Lord Jesus becomes but the part, albeit possibly the chief part, of a mighty whole; but one which is essential, indispensable, conformable in some sense even to nature, and most undeniably consonant with reason. If Jesus Christ was this, then it is no wonder that He rose again from the dead; but the greatest and most impossible wonder of all would have been that He should not rise, that Death should have had final dominion over Him. Death was His creature, He was its Lord. The resurrection showed unmistakably the relation of the creature to the Lord, and if you get rid of the resurrection of the Lord Jesus, then you get rid of the abstract superiority of life to death; you have the enjoyable prospect before you of death without end as the ultimate lord of all, as the goal of all existence, and the extinction of all personal hope.

And here it was that the apostles had such a marvellous vantage-ground on which to place the engines wherewith they were to move the world. They had the conception of a *Christ* to work with, a conception which was a unique fact in the history of the world, just as much as the republic of Rome or Athens was a fact. They had this conception, the abstract possibility of the existence of such a person in the national mind of Judaism, and even in the national mind of Greece and Rome, and having this conception it became comparatively easy for Peter to tell the multitudes from all nations assembled in Jerusalem on the day of Pentecost that God had raised up Christ, having loosed the pains of death, because it was not possible that *He* should be holden of it.[1] There was an appeal here, in the minds of those men, to a sense of what was fit and natural, and they could not help seeing it. And therefore they accepted the resurrection as being itself the key to many mysteries which would be unsolved without it, as explaining more than it required to be explained, as proving the confirmation and evidence of a hope which without it could never be proved, and which must vanish in despair.

Nor was it otherwise with St. Paul. In writing to Corinth he could say of Christ, the ideal man, that He rose again the third day *according to the Scrip-*

[1] Acts ii. 24.

tures. Had it not been for those Scriptures the resurrection of Christ would simply have taken its place among the exceptional, and abnormal, and highly irregular facts of science, and observation, and experience, which could only establish its claim to be accepted according as the evidence advanced was or was not deemed satisfactory by the individual to whom it was presented. But seeing that there were written documents of vast antiquity, which had been the cause of remarkable anticipations being cherished and maintained, not only by the Jewish nation, but by the world at large, in which it was affirmed, for example, as we read this morning, that the Lord God would *swallow up death in victory, and wipe away tears from off all faces;*[1] or, as we shall read this evening, *Thy dead men shall live, together with my dead body shall they arise: awake and sing, ye that dwell in dust, for thy dew is as the dew of herbs, and the earth shall cast out the dead;*[2] we can readily understand the fulfilment of the sequel, *It shall be said in that day, Lo this is our God, we have waited for Him and He will save us; this is the Lord, we have waited for Him, we will be glad and rejoice in His salvation.*[3]

For, given this preliminary faith in the Divine word; given those natural yearnings and irrepressible hopes to which even that word appealed, it became then not a mere dilettante abstract question as to

[1] Isa. xxv. 8.
[2] Isa. xxvi. 19.
[3] Isa. xxv. 9.

whether or not God could or would or should raise the dead, but whether or not, under the special and highly exceptional circumstances of this particular case, as one part of the far-reaching and elaborate plan of a mighty and gigantic whole, and as the fulfilment of an ancient promise which was confirmed by the oath of God, He had raised the dead;—it became then a question as to whether or not that word could fail, and whether or not the resurrection of Christ had once for all fulfilled it.

And this, my brethren, is our position now. We have, to take one instance, those magnificent chapters of Isaiah which are the customary spiritual food and sustenance of Advent. We can see for ourselves what it is they proclaim. They need no commentary to enable us to take in their broad and patent message, for whatever obscurities we may find in them—and they are many—they are after all so plain that it is as if they were engraven upon rocks, that he who runs may read them while he runs, without a pause or break. And of these we know, as a matter of undeniable fact, that they were written for centuries before Christ came. They tell us, then, in the name of the Lord, what it is the Lord will do—not brute nature or blind chance—but what God, the living God, and the Lord of nature, will do for dying man. The only question then for us to determine is, Will He do it, and has He done it? If Christ is risen He has done it, and He will do it again. If Christ is not risen, then we not only have to do violence to, in order to explain away, all the varied tissue of converging evidence which shows—and for ages has been understood to show—that He did rise again from the dead ; but we have this inexplicable fact to account for—the existence for long ages of written testimony which declared that after the Lord's servant had been led as a sheep to the slaughter, and had made His soul an offering for sin, He should see His seed and should prolong His days, while the pleasure of the Lord should prosper in His hand;[1] as well as this other undeniable fact, that upon the authority of this testimony to persons who knew it had not been fulfilled, but anticipated its fulfilment, the Apostles went forth, proclaiming that Jesus had risen from the dead the third day according to the Scriptures, and declared Him on this ground to be the Christ; and that on their testimony He was accepted as the Christ and the world became Christian, because men had in their hands the cypher and the key to it, the impression and the seal which corresponded to it, and because without this fact the cypher was a cypher still, and the impression was a thing of chance, on which the stamp of no seal had come.

[1] Isa. liii. 7, 10.

XVII.
THE THIRD DAY HE ROSE AGAIN FROM THE DEAD.

And that He rose again the third day according to the Scriptures.—
I COR. xv. 4.

A SUBJECT like that of our Lord's resurrection may well be allowed to occupy us for a longer period than some others, and there were points upon which we did not touch in the last discourse. When, for example, it is said that *He rose again the third day according to the Scriptures,* there can be no doubt that the proclamation of any such fact receives additional testimony when it is shown that for ages before Christ came it had been distinctly promised in Isaiah that *the earth should cast out the dead.*[1] It might, of course, be affirmed that such language was merely poetical and was not to be taken literally; but when an historic fact is declared to have taken place in literal agreement with such language, it may surely be required not only to disprove the fact, but also to show cause why the language should not be taken literally before it is disproved. And if, for a variety of reasons, there is ground for accepting the fact, a strong presumption is under the circumstances

[1] Isa. xxvii. 19.

thereby created, that the language of the prophet spoken in the name of the Lord was to be understood to the fulness of its possible meaning. I do not wish to imply that these words, *the earth shall cast out the dead*, are those upon which alone or principally I should rest the antecedent probability of our Lord's resurrection, but that they, among many others, vividly illustrate the general truth exemplified by His resurrection.

The words of the text, however, are joined with others already commented upon, *and that He was buried;* and the expression, *according to the Scriptures*, may be reasonably interpreted as applying to both. The question then occurs, To what is it that this expression does refer? Is it to our Lord's burial and His resurrection alone, or is it to His resurrection the third day? Does the apostle mean to say that had He lain in the grave more than three days the Scripture would have been broken—that had He lain there less it would not have been fulfilled? or is he content merely with the more general statement that, by His resurrection from the dead, the Scriptures were fulfilled? The question is by no means an unimportant one in the present day, because it bears directly upon the manner in which the Scriptures are to be regarded. If, as a matter of fact, Christ our Lord in minute particulars fulfilled the Scriptures and was careful to do so, then there can be little doubt that such minute attention to them is important and even required.

And thus the Scriptures are raised to a somewhat different level, and one in which these smallest particulars are worthy of our consideration. If, on the other hand, we may rest content with a mere vague and general agreement with their spirit, then they remain upon a lower elevation, and one on which they approximate more nearly to the ordinary literature of mankind. Here it may be enough to say that the pervading spirit of the Old Testament and the New are alike; that one is nothing more than the higher manifestation of the other, and that the one was commended to mankind because it was not altogether original but had been partly anticipated of old .If, on the other hand, there is evidence that St. Paul assumed a different ground from this, and if from the representations of the Evangelists there is proof that our Lord did also, then we can hardly fail to conclude that this view of the ancient Scriptures was not only that which was taken by themselves, but also that which they were desirous to commend to us. And I think from the way in which the writer says, *and that He rose again the third day according to the Scriptures*, he does mean to be understood to say, that Christ not only rose from the dead according to the Scriptures, but that His rising the third day was anticipated by them and fulfilled them. Let it be observed, then, that I am not now advancing St. Paul's opinion as binding upon ourselves, but only endeavouring to ascertain what that opinion was. How far it may be a rule for us is a subsequent consideration; we want now to determine what it was, and if possible to justify it.

Assuming then that he believed Christ's rising from the dead on the third day was expressly provided for by the Scriptures, what were the Scriptures to which he referred? First, I think, we may reply with certainty the 16th Psalm, *For thou wilt not leave my soul in hell; neither wilt thou suffer thine Holy One to see corruption.* This Psalm had been in existence for ages. St. Peter had shown before that understanding David's language, as the LXX had understood it, of corruption, it was impossible that that language could apply to him. If, therefore, it had any meaning at all, it must apply to someone else, and he asserted that it applied to Christ. But if the Lord would not suffer His Holy One to see corruption, doubtless a limit was assigned, by the very choice of that expression, to the time which His human body could, in the course of nature, be held by the grave. Probably in such a climate as that of Palestine three days would be this limit, and if so, the language of Scripture would demand that the resurrection of Christ should not be longer delayed, supposing that language should be rigidly adhered to. An antecedent probability existed, therefore, in prophecy, that Christ should rise from the dead within such a time that His natural body, left to itself, would have succumbed to the operation of natural law. But out of the mass of the prophetic writings, who, before the fact, could have anticipated such an event as probable? Verily no one. And it is precisely in this inherent improbability that the strength of the proclamation lay, when it was shown to be—as it clearly was—in accordance with the Scriptures. It is futile to maintain afterwards that David's language could have had no reference to Christ, and yet profess to accept the resurrection, because here is the statement which, at all events when thus interpreted, corresponds exactly with the fact. We may deny the fact, but we cannot deny it on the ground that it failed to justify the language. We may deny the possibility of the Psalmist's language referring to Christ, but we cannot deny the coincidence of correspondence between the two. And this coincidence becomes the more remarkable, and acquires indeed a degree of independent strength, when we see that to them who were most familiar with the language, the fact of its correspondence with the event came home with the force of irresistible conviction. Granting the necessity that the Scriptures must be fulfilled, here was their fulfilment. Now they had a depth of meaning which they never had before, and which they could not have till the time that they should be fulfilled had come; but after the arrival of that time, and the course of events had thrown a flood of light upon them, it was too late to say that their original capacity for any such meaning was a mistake.

There was, however, another wonderful prophetic book, which had been in existence for many centuries, whatever its origin and however it had been interpreted. This book was the narrative of a reluctant prophet, who was charged with a message that he refused to deliver, who became the prey for three days and nights of a sea-monster, and was saved by a mighty salvation, in order to execute the office which had been entrusted to him, and who, by his discharge of it, became the means of preserving alive the inhabitants of a heathen city, which was second to none among the great cities of the ancient world. We are told on the authority of St. Matthew and St. Luke that our Lord used the history of this prophet as a parable of His own, declaring that the sign of the prophet Jonas was the only sign that should be given to the men of that generation, and saying, according to St. Matthew, *that as Jonas was three days and three nights in the whale's belly, so the Son of Man should be three days and three nights in the heart of the earth.*[1] Here, then, it is probable that we have the Scripture authority for the third day. More than three days the letter of Scripture did not demand; anything less than the third day would have been in violation of it. We are told, moreover, on the high authority of Lightfoot, that a portion of three days could be spoken of in the Jewish acceptation as

Matt. xii. 40.

three days, and there are in Biblical language examples of such a method of computation; so that the resurrection on the third day has become an integral part of the Christian Creed. Christ having been buried on the Friday, having rested in the grave on the Sabbath, and having risen from the dead on the first or Lord's day, was in the heart of the earth a portion of three several days, and rose from the dead the third day. It is probable, however, that our Lord intended a very much closer parallel to be observed between Himself and Jonah the prophet than the minor one of the three days and nights. However the history of that prophet was regarded by the men of his time, there it was as a substantive portion of their literature. It recorded a marvellous deliverance. Even if the record were not taken as history, which it undoubtedly was, that would necessitate its being taken as a parable, and that would further necessitate a meaning being found for the parable. What was its meaning? No one could say. Christ's resurrection would provide a meaning, and such a meaning as nothing else could give. The prophet, moreover, had spoken of his own deliverance as a deliverance from the belly of hell, or Sheol. *Out of the belly of hell cried I, and Thou heardest my voice.*[1] Christ was to be delivered from the jaws of hell, because it was not possible that He should be holden of its pains. But above all as Jonah's message was

[1] Jonah ii. 2.

only fruitful after his resurrection, so Christ's message would go forth with far greater success after His resurrection than before it ; and as the preaching of Jonah had a great effect upon the Gentile city of Nineveh, so the gospel of Christ would have a success among the Gentiles that it lacked among the Jews, and thus become a sign to the men of that generation, as the prophet had been to the men of His own.

There is yet another passage, occurring in Hosea, that was probably remembered in this same connection : *Come and let us return unto the Lord, for He hath torn and He will heal us ; He hath smitten and He will bind us up. After two days will He revive us, in the third day He will raise us up, and we shall live in His sight.*[1] What was the primary meaning of the prophet here it is impossible to say, but given a general reference to Christ in the scriptures of the prophets, it is not hard to discover room for a special one here. If all the promises of God in Christ are Yea, and Amen, we can nowhere find this promise so fulfilled as in the resurrection of His Son the third day. But be that as it may, here we have the aggregate of those Scripture passages out of which, and out of which alone, the doctrine of Christ's resurrection the third day could have been constructed. This was the kind of foundation the disciples had to build upon, if they were so minded to invent the story of their Master rising again. It must be confessed not a very hopeful and promising one ; nay, we

[1] Hosea vi. 1, 2.

may confidently say it was not one that could possibly have suggested itself to such men, prior to the fact; but after the fact had occurred we may readily perceive that the correspondence between it and the written monuments of Scripture was much closer than could have been supposed or anticipated, and being so close, we can understand why it was that St. Paul taught the Corinthians that Jesus Christ rose from the dead the third day *according to the Scriptures*. We must not forget, however, that of this very message here summarised he says, *I delivered unto you that which I also received*. He throws us back therefore on One beyond Himself, and we know who that is.

We know, moreover, that it was our Lord's habit to teach His disciples that the Scriptures referred to Him, and were fulfilled in Him. We cannot say that we know anything of our Lord's teaching, if we may not determine that He taught thus; and even in the solemn moments verging on His agony and death, we find Him saying, *Thinkest thou that I cannot now pray to my Father, and He shall presently give more than twelve legions of angels, but how then shall the Scriptures be fulfilled that thus it must be?*[1] These were not the Scriptures of the New Testamant, but the Scriptures of the Old. They were the very identical ancient documents of the Jews, which we now have in our hands, and which are so vehemently assailed in the present day. It is impos-

[1] Matt. xxvi. 53, 54.

sible, then, for us not to see that both our Lord and His apostles assign to these Scriptures a degree of authority and certainty which must be maintained intact, if their own language is not to be rejected. This is one of the landmarks by which we must direct our course. It cannot be that we are to regard these Scriptures in such a light as will make it incompetent for them to be the inviolable writings which Christ represented them to be. On the contrary, we are clearly warranted in saying, there is that in the Scriptures of the Old Testament which made them the vehicle of a special Divine message to man, and which still makes them so, notwithstanding men's rash and destructive conclusions with respect to them. And seeing that these conclusions are oftentimes based upon conjecture and not at all upon demonstration, it is they that must suffer themselves to be corrected by our Lord's teaching, and not our Lord's teaching that must be made to yield to them. If there was any reason whatever for His continually-expressed conviction, to call it by no higher term, that the Scriptures referred to Him, then they could only do so because they were instinct with a Divine life and fraught with a special Divine blessing. It was not fortuitous that David had spoken as he did in the 16th Psalm; it was not fortuitous that the history (or, if you will, even the legend) of the prophet Jonah had been preserved, that it existed in the Jewish literature and was classed among the twelve minor prophets, recording a marvellous deliverance for a no less marvellous end; recording the salvation of a people upon repentance by the preaching of a man who had been rescued from the jaws of death after a three days' entombment; it was not altogether without meaning or fortuitous that the prophet Hosea had spoken as he had of God's raising up Israel the third day. There was a predetermination in all this; the threefold testimony of these three writers, of various ages, was designed as a threefold cord, not easily to be broken, and though it could not be affirmed of any one that he directly contemplated the resurrection of Christ in writing as he did, and though it is impossible to prove from the nature of things that the combination of the threefold testimony was designed by God to point to this end— just as it is impossible to prove that the mechanism of the human eye or ear points to the working of a designer; yet, when we have the evidence before us, so clear and patent as it is, there is no little difficulty for the prepared, in one case or the other, to resist the conclusion that eloquently suggests itself. And when, in addition to all this, we have the express declaration of Jesus Christ that all things must be fulfilled which were written in the law of Moses, and in the Prophets and in the Psalms, concerning Him, it becomes nothing less than wilful and determined obstinacy which resists it. The fact is after all, and the more we ponder it the more the truth of it will force itself upon us, that we may argue about these things till we are weary, but there is a preparation of heart required for the acceptance of the reasonableness of Divine truth. Unless we are willing to see our God when He reveals Himself to us, we shall not see Him. It is not within the power of any human being to show Him who cannot show Himself to those who will not see. And this it is that is so extremely distasteful to man, because it appears to take the power of faith out of his own hands. We have not of ourselves the power to judge aright, when that judgment is to show us our vileness and nothingness in showing us the glory of God. We need to come to the fountain of light, not only that we may see light, but that we may receive the power to see it. God has spoken by His Word, in spite of all the difficulties attending the determination of the way in which He has spoken, as He has spoken of nothing else. The evidence of this is the way in which Christ said that that Word must be fulfilled, and the way in which He fulfilled it. We cannot call ourselves Christians, and yet deny the one or the other. If we are prepared to accept Christ, and the teaching of Christ, then we shall hail with gratitude the tokens which were given before of Him, like coruscations of roseate light in the eastern sky, heralding the advent of the lord of day. We shall know that as these infallibly betoken the glory that is to follow, so the longings and aspirations and mysterious anticipations of prophecy and psalm and law were ordained as the natural and becoming harbingers of the advent of the Sun of Righteousness, who should arise and shine with healing in His wings, unto and upon all those, but only those, who waited for His coming, and were glad at His approach.

XVIII.

THE THIRD DAY HE ROSE AGAIN FROM THE DEAD.

If thou shalt confess with thy mouth the Lord Jesus, and shalt believe in thine heart that God hath raised Him from the dead, thou shalt be saved.—ROM. x. 9.

THERE is yet another aspect of the Lord's resurrection which we must not omit to consider before we proceed to treat of the next article of the Creed, and that is its practical bearing upon life and action. The ministers of the Gospel are frequently taken to task because they represent Christianity too much as a creed and a system. The only theology which finds favour with the popular literature and the popular thought of the present day is that of morality. An article on the English pulpit in the *Quarterly Review*, which has attracted considerable attention, expresses the opinion that drunkenness, for example, among other vices, might be profitably treated by the Christian preacher. I confess that I fail to see this. A discourse upon drunkenness, for instance, in this place, would, I fancy, be more ill-timed and inappropriate than you probably regard many of those to which you are invited to listen.

To be sure, if we could get together all the drunkards, there would at least be an opportunity of preaching to them—with what success one might; as in fact the first requisite for preaching to any purpose is to secure·a congregation who are willing to listen and to learn. This, however, by the way. I have intentionally selected an extreme case, to give the greater point to what I want to say, which is, that the popular mind, for the most part, can only appreciate Christianity as an ethical system. The same writer observes that considering the multitude of sermons that are preached in this land every week, the effect produced is, comparatively speaking, *nil.* I beg entirely to differ from him. God knows that the appreciable effect is small enough, but who shall calculate the effect which it is not in the power of man to appreciate; which would only begin to be appreciated if for a single month every pulpit in the land were dumb? Though Christianity of course rules the whole province of morality, it is itself something other than moral; and this cuckoo cry of morality seems to me to indicate that the age has not learnt one of the first lessons of the " Pilgrim's Progress," that morality is a miserable substitute for the Gospel. The more legitimate conclusion is, that if our morality is defective, as it conspicuously too often is, then our Christianity is more defective still. It is not that morality is to displace Christianity, but that Christianity is to develop and to regenerate morality.

It is impossible, therefore, but that Christianity

must be a creed and a system; the very essence of it is the person and life of Christ,—the very essence of this is a series of exceptions and unique facts. If we cannot have a Christianity without Christ, which one would imagine was a truism, then we cannot have a Christ without having what is exceptional and unique in human life and history. We cannot have a Christ, for example, who is dead as other men are dead; who is living only as Socrates is living, in the spirit and influence of his teaching; who has risen from the dead only as the teaching of Socrates rose from the dead after he was poisoned; who has no other relation to the Father's home, or to us on our way thither, than Aristotle, or Archimedes, or Roger Bacon. And the men of this generation and the people of this land will before very long have to decide for themselves whether or not this is the Christ that they will have,—whether Christ only differs from other men by the bare superiority of His teaching, when they may be pleased to consider it superior; or whether, apart altogether from the abstract merit of His teaching, of which we are judges, He has in Himself and of Himself something to give and impart to us which we can only find in and derive from Him. And if Christ has the power over death which His resurrection proclaims Him to have, then He has this exceptional and unique gift.

We take, then, this statement of St. Paul as expressing the practical complement of the fact of the resurrection which has engaged us hitherto, and shall endeavour to unfold it now. When he wrote to the Romans he did not say, "All you have got to do is to lead moral lives; to be decent, respectable, truth-speaking, truth-loving; honest and upright as men of business, in your intercourse with your fellows; sober, temperate, and chaste in your management of yourselves; prudent and careful in your management of your households; not getting into debt, but living strictly within your means, and according to your station; discreet and just in the management of your children, seeing that they are well and wisely educated up to the requirements of the time," and a mass of the like judicious and timeserving counsel. He did not say this, or anything like this, however much what he did say may have involved this, and far more than this; but what he did say was (and it was thus, you observe, that he characterised his own preaching), *If thou shalt confess with thy mouth the Lord Jesus, and shalt believe in thy heart that God hath raised Him from the dead, thou shalt be saved.*[1]

Now when this message is fairly and adequately considered, it will always have, to the popular mind, the appearance of being fanatical. It is impossible to deal honestly with the apostolic language and not find in it this unmistakable flavour of fanaticism; because what does the writer say? *Thou shalt be saved.* Then the men to whom he wrote wanted saving. He had the offer of salvation; he came

[1] Rom. x. 9.

professing to teach them how they might be saved. Of course it is a further question what salvation means—how we are to understand the word. I will come to that by-and-bye ; what I want to implant in your minds now is that the Romans were assumed by St. Paul to be men who were in need of being saved, they were lost men without that which he had to give them. There can be no mistake about it. If language means anything, then his language means this. And he said, moreover, that the Lord Jesus could save them : that by certain a relation to Him they would be saved : not that by being moral men they would be saved ; not that by being good citizens, good fathers, good subjects, good husbands, good masters, good servants, and the like they would be saved ; but by confessing with the mouth and believing with the heart. Now if confessing with the mouth and believing with the heart is equivalent to being good citizens and the like, they are convertible terms ; then you may of course substitute the one for the other, but not otherwise. And I think that no man in his senses can say that they are convertible terms, or suppose it for an instant. If, therefore, what St. Paul preached was the Gospel, that which would substitute this for it cannot be the Gospel ; if one was Christianity the other cannot be.

How, then, shall we understand this crucial word, being saved ? Are we to approach the matter with the awful preliminaries of the bottomless pit and the everlasting fires of hell ? *St. Paul does not do so.* Some men cannot get on without hell. There is a substratum to all their theology, implied or understood, of hell fire. Their gospel is paved with the "burning marle" of the lost Archangel's dwelling-place. This is one of the irreparable mischiefs done to English theology by the immortal poem of Milton. Surely it is possible to get a better idea of salvation from the analogy of what we know and have experience of, than from that which we know not, and are unable to form any probable conception of. Surely in order to understand or appreciate the dealings of God, it cannot be requisite first to attempt to sound the depths and survey the horrors of the abode of Satan. Is it not possible to save by the administration of daily food, without first having a vivid apprehension of all the conceivable horrors of starvation? Is it not possible to save by the constant and careful preservation of health, without being first exposed to the hair-breadth escape from some perilous illness ? And is not one the normal and the other the abnormal condition of things ? Is it not possible, then, to land a man safely at the very gate of heaven, without first hanging him in mortal terror of his life over the seething abyss of hell ? And if it is, why should we insist upon the one method being followed in preference to the other? Nay, further, is it not possible to save in the highest and noblest sense by a wholesome and judicious education, in which the mind is stored with sound and healthy knowledge, and imbued with germinal wisdom, and noble sentiments, and beautiful images, instead of first doing irreparable damage by rendering the mind familiar with the odious features of vice, in order that we may have the glory of a somewhat ambiguous reformation? Is it otherwise with the Christian doctrine of salvation? Man, as he is, in his lost estate, is a being unsaved. This is the doctrine of the Gospel, and surely it is one which is indisputable. Christ professed to do what the greatest of the heathen philosophers had been proved incapable of doing, namely, to regenerate the heart of man. Wherever, therefore, the Gospel came, whether to intellectual Athens, or to imperial Rome, or to sensual Corinth, its message was precisely the same. "Under certain conditions thou shalt be saved. As it is, thou art not saved. And everything testifies to the fact. Thy wisdom has given thee no certain knowledge of God; thy teachers have exemplified the futility of their own wisdom; thy social condition is hopelessly and irremediably corrupt. Here is that truth which will make thee wise unto salvation and give thee life, *Believe on the Lord Jesus Christ, and thou shalt be saved.*" And it is not otherwise now. Granted that there are most lamentable plague spots on the surface of our social existence, that our moral condition is vitiated with the foulest blots; granted that the spectacle presented by the Christian Church is sufficient to make every wise man sigh, there is yet this conspicuous difference between the condition of the modern and the ancient world, that our evils exist, not because the precepts and principles of our religion are, but because they are not, carrried out. It is in spite of our religion that we are what we are ; because we give the lie to our belief in our practice ; because there are parts in the mass of society which the leaven of the Gospel has failed to penetrate, where it has encountered insuperable opposition. The Gospel was to be preached, not as something which was to make men wise and good in spite of themselves, and their depravity, and their unbelief, but for a witness, simply a witness, unto all nations.[1] The witness of the Gospel is that men as they are (and by men, brethren, I mean myself and you, we are no exception, Christians without Christ are exactly like other men), I say the witness of the Gospel is that men as they are, are unsaved. Surely the state of London at Christmas time, the state that is of the lower strata of society in London, whose chief notion of a holiday is the flinging away of all restraint, and the running riot in every way that brutal appetite suggests, is enough to show this. And what is exhibited in the most conspicuous manner in the lowest masses, is felt to be no less true virtually of himself by the conscience of the disciplined and educated Christian, that apart from Christ he has no life, and therefore is not saved. And what is more, the disciplined and educated Christian feels,

Matt. xxiv. 14.

also, that it is no mere alteration of conduct, to whatever extent it may be carried, that will save him, because it is not only in what he does, but in what he is, and chiefly in what he is, that he requires to be rectified. It is here that the Gospel of Christ seems to me to join fatal issue with those professed Christians who exalt the human will as the standard of perfect action ; who represent the man who determines to be good, and has moral energy and self-control sufficient to enable him to act on his determination, as being that which he determines to be, or if not, as having only himself to blame. Because the Gospel seems to me to declare plainly that, granting all this is not only resolved but achieved, there is still room for the absence of that which it proclaims, namely, spiritual life by Jesus Christ. The Gospel of Christ does not say, Do this or that definite thing, and it will be well with you; because in such a case all that can be said is, Do this or that and it shall be done, leaving thee exactly where thou wast before; but it does say, Believe and *thou*, in thine own incommunicable indivisible personal essence shalt be saved : thou shalt be made whole, just there, where to thyself thou art most conscious of defect, most sensible of having the territory of thy personality invaded and usurped. And if the Gospel of Christ does say this, as it manifestly does say here, I conceive that that is a misrepresentation of the Gospel which says anything else, which implies that the Gospel is a gospel of morality, and that its ministers are wrong when they proclaim it as a creed or a system. That it is not *only* a creed or a system, is as evident from the tenor of these words as that it is not only morality. But the fact is, that the Gospel of Christ professes to give man life, a life which, without it, he is destitute of, and cannot have ; and this life it professes to give, not as the effect or reward of doing something, but as the consequence of believing a definite fact, namely, the resurrection of Jesus Christ. And yet not as the consequence of believing this fact only as a fact, like the conquest of this country by the Romans, or by William of Normandy, for there have been thousands who never doubted this fact, and yet have never been the better for believing it,—but of believing it in the heart, that is to say with the innermost centre of the personal being, with all the faculties of the spiritual essence. For nothing is more true than this, that the Gospel not only revealed new facts to man, but also revealed new capacities in man—discovered to himself the possession of new faculties, which before had lain dormant for the want of analogous objects on which to exercise them. So the Gospel said, " Here is the resurrection of Jesus Christ, a fact for the heart, and not for the understanding, to lay hold on and apprehend. And the heart that is conscious of the want of life, may find life in this fact." Only here again it must be borne in mind that the fact is to be apprehended, not merely as a bare fact like one of those already mentioned, which being once over, is removed farther and farther into the past by the flight of time, but as a fact of which the significance is perpetual, and ever fresh, as—*if thou shalt believe in thine heart that God hath raised Him from the dead*—it is indefinite in its operation without regard to time. It must be brought home to the heart as a recent work wrought by God, a work that is specially redolent of the present God, and expressive of His will and favour. For the resurrection of the Lord Jesus is the highest exponent of the law of Divine life in its relation to man. It brings the life of God present to the soul of man, in the person of a living man, whose physical constitution has cast out death, and is the centre and source of life. Can it be that this is a carnal view of the Lord's new life? Is it not that any life which left His body in any sense a prey to death, unredeemed from the power of the grave, must be an impalpable life which we cannot grasp, or which, if we grasp it, leaves us as it finds us, dead; and must not such a view be essentially inferior to one which sees in His triumph over death a reality, and not a metaphor, a blessed fact and not a shadowy idea? Whereas the belief in Jesus Christ, as one who was dead and is alive, is a belief that is fraught with life to the heart of man; which brings with it inextinguishable hope, which grows brighter and brighter as life wanes and years pass by, and friends drop off or change; which survives the vicissitudes of perpetual and ever-recurring decay, and kindles a torch which shall burn for ever at the smouldering ashes of mortal joy, and makes the heart of the old man young, and the courage of the feeble strong : while in the contemplation of human sin, of that which stares one in the face without, and of that which the heart is privy to within, it is this and this alone which can give the assured hope of salvation, which can say with definite and unfaltering tones, *if thou shalt confess with thy mouth*—for what is the secret conviction of the heart without the open confession of the mouth ? it is worth but little more than such open confession without a corresponding inward conviction,—but *if thou shalt confess with thy mouth the Lord Jesus and shalt believe in thine heart that God hath raised Him from the dead, thou shalt be saved:* not merely put in a state which may ultimately lead to salvation, or which may possibly not, but *saved* alike with a present and with an everlasting salvation, the salvation of those who make the Lord, the Rock of Ages, their everlasting hope; a salvation which gives peace and joy here, which gives victory over sin, and mastery over self, and confidence even in despair here, and which, for the endless future of the world beyond the grave, is content to rest securely on the unfailing word of Him who says, *Because I live, ye shall live also.*

XIX.

HE ASCENDED INTO HEAVEN.

He that descended is the same also that ascended up far above all heavens that He might fill all things.—EPH. iv. 10.

THIS passage is valuable, as showing that the fact of our Lord's ascension was part of that scheme of oral instruction which had been committed to the Ephesians, or whoever the persons were, to whom this epistle was sent by the Apostle Paul. The allusions to that event in the Gospels are very few and very brief. St. Matthew and St. John have not recorded the fact. So that it might have been supposed by some that the belief in our Lord's ascension was not part of the original mass of tradition respecting Christ, were it not that here for example, and again in the first Epistle to Timothy,[1] and several times in the Epistle to the Hebrews,[2] clear incidental reference is made to that event. We cannot therefore for a moment doubt that the ascension into glory was among the several incidents in our Lord's life, which from the first were inculcated and believed by the Christian teachers and the Christian Church. And in fact it follows as a natural and a

[1] 1 Tim. iii. 16.   [2] Heb. i. 3; ix. 24; xii. 2., etc.

necessary sequel to our Lord's resurrection. He shewed Himself alive after His passion by many infallible proofs, being seen of the disciples forty days, but only forty days, and speaking of the things pertaining to the kingdom of God.[1] When these days were accomplished He was seen no more. Why not? Having risen from the dead, He could *die* no more; but He was to be *seen* no more. Where, then, was He? The most natural answer is that He had ascended up where He was before.

We may observe, then, that the comparative silence of the Gospels about the ascension is a strong collateral evidence of its truth, under the circumstances, rather than the reverse. If the Jesus, of whom they spake, were He who they said He was, it would follow naturally and obviously that He had returned to the bosom of the Father. He had said that a certain nobleman went into a far country, to receive for himself a kingdom, and to *return*.[2] He had spoken of sitting on the throne of His glory to judge all nations,[3]—the fact of the ascension was involved and implied in these and similar utterances; and therefore seeing that in itself it was an event so marvellous, it is plain that the Gospel writers, if they wished only to record the marvellous, would have recorded the ascension. Whereas two Gospels only have mentioned it, and that in the briefest possible manner.

[1] Acts i. 3.
[2] Luke xix. 12.
[3] Matt. xxv. 31.

Again, we observe further, that we have now taken final leave of the natural, the human, and the earthly in the Christian Creed, as in our Lord's life. We have now entered on the supernatural, the heavenly, the Divine, and shall henceforth there remain. If rising from the dead is a miraculous and supernatural act, so also is ascending into the the heavens. It is impossible to regard it otherwise. We must altogether explain it away, and resolve it into pure metaphor, if it is to cease to be miraculous. But it is perfectly plain from the several accounts in St. Mark, St. Luke, the Acts of the Apostles, and the various allusions in the Epistles, that the disciples regarded the ascension of their Master in the simple manner that their own senses bade them. The chosen had seen Him go up into the heavens, a cloud had received Him out of their sight. The vision they beheld had been interpreted to them[1] by angels; it was impossible for their plain, simple, matter-of-fact and unsophisticated minds to imagine or conceive any other method of understanding the fact,—it was contrary to all laws of nature that a human body should ascend into the air. The human body of their Master in their own sight had done so, and that was enough.

And it should be enough for us. Account for it we cannot, believe it we may, get rid of it we dare not, if we are willing that the simple faith of the first Christians should be ours, or should govern

---

[1] Mark xvi. 19; Luke xxiv. 51; Acts i. 9·11.

ours. The Lord Himself appears to have represented His own ascension as the greatest effort of faith for those who were unspiritual. When some of His disciples murmured at His teaching about the mystical union between believers and Himself, which He spoke of as eating His flesh and drinking His blood, and exclaimed *This is a hard saying, who can hear it,* He replied, *Doth this offend you, What and if ye shall see the Son of Man ascend up where He was before. It is the spirit that quickeneth, the flesh profiteth nothing; the words that I speak unto you they are spirit and they are life.*[1] He therefore not only leaves the mystery in its undiminished vastness and obscurity, but virtually supplies the key for its solution. The ascension of Christ, like all the other supernatural acts of His life, appeals to a new organ in man,—an organ of which some men appear to be entirely devoid and destitute, —the spiritual faculty. Where this organ is found, there is the capacity for embracing such acts and words as present insuperable obstacles to the merely natural, material, intellectual tendencies of the mind. If we were to see a man profess to ascend into the air now, we should at once know it was imposture or delusion, or the like. When the Christian says He ascended into heaven, he not only knows that this was literally done, but never for a moment thinks of resolving it as he would resolve it now. Why not? Because with Him it is a foregone conclusion, that

[1] John vi. 60-63.

the person so ascending was the Lord of heaven and earth. Given the premises which are indispensable, and the inference naturally follows without effort and without dispute ; but it is surely disingenuous to attempt to explain away the accidents, while at the same time not openly denying the premises ; and still more so to reject the accidents for the express purpose of denying the premises. The inevitable consequence of such a course must be to leave this world without its manifested God.

Now, to the Christian, the ascension puts the coping-stone to the edifice before constructed. It is the coronation of the Lord of life ; but like all the other acts of His personal history, it is the very opposite to what we should expect in earthly things. There was no pomp or splendour about His ascension. It was quiet, unobtrusive, unobserved of any multitudes; unwitnessed by the world at large; unaccompanied by those accessories of greatness and glory which so powerfully affect the ordinary mind. All the greatest acts of God are secret and unobserved. What human eye detects the first pulse of life that beats in the germ of the sprouting acorn that is to produce the oak? Who knows where is hid the reserve of power which moves and guides the universe? Very few were aware when the Child was born in Bethlehem which was to be the King of the Jews. Few, comparatively speaking, watched His death. No one was present at His resurrection. Eleven men only saw Him ascend into heaven.

This is of a piece with the unobserved greatness and majesty of God.

When the traveller crosses the western ocean he may sail for days without seeing a ship; but meanwhile the sun comes forth in his splendour and sets with majestic glory in the distant wave, and as the spray dances in the sunbeam, and the prow of the vessel cleaves the billow, the prismatic colours of refracted light sport gaily and joyously over the surface of the deep. For whom is all this? Is this miracle of nature wrought for him? Perhaps no eye but his observes it—and oftentimes he observes it not—yet the wonder is not withheld. The Lord rejoices in His works, whether man is called to witness, or cares to witness, them or not. Surely, then, the majesty of Christ is seen in the comparative silence and solitude of His mightiest works, and He was likest unto God when He rose from the dead with no mortal eye to witness His resurrection, and ascended into heaven in the presence of eleven only of His chosen ones, and not even of His mother.

But seeing that He left not Himself without witness when He ascended up where He was before, it is clear that He intended us to derive some lessons of instruction and comfort from the fact. Let us reverently ponder these.

The first undoubted lesson to be learnt is this. The exaltation of the human nature in the person of its head, *He ascended up into heaven.* What and where is heaven? It is other and higher than earth. It is where our Father is who dwelleth in heaven. It is there that Christ is gone, whatever and wherever that is. The connection is thus clearly established between us in our human nature and the central dwelling-place of God. Be it observed, however, that this is a truth which we must be careful of dealing with, according to the natural limits and laws of our mind. As we have said, it is a spiritual truth, to be apprehended spiritually, to be grasped only by the spirit.

Again, we know how easy it is for us to become engrossed in the affairs of life and circumstance. We know when this is the case how completely non-existent all other things and places and persons are to us. We know how thoroughly this is the case, from the fact of our insular position, with us as a nation. How comparatively rare a thing it is for an Englishman to speak any language except his own. What a common thing it is abroad to meet with people who speak at least two or three. We know also that the human mind is so constituted, that when its attention is exclusively directed too intently to one small area of business or routine life in this manner, the health gives way. And therefore in this high-pressure existence in which we all live here it becomes absolutely essential that the strain of continuity should be broken from time to time. It often happens that the best and the only thing we can do is to get away out of the reach of the tentacles of our common life, where letters cannot find us, and familiar faces cannot bring with them the train of harassing and painful associations; where change of scene and change of incident, and an entirely new adjustment of things, and a re-disposition of time may not only relax the tension of the over-wrought mind, but likewise call into exercise as it were a new combination of mental nerves and muscles. Every man of action has felt and is doomed to feel this. Such a malady, the inevitable consequence of a highly artificial life, imperatively demands the natural remedy of rest and change, and the direct influence of natural scenery. That is to say, it is good for man that he should be conscious of another life and of other scenes than those in which he daily mingles. And this is undeniably one great lesson of the Lord's ascension. That has opened to our faith and to our imagination the existence of another world in which One who shares our nature and is clothed in our flesh lives and reigns. He has invited us to come to Him there. He is gone before to prepare a place for us. He is ascended into the heavens that we may also in heart and mind thither ascend and with Him continually dwell. He who knows our nature, knows that it is good for us to have before our mind the definite existence of a place where He is, where for the present we cannot come except by faith; but where, nevertheless, we may now by faith dwell with Him, and where hereafter, the promise is, that we shall be with Him for ever.

The ascension of Christ, then, shows us the *wisdom* of living elsewhere and otherwise than in the present, the temporary, and the local. It gives us a better prospect, a higher aim, a more glorious hope. Mankind are not ignorant of the principle herein embodied. To be able to live in many circumstances, to move naturally and easily from one experience to another, from one engagement to another, from one interview to another, is the mark of a comprehensive, an able, and an agile mind; but when the change is simply from one department of the present or the local to another, though the powers of the mind may be refreshed, the spirit is not recruited. What we want is an increase of spiritual strength. We want to renew our youth like the eagle's. This is to be done only by refreshment of the spirit, by recreation from the spiritual reserve of the eternal world.

But what are those to do who have the like strain with ourselves, but can know no change and enjoy no relaxation, who are the victims day after day of the perpetual harass and irritation of small annoyances which are like the continual droppings of water that wear away the marble, who are chained by the links of association to some oppressive and exacting thought which is continually recurring, and the recurrence of which is pain; but who, unlike the wealthy and the free, are forbidden the solace and refreshment of relaxation, simply because they are neither free nor wealthy, and cannot shake off the weight of carking care? I say, what are such to do?

And to them I would reply, Whatever the trouble is which weighs upon you, whether family care or pecuniary difficulty, or business responsibility, make a conscience of forgetting it, let not that reflex action of the mind, by which it contemplates itself and its own position, be encouraged or permitted. While, therefore, you give the requisite amount of mental effort to the work immediately in hand, let that be all you give; shake off the recurrent and reflective action by which the mind broods on the subject that engages it. Determine not to think of it. Let the words of the old song, "My mind to me a kingdom is," be the maxim of your conduct. Resolve that your thoughts shall only run as you deem it expedient they should run. You have done your duty, that is assumed; I only speak to those who desire to do their duty—others, the idle, the indifferent, the inearnest, the frivolous, I am not concerned with—you have done your duty, you can do no more: leave the rest to God. He knows better than you do the way that you take. It is His prerogative to create light out of darkness. There is no use in your taking thought, and indulging care. You cannot add one cubit to your age, you cannot make one hair white or black. Care will take away many cubits from your age, and will turn your hair white before its time. The hour will run on just as slowly, just as rapidly, whether you take anxious thought or not; every hour will have its sixty minutes, neither more nor less; every day will bring its night, and every night will usher in the morn. Cultivate, therefore, as a religious duty the habit of obliviousness. When you have done your work, dismiss it.

And what if, as sometimes happens, your work is never done? Then, one thing at a time. Do not mix up the work of to-morrow, with the duty of to-day. To-morrow may never come, and then some one else must do its work. Work was made for man, and not man for work. Man was made for heaven, and that is where Christ is gone, and that is the home of the ascension.

It is not an unlovely thought that one of the first scriptures that are read in the new year,[1] according to the new table of lessons, is the detailed narrative of the ascension by St. Luke in the Acts. At such a time we ascend, in spite of ourselves, to a higher elevation. So much more of life is behind us, so much less before us; and Christ also has ascended, He is gone up on high, He hath led captivity captive, and received gifts for men, yea even for his enemies, that the Lord God might dwell among them. Never had these marvellous words such meaning as after that scene on Olivet. But we misunderstand that great event, if we think that He is gone up that He might go away. He is gone up that the Lord God might dwell among us. In St. Paul's wonderful language, *He that descended is the same also that ascended up far above all heavens*,

[1] Preached on the first Sunday in the New Year.

that He might fill all things. Place and space are no conditions of the spiritual, any more than time is. Higher or lower, as we measure by an earthly standard, are not applicable to that world which is imperceptible to the natural eye. Christ ascended that He might fill all things ; not that He might vanish, but that he might pervade. Mary Magdalene was bidden not to touch Him, because He was not yet ascended, the necessary verbal inference being thus left, that there was a sense in which she might touch Him more readily after His ascension, and if the purpose of His ascending was that He might fill all things, this would be intelligible. We dare not speculate upon the effects of His ascension upon the conditions of His risen body, but we know this, that there are no limits to His presence,—a presence in many ways more real and more effectual now than in the days of His flesh, when His presence was conditioned by the limits of time and space.

If we thus apprehend the presence of our Lord, we shall find in all the trials and cares of life that we have a very present help in trouble, and shall know that One who hath triumphed over death, and ascended with His risen body into the heavens that He might fill all things, is not only willing but able, not only able, but willing, to succour and to save all those who came unto God by Him, seeing He ever liveth to make intercession for them.

XX.

AND SITTETH ON THE RIGHT HAND OF GOD THE FATHER ALMIGHTY.

Who is he that condemneth ? It is Christ that died, yea rather, that is risen again, who is even at the right hand of God, who also maketh intercession for us.—ROM. viii. 34.

WHEN we bear in mind that this passage was probably written before any one of our present gospels was in existence, it is very interesting to note how the writer had fully embraced a fact relating to the person of Jesus Christ, which is directly stated only in the gospel of St. Mark. We are there told that *after the Lord had spoken unto them he was received up into heaven, and sat on the right hand of God.*[1] In the epistle to the Colossians St. Paul says, *If ye then be risen with Christ seek those things which are above, where Christ sitteth on the right hand of God.*[2] In the epistle to the Hebrews we read that, *when He had by Himself purged our sins, Christ sat down on the right hand of the majesty on high;*[3] and again, *We have such a high priest, who is set on the right hand of the throne of the majesty in the heavens;*[4] and once more, *Who for*

[1] Mark xvi. 19.
[2] Col. iii. 1.
[3] Heb. i. 3.
[4] Heb. viii. 1.

the joy that was set before Him, endured the cross, despising the shame, and is set down at the right hand of the throne of God.[1] And lastly, in the first epistle of Peter, *Who is gone into heaven, and is on the right hand of God, angels and authorities and powers being made subject unto Him.*[2] This is the aggregate of scriptural allusion in the New Testament to that declaration of the Creed which we are now to consider.

And this present passage in the Romans joins with the session of our blessed Lord on God's right hand, the statement about His making intercession for us, which has no other parallel in Scripture but the similar statement in the Hebrews, *Wherefore He is able to save them to the uttermost that come unto God by Him, seeing He ever liveth to make intercession for them.*[3] To my mind the solitary occurrence of this direct assertion about our Lord's intercession in the two epistles to the Romans and the Hebrews would go a long way towards producing the conviction that the same writer was the author of both; this, however, by the way. We have several allusions to our Lord's present position of glory on the right hand of God. Usually this is represented as one of session; but on one remarkable occasion, namely the martyrdom of Stephen, we are told that he *saw the glory of God in the opened heavens, and Jesus standing on the right hand of God.*[4] We have

[1] Heb. xii. 2.
[2] 1 Peter iii. 22.
[3] Heb. vii. 25.
[4] Acts vii. 55, 56.

only two allusions to His intercession for us, and one of them is this. In the Creed there is no mention of the Lord's intercession, but we cannot separate it from the thought of His present position, nor indeed His present position altogether from the thought of His intercession, and therefore it may be well to combine the two in our meditations to-day.

When I say that there are only two allusions to our Lord's intercession in the New Testament, I mean express allusions. We have in the Hebrews such a statement as *Christ is not entered into the holy places made with hands, which are the figures of the true, but into heaven itself, now to appear in the presence of God for us*;[1] and in the first epistle of St. John, *If any man sin we have an Advocate with the Father, Jesus Christ the righteous*,[2] and the like. To the ordinary mind this will appear like a repetition of the same idea, but to the careful student of the exact declarations and language of Scripture the difference will be worth noting.

We proceed, then, to the consideration of the subject in hand; and we must first observe that we are dealing now with a matter altogether beyond the scope and apprehension of our natural faculties. We cannot see Jesus Christ now; no exercise, therefore, of our natural faculties will inform us where He is or what the conditions of His present existence are, any more than you or I can divine the nature of a particular country which we have never visited

[1] Heb. ix. 24. [2] 1 John ii. 1.

When Sir Roderick Murchison told Livingstone what geological formations he would find in the centre of Africa, he hazarded an assertion which was based on a scientific induction of facts, and which was consequently verified. Had the assertion proved false, his science would have been at fault, and the error would have been capable of detection. But there is no analogy between the geological formations of Africa and the state or accidents of the kingdom of heaven. No bow which is bent on earth will project an arrow into the dwelling-place of God, and induction fails us here. We may argue for ever, but our conclusions will be invalid and void. Archimedes used to say that had he where to place his engines he could move the world : with equal truth we may say that we cannot map out the geography of heaven, simply because we have no instruments or lenses which will carry or reveal so far.

But it must be borne in mind that the facts we have already contemplated, which, as we have seen rest on a basis of evidence so conclusive, throw great light on those of which we have yet to treat. If Jesus Christ is, as we believe Him to be, the human manifestation of the Divine Being, then that circumstance must materially affect all that we are told of Him after He left this earth. The conditions of Christ's present existence are not difficult to apprehend because we have exalted Him too high, but because we have not exalted Him high enough. We are dealing with One, whose glory is infinite, and commensurate with nature and with space; we are not dealing with a man, the conditions of whose existence were limited by the limitations of our natural life.

When we are told that Christ ascended into the heavens, we must not forget who Christ was, and we must beware of interpreting His ascension by the degrees of higher and lower, but must remember that ascension is a spiritual act, pertaining to the spiritual body, and that it transcends the conceptions of the imagination or the intellect, as much as the spirit transcends the mind. If we are told that Christ is at the right hand of God, we must correct the thoughts suggested by the sober undoubted truth, that God is a being without body, parts or passions, and that He has no right hand on which to sit, whatever the literal expression may be designed to teach us.

This, as it seems to me, is one of the purposes intended to be served by the Revelation of St. John. Read in the first chapter the vision of our Lord in glory, which was vouchsafed to His servant John, in the isle of Patmos, and see how the right hand of power is interpreted thereby. "*And when I saw Him, I fell at His feet as dead, and He laid His right hand upon me, saying unto me, Fear not, I am the first and the last; I am He that liveth, and was dead, and behold I am alive for evermore.*"[1] Here is the right hand of power in an altogether different

[1] Rev. i. 17, 18.

aspect, not an aspect of locality, but an aspect of condition, an aspect of exaltation and glory.

And let it not be said that such a subject is unprofitable because it is beyond our powers to comprehend it. I am well aware of that. I do not profess to comprehend it, but I know how impossible it is for the human mind not to exercise and to vex itself about the questions that arise out of this and kindred matters, and how from the mind being so exercised very serious obstacles may arise to faith, and my object is, if possible, to remove these and similar obstacles. The right hand of God must be apprehended as a spiritual condition, not as a local position. It expressed to the Jewish mind the highest possible conceptions of glory, majesty, power, dignity and the like. But what to the Jewish mind may have been an assistance to the conception, may be an impediment to ours. Let us not suffer the bondage of the letter to become so to us, but seek to be delivered from it by the freedom of the spirit.

There is one interesting remark, however, to be made here. We know that St. Paul was present at the death of Stephen. There is every reason to believe that he was powerfully affected by that scene. We are told he was consenting unto his death, that he was standing by, and kept the raiment of them that slew him. He does not seem to have taken an active part in it. The seeds of conviction which germinated afterwards on the journey to Damascus were, in all probability, sown at the death of Stephen, and there are sundry indications of the influence wrought by the defence of Stephen on the apostle's mind. We seem from time to time to come across verbal reminiscences of that speech. I believe this is one of them. Among the books composing the New Testament, this expression in the Romans is probably the earliest reference to our Lord's session we can find. But though the Acts may have been written later, it is clear that the events recorded in the seventh chapter must have happened earlier, and in point of time there is no statement of the truth in question so early as that in the dying words of Stephen.

Believing therefore, as we do, that the vision vouchsafed to the first martyr was an actual revelation, and believing that, under the circumstances there was, humanly speaking, adequate cause for such a revelation to be vouchsafed, we are led up at once not only to the probable source of St. Paul's various statements, about the condition of our Lord in glory, but also to the actual foundation of those statements not in the voluntary speculations of the human mind, but in the true and actual revelation of the glorified Son of God. We can only know where and how He is now—what was the position He assumed after His ascension, by His graciously vouchsafing to reveal it. If He has revealed it, then we know it with the assurance of absolute certainty. And that he has revealed it we have the authority of St. Luke in the Acts, for the fact, together with the possible reminiscence of the event recorded in the words before us.

For it can hardly be needful to allude to the verbal discrepance between Jesus sitting at the right hand of God, as He is commonly represented, and His standing there as Stephen saw Him. The vivid change of attitude has always been thought, and rightly, to denote that accession of interest which might fitly be supposed to characterise the Lord's position as witnessing the death of His first martyr, a thought which has found expression in our own collect,[1] which speaks of Jesus as "*standing* at the right hand of God to succour all those who suffer for Him."

For those eighteen centuries past, the Lord has not been, if we may so say, an unimpassioned or at all events an unconcerned spectator of the fortunes of His Church. But every deed of blood, and every act of faith, has had Him for a witness and a succourer, not indeed by restraining the lawlessness and fury of the adversary any more than it was restrained at the death of Stephen, but by sending forth supplies of spiritual strength and consolation with the foretaste of glory which was given then, and by making, as was notably the case then, the blood of the martyrs to be the fruitful seed of the Church.

But there is yet another thought which we must not pass by, which is that of our Lord's intercession

[1] For St. Stephen's Day.

on our behalf, which is sometimes, as here, conjoined with that of His session at God's right hand. This also I feel sure is open to misconception, and is likely to lead to fatal and pernicious error. The notion, I fancy, which is commonly derived from our Lord's intercession, is one which as it seems to me can only do dishonour to the glory of God, or at least which may serve to bring apparent honour to Christ, at the expense of the honour due to God. The idea of intercession is too apt to suggest that of an offended and angry being, who is only with reluctance won over to lay by his wrath upon the intercession of another being, who is intrinsically more merciful than he. I would not hesitate to say that I can only regard this as a notion at once unworthy of the nature of God and of the work of Christ.

It may help us to a better conception of this matter, if we bear in mind that the same expression in a yet stronger form is applied by St. Paul in the same chapter of this same epistle to the work of the Holy Spirit which is here applied to Christ; when he says *the Spirit itself maketh intercession for us with groanings which cannot be uttered.*[1] I am not aware that any one has ever misconceived of the Spirit's office in a similar way from the application of this expression to it. We never imagine that any natural reluctance on the part of God is overcome by the Spirit's intercession on our behalf. Then

[1] Rom. viii. 26.

why should we imagine it of Christ? Is not the Holy Spirit the very gift of God, and how can the gift be mightier than the giver, or how should it prevail against the giver? Was it not God that sent the Son to be the Saviour of the world? How then can that be a just and adequate representation of the work of Christ, which conceives of it as a salvation out of the hands of God, rather than a salvation by bringing back to the love of His mercy and grace.

Again, another passage in the epistle to the Hebrews already referred to, is not without its bearing on this matter, that, namely, which speaks of Christ entering *into heaven itself now to appear in the presence of God for us.*[1] Surely it is this which contains the key to the whole matter. We are on earth, God is in heaven. We have not as yet access to heaven, but we have One three in substance of our nature to appear on our behalf; He is our advocate, our intercessor, our representative, our substitute; He is all that these words feebly endeavour to express, and more than all that they convey, but we must beware of suffering the language chosen to bind us in a servile manner to the rigid significance of the letter, otherwise what was designed as a help will only becom a hindrance.

I speak, of course, mainly for myself. I cannot answer for others. It is possible that you may have no experience of the same difficulties. To me a too

[1] Heb. ix. 24.

literal acceptation of such terms as intercession, advocate, and the like, would have the effect of throwing so much of the haze of uncertainty and inefficiency over the work of Christ as would suffice practically to rob that work of its real completeness. And this I believe to be at once fatal to that acceptance of the Gospel message, which is essential unto life, and also to be out of harmony and agreement with analogous statements of holy Scripture, which are surely characteristic of its general tenor.

For example, in this very chapter, full as it is of glorious hope, we have this assurance to start with. *There is, therefore, now no condemnation to them that are in Christ Jesus,* and again here, *Who is he that condemneth?* Verily, if there is one thought which the writer is anxious to bring home, it is this, the very elimination and abolition of condemnation. But if condemnation is done away, and if there is none to condemn, where is the place for further advocacy or intercession? Certainly nowhere, if by such advocacy and intercession is implied any the smallest degree of reluctance on the part of God yet remaining to be overcome.

But it is not so, for Christ's is a finished salvation. The pardon He administered was a pardon absolute and unconditional, a pardon which is neither to be revoked nor suspended, which is not to be more free and complete hereafter, but is free and complete now. And, therefore, His advocacy and intercession is not something ambiguous, tentative, ineffectual, incomplete, but an eternal, infinite, and complete intercession, partaking of the essence of all His work.

And I know no truth so important to enunciate and inculcate in the present day as this. The high priesthood of Christ is an accomplished high priesthood, exemplified and attested by His position at God's right hand as the eternal mediator. There remaineth no more offering for sin as there remaineth no more condemnation in the conscience. It is an evil day for the Church of England, and an evil day for the Church of Christ when there is any hesitation or uncertainty on this matter. Sin is either put away, or its defilement remains. The death of Christ, either put it away once for all, for each, and for all of us, or it failed to do so and left some of it for us to put away ourselves, by the monstrous paraphernalia of sacraments, confession, penance, priestcraft, and what not.

We must determine, brethren, in this our day, which of the two Gospels we will believe ; the Gospel of Christ, who offers us a full and free pardon upon the exercise of direct personal faith in Him, or the gospel of the priest, in which forsooth Christ will communicate Himself to us through His Church, that is to say, not immediately as Himself the one only mediator between God and man, to whom not priest, saint, angel, archangel, or virgin mother may be added, but as mediating through an endless succession and continual repetition of sacraments and ordinances, if so be at the last we may perchance attain to the fulness of that assurance, which, if it is ever ours must be ours eventually by the exercise, sooner or later, of direct personal faith in Jesus Christ.

In distinct and decided opposition to such a theory, as I believe, was the glorious fact revealed of Christ's eternally complete and never failing intercession at the right hand of the majesty on high, in the contemplation of which the apostle asked, *Who is He that condemneth? It is Christ that died, yea, rather that is risen again, who is even at the right hand of God, Who also maketh intercession for us,* heaping image of confidence and assured hope upon image; and with reference to which our Lord Himself said it should be the special work of the Holy Spirit to *convince the world concerning righteousness*, because of His own permanent entrance into the presence of God for us: *Of righteousness, because I go to my Father and ye see me no more.*[1]

[1] John xvi. 8, 10.

XXI.

FROM THENCE HE SHALL COME TO JUDGE THE QUICK AND THE DEAD.

Because He hath appointed a day in the which He will judge the world in righteousness, by that man whom He hath ordained, whereof He hath given assurance unto all men in that He hath raised Him from the dead.—ACTS. xvii. 31.

IT is instructing to notice that those epistles of St. Paul, in which perhaps more than in any other, he makes allusion to the coming of Christ, were the epistles to the Thessalonians, which in all probability were written shortly after his speech at Athens, here recorded in the Acts. Possibly the persecution to which he had recently been exposed in Macedonia, had had the effect of turning his thoughts to the time of retributive justice which he felt would surely come. However this may have been, there is at all events, a striking coincidence in the line of thought presented to us in the letters and the speech.

The statement in the text, moreover, is further remarkable in this respect, that it bases the declared certainty of the judgment to come upon the assured fact of the resurrection past. The doctrine of a judgment to come, is not peculiar to Christianity, traces of it are to be found in other religions as well ; but the announcement of the resurrection of Christ, is of necessity peculiar to Christianity, and therefore the announcement of judgment to come which is based upon it, must be so likewise to such an extent, and in that particular. The notion of judgment to come, as an element of what may be called natural religion, is suggested by, and springs out of the notion of human responsibility, of which I fancy it is extremely difficult to divest the mind. All must admit that in a sense we are all responsible. For example, we are all responsible to society, and if we violate the precepts of society, society will make us feel our responsibility. We are all responsible to ourselves. There is a duty we owe to ourselves, and every transgression of excess committed will force us to acknowledge we have failed to discharge it. And then it will be difficult for our thoughts the meanwhile to be neither accusing or else excusing one another. But when we get so far, as it seems to me, we cannot help getting farther ; it is not easy to avoid taking the next step, that wherever there is duty, there must be one to whom it is due ; that if we have failed in our duty to ourselves it is not we who established that line of duty, or so constituted ourselves as to be sensible of dereliction from it; that in fact the sense of violated duty points us to a code of duty external to ourselves, which we did not invent, but to which we owe allegiance, and that as we did not invent this code to which conscience testifies so neither did the code invent itself; that it is the result of an arrangement and adaptation by which we are bound, and which if it is to be referred to nature then shows that we are responsible to nature rather than to an imaginary code ; in short, it seems to me that however we define or explain our responsibility, it is hard indeed to get rid of the fact that we are responsible : the thing does not admit of denial whatever we do with the word.

Surely, then, it is impossible not to see that a foundation is laid in human nature for the doctrine of a judgment to come, which has approved itself to many nations, and been expressed in many creeds.

For, given the fact that man is responsible to some one who is the author of duty, and that this responsibility is continually revealing itself—though indeed in an uncertain and irregular manner—in human life, it seems to be necessarily demanded in proportion as the fact of responsibility is felt and acknowledged, that the meaning of the fact should ultimately be revealed both to the personal conscience and to the world at large. What is every court of judicature but an earthly and very imperfect shadow of a perfect and Divine reality. The judge pronounces a sentence, but his sentence, though final as regards this life and present phase of things, is not final as regards the inner world, which the several stages of the procedure have revealed and implied, nor even as regards the ultimate ends of justice. How few are the criminals who are in any degree bettered by the terrible discipline of crime and its attendant punishment; but surely the ultimate ends of justice must be not merely punishment, but reformation. A man is not really judged in his inner being unless he has been made not only to feel and confess he has done wrong, not only obliged to render such recompense as the law may demand and his own ability provide, but also has been set right in himself and delivered from the evil which has enslaved him. It is obvious that this must be the ultimate purpose of Christianity as a remedial system, but it is no less obvious that such purpose cannot be attainable here; if, therefore, it is to be attained at all, it must be attained hereafter. And surely this is a hope which is not excluded from, but encouraged by the thought of the Christian judgment.

There are, however, many associations connected with that doctrine, as it is commonly apprehended, which, I think, are calculated to bring it into discredit, and which do not appear to be warranted by the teaching of Scripture. Let us consider, then, what that teaching is. First we have the personal return of Christ—*From thence He shall come:* that is to say, from the highest heaven whither He is ascended, and from the right hand of the Father where He sits. Then are we to understand that Christ will ever cease to be at God's right hand? are we to understand the highest heaven will cease to contain the personal body of the Lord? These and similar questions, which appear to force themselves on the reflective mind, go far towards convincing me that we really know very little of this matter because we have been told very little. We may certainly determine that we know nothing but what we have been told; and if it shall appear, as it certainly does, that much of what we have been told cannot possibly be understood literally, then, we can only decide that we know less than we thought we knew. In the face, therefore, of the transcendant difficulties of the whole subject, the best course seems to be to cling fast to what we have been told and to add no more. For instance, we have been told over and over again that Christ shall return to judgment, but we have not been told what that means or what we are to understand by it. Undoubtedly we have been led to suppose that whatever it means it did receive a partial and preliminary fulfilment at the destruction of Jerusalem, and this fact cannot but serve to modify to some degree the sense in which we interpret the return of Christ. Still I do not see how it is possible to do away with so clear a statement as that of the angels at the ascension, *This same Jesus which is taken up from you into heaven shall so come in like manner as ye have seen Him go into heaven.*[1] The return at the siege of Jerusalem was in no sense a fulfilment of this language, whatever else it was. I hold, therefore, that both by the language of Scripture and that of the Creed, we are shut up to the belief in a

[1] Acts i. 11.

personal return of Christ of some kind. He has too often given us to understand this Himself, in a variety of ways, to leave any impression but one upon the mind. When, however, we are told that He shall appear in the clouds of heaven, *in flaming fire, taking vengeance on them that know not God and that obey not the gospel of our Lord Jesus Christ*,[1] and the like, I am free to confess—and I do so in all humility before God—that I do not know what such language means, partly because of other language in Scripture to which manifestly no less deference is due, and partly because the logic of events appears to have warranted another interpretation than the severely literal one.

The question, my beloved brethren, is just this, Are we bound by the teaching of Scripture to expect a tremendous physical catastrophe of stars falling, and heavens shrivelling like a parched scroll, and mountains falling, and seas dividing and the like, or are we taught by the analogy of Scripture, and of nature, to believe that the end will come rather as the beginning came, silently, gradually, imperceptibly, as when Simeon took up the infant Christ in his arms, and that its likeness to the descriptions given must be sought rather in the marvellous contrast finally presented, than in the accidents by which it is brought about.

And whether I am right or wrong, I do not hesitate to say that my own faith would be much

[1] 2 Thess. i. 8.

more easily confirmed if I thought this was the tenor of Holy writ, than if I supposed that the pictorial description of the day of judgment popularly and traditionally received, was to be literally and minutely fulfilled.

And I will tell you why. Christianity it appears to me has revealed God to us. We no longer worship an unknown God. We no longer worship a God whose presence is restricted to place. We have been told on the highest authority, that God is a Spirit, and that we must worship Him in Spirit. Christianity as it seems to me, is the revelation of God in the present, in the personal phenomena of human life, in birth, in marriage, in death, in joy, in sorrow, in pain, in suffering, in trial, breavement, affliction and the like. Christianity is the revelation of the Divine in man, through the manifestation of One in whom the human and the Divine are permanently, indissolubly, completely, and exceptionally united. We do not wait for the perception of a material God, or the entrance into a material heaven, but for the fuller and more complete realisation through the Spirit of the nature and the character of God, and for, no doubt, the physical perception of the person of Christ. When this physical perception is vouchsafed to us, our eyes will *see the King in His beauty*,[1] and so far He will at all events have come to us. But when we say that He shall come, and come from heaven, we must not fail to re-

[1] Isa. xxxiii. 17.

member who it is that shall come, and where and what the heaven is, from whence He shall come. It is not the unknown God who shall come, but the God whom we have learnt to know through His manifestation in Jesus Christ. And as heaven is not a physical, earthly, or material place, so we do not look for the invasion of one physical material place by the accidents of another, for the intrusion of another and an unknown physical world upon our present and known world, but for the more direct and immediate presentation of the present spiritual and eternal world, to the conscience and the sense of the redeemed and glorified Christian.

Our Lord Himself has led us to suppose that His manifestation at the last will assume a very different character to those who already know Him and to those who knew Him not. To the former He says, *And when these things begin to come to pass, then look up, and lift up your heads, for your redemption draweth nigh.*[1] That this world and this life is not our all, none knows better than the Christian, and none hopes more ardently than he. What shall be the conditions of final transition from the one to the other, no one knows, nor, as it seems to me, has Holy Writ revealed; but this transition is surely identical with the coming of Christ and the day of judgment.

Does all this seem hazy and unsatisfactory to you, my friends? If it does, then, I counsel you to reject it; only if it seems to remove some of the difficulties

[1] Luke xxi. 28.

that beset the popular and material notions of a tremendous and final catastrophe, and to shed a gleam of light on some of the most perplexing statements of Scripture, then do I venture to offer it to your contemplation.

We do our Christianity great violence, when we believe that Christ is absent, or forget that He is present, or cease to realise the dispensation of the Spirit, which alone can help us to perceive Christ; and if to anyone Christ shall come to judgment, it will surely be to those who have had Him pleading with them all their lives, as a present and living God and Saviour, whom they in their dulness and blindness have refused to hear and to perceive.

While however, as it seems to me, Christianity has given us no definite notion or idea as to *how* Christ shall come, or what shall be the unmistakable signs of His coming, it has placed the fact of His future manifestation to the world at large, on the firm and solid basis of His resurrection as a past and veritable fact. And we can no more question the one, than we can doubt the other. His resurrection is by all Christians an acknowledged fact, historic and indestructible. The Christ, then, who was once seen by mortal eyes, shall by mortal eyes be seen again. How we cannot tell. The language of Scripture may be unintelligible as it often has been, and I believe is until it has been fulfilled, but that a time shall come when not only believers shall see Him to their joy, but those who do not believe in Him, shall see Him to their confusion, admits, I conceive, of no shadow of doubt, being established as St. Paul says, or seems to say, no less by the Divine Word than by the natural inference from facts.

And this time shall be the consummation of the ages, and the day of judgment, when He shall come to judge the quick and the dead. The more we ponder it the more inconceivable and unintelligible it becomes. Who are the quick, or who shall they be? Those who are alive at His coming! What a stupendous thought, and how impossible to grasp or shape it! And yet, what is the alternative? Certainly no less difficult of conception,—either that the present state of things shall go on for ever and for ever in all essential aspects as it is, or else that the race shall die out, and the poet's vision be realised of a last man :—

> "I saw a vision in my sleep
> That gave my spirit strength to sweep
> Adown the gulf of time;
> I saw the last of human mould,
> That shall Creation's death behold,
> As Adam saw her prime."

Now in the abstract it is impossible to conceive of either of these alternatives as being realised; whereas the statement that the one man ordained by God to be the judge of quick and dead shall come to judge them, is in itself antecedently probable, and is certainly not in the abstract inconceivable, however impossible it may be for us to determine or conceive the conditions under which it shall take place.

We arrive, then, at this result, that as the declaration of Scripture that there shall be a future judgment is based on the instincts of human nature, and corroborated by the verdict of the human reason, when compared with the only alternatives possible to our conception, so the very obscurity of Scripture, which we cannot but acknowledge, must be regarded as due to the inherent obscurity of the subject, and the absolute impossibility of making it plain to our apprehension, rather than to any other cause. Such a result may appear to be superfluous to those who are willing to accept the statements of Scripture, whether they are intelligible or not; but it will hardly be deemed so by those who would be thankful to accept the Scripture statements if only the preliminary obstacles of rational thought arising out of those very statements themselves, could be satisfactorily removed.

And for the rest, brethren, it is a solemn matter, which time itself will, before long, reveal to all of us. If the history of Jesus Christ is not all a fiction, which it most unquestionably cannot be, then we shall each of us, before very long, behold Him. In Him will be revealed to us the tremendous significance of that inextinguishable sense of responsibility which burns within us. If His own word is true, then He is the ultimate person to whom we are responsible. He it is to whom duty itself is due. There may be this and that owing to our fellow-creatures, this and that due to ourselves, but beneath and beyond it all there is concealed and yet revealed an obligation which is due to Him. He it is who has bound us by this obligation—me to preach, you to listen, one and all to do the work which what we call chance and circumstance, profession and vocation, has given us to do. We all acknowledge certain duties—duties to our parents, children, brethren, employers, servants, and the like. Will it not be a great assistance to every earnest mind among us to set the Lord Jesus Christ always before us, the crucified, risen, and ascended Lord, as the taskmaster of our work, the adjudicator of our reward, to look to Him as the one Being whom we strive to serve, knowing that He is not, like our fellow man, hard to please, but that He accepts the pure intent and the humble effort, that He does not reap where He has not sown, nor gather where He has not strawn; but that, to every one who seeks His grace, and desires His favour, and relies upon His strength, and believes in His love in life and in death, He will say in the judgment, *Well done, good and faithful servant, enter thou into the joy of thy Lord.*[1]

[1] Matt. xxv. 21.

XXII.

FROM THENCE HE SHALL COME TO JUDGE THE QUICK AND THE DEAD.

Because He hath appointed a day in the which He will judge the world in' righteousness by that man whom He hath ordained, whereof He hath given assurance unto all men in that He hath raised Him from the dead.—ACTS xvii. 31.

THERE are two main thoughts which, though closely connected, are yet separate, which are suggested by the article of the Creed we are now considering, namely the personal return of Christ and the future judgment. The former of them chiefly occupied us on Sunday last. To-day we will concern ourselves more especially with the latter.

It is very frequently said that the strongest argument for the reality of a life to come is supplied by the inequalities of the present life. It is thought that the conspicuous injustice of the existing condition of things can only be redressed by the further advantages of another life, in which a different system will prevail. At the same time, it is part of the popular doctrine, which reasons thus—that the judgment to come will decide irrevocably what the character of that life is to be.

But first, I do not think that the popular expedient of calling the future life into existence to redress the balance of the present derives any sanction from the teaching of Scripture. It is at the best but a human inference drawn from it. We have, indeed, in the parable of the rich man and Lazarus the words, *Son, remember that thou in thy lifetime receivedst thy good things, and likewise Lazarus evil things, but now he is comforted and thou art tormented*,[1] which may perhaps appear to favour such a notion; but it may be fairly questioned whether these words are intended to teach it. And secondly, though what they do teach, which is equivalent to the hope suggested by the familiar promise that the Lord God shall wipe away tears from off all faces, is the legitimate and most blessed consolation of the Word of God, this is altogether very different from the argument in question. For, granting that our present brief existence here is to be succeeded by an eternal and unalterable existence hereafter, I would ask, "How is it possible that any just compensation for anything temporal can be supplied by something which is eternal? how is it possible that the finite can be in any sense commensurate with the infinite?" St. Paul says, *Our light affliction, which is for a moment, worketh for us a far more exceeding and eternal weight of glory:*[2] that is intelligible. The present pain is a way to the future glory. The cross is the path of life, death is the gate, and the condition of bliss,—all that we admit.

[1] Luke xvi. 25. [2] 2 Cor. iv. 17.

But in every case, be it observed, the less leads on to the greater just as the seed produces the plant, and the bud unfolds the flower, but it cannot be pretended in any case that there is an equipoise or equivalent. Who would not purchase, and gladly purchase, endless felicity by the endurance of pain which must shortly have an end? Who would not go through any amount of suffering if with the suffering he could have the positive assurance of eternal joy? One would necessarily surpass the other as a grain of sand is outweighed by the sun in the heavens. It would be absurd to say that the one counterbalanced the other.

But this is far more apparent when we contemplate the alternative case. What would be the value of a life spent here filled to the overflow with all that life could give—with health, wealth, ease, honour, luxury, prosperity, fame, power, eminence, and the like, even supposing that the enjoyment of all these things were protracted to the utmost possible limit of human existence, if all were to be succeeded by an eternity of hopeless and unutterable misery? Would there be anything like a *counterpoise* in the one to the other? Unquestionably not. I venture to say that there is no one in the whole world who would consent to the enjoyment upon such conditions of the utmost that the world and its fulness could give. There is no one who, upon having placed fairly before him the two alternatives, endless bliss and endless woe, and placed in such a way that their reality could be somehow appreciated, and not merely believed in as a tenet, would not gladly forego present enjoyment and pleasure of every sort and kind, and submit to present degradation and suffering, rather than encounter the one or lose the other.

But, as a matter of fact, the instances in which this extreme position of good or evil is realised in life are very rare, and consequently it is obvious that if in the most extreme cases the notion of a counterpoise utterly fails, it cannot possibly hold good in any cases that are not extreme ; that is, it offers no solution whatever of the ordinary inequalities of life to throw into the scale for their adjustment the prospect of a future endless life in which they will be reversed.

I confess frankly, therefore, that to my mind the ordinary argument that there must be a future state in which the inequalities of the present one will be rectified, fails utterly to come with any force, if that future state is to be, as it is assumed to be, one of unending bliss or woe. You will say then, do you mean us to infer that under colour of dealing with the subject of judgment to come, you are endeavouring to destroy the notion of an unalterable future state of existence? To which imaginary question I reply emphatically, No. I am doing no such thing. I am not at present going to touch that question, if I touch it at all. What I want to show is simply that the argument for a judgment to come which shall rectify all that is wrong here, will fail to satisfy any one who reflects that the permanent readjustment of things upon a reversed basis would offer no adequate compensation. To substitute for temporal misery eternal felicity, and for temporal felicity eternal misery, would surely be at the best but a very clumsy way of rectifying the evil of this world. Whatever cause the ideally good might have to be satisfied with their lot, the ideally wicked, as it seems to me, would have fair ground for impugning the justice of God. And such a conclusion, if it is sound, need give us no alarm, supposing that the misapprehension from which it springs is the result of our own systematic theology and not of the teaching of Scripture.

Now here again we must observe that the subject is one of profound and hopeless obscurity, nor do we pretend for one moment to throw any light upon it, except so far as we can gather light from Scripture itself. Neither are we about to propound any other theory which is to replace the popular one; we desire rather to disabuse the mind of theories altogether. It is against the popular theories and the popular notions of a rigid and inflexible system that we protest, because we are conscious of their baneful influence upon the free action of our faith and desire to substitute for them the simple elemental principles of Holy Writ.

And these, as it seems to me, are few and obvious. For example,. there comes first of all that grand foundation principle—the spontaneous utterance of the father of the faithful, and the guiding star of his own faith and hope, *Shall not the Judge of all the earth do right?*[1] to which may be added the correlative question, "Is it possible that He can do wrong?" Each of these questions admits of but one answer. Then, if that is the case, the restless and perplexing debates of our own mind may surely have an end. The Judge of all the earth cannot do do wrong—He can only do right. That is the first principle.

. Then follows the second, which seems to me to be no less plainly taught in Scripture, even if it be not explicitly enunciated. And it is this: God's notion of right and wrong can only be the complement of ours. Ponder that. I do not say that our notion of right and wrong must necessarily be the measure of God's, for that may be open to question; but I do say that God's notion can only be the complement of ours. And I will shew you presently what I mean; but first I want you to apprehend the opposite principle—which is frequently adopted in the place of this,—which is that God's notion of right and wrong must be something essentially different from ours; that we can form no idea of what to the mind of God would be either right or wrong; that we can frame no adequate conception of the Divine justice. Now, these are the two antagonistic principles which lie at the root of all our misconceptions on the matter before us. And I do not

[1] Gen. xiii. 25.

hesitate to say that this last principle, while it appears to be the more humble-minded and pious of the two, is in itself most pernicious and absolutely fatal, not only to our worship of God, but to our acceptance of His Word. How can I worship a God of whom I do not know but that His conception of justice may be something diametrically opposed to mine? If He has the absolute and arbitrary determination of what is right and what is wrong, how can I have any confidence in my approach to Him? And what is more, how can His revelation have any ground of approach to me, if it does not appeal to those very notions and elemental conceptions of right and wrong which He has Himself planted in my moral nature? It is because He has endowed me with a moral sense, which however imperfectly and inadequately reflects His own, and is not opposed to it, that He by His Word can find in me a foundation on which its acceptance may be built. Surely to every thoughtful mind this can only be self-evident. God's Word is God's Word, not because it contradicts my sense of justice and right, but because it fufils and confirms it. What else does our Lord imply when he says, *Yea, and why even of yourselves judge ye not what is right?*[1] and again, *Judge not according to the appearance, but judge righteous judgment?*[2] Is not this the very accusation that He brings against the Jews when He tells them, *Ye seek to kill Me because My word hath no place in you?*[3] They had

[1] Luke xii. 57.   [2] John vii. 24.   [3] John viii. 37.

quenched the natural God-given light of justice and right within, and so were incompetent to judge of Him ; but not because His sense of right was one which was essentially opposed to any they could attain to.

Having then arrived at these two elemental principles, first, that the Judge of all the earth can only do what is right, and that His idea of right must be the complement, not the contradiction of ours, we go one step further, and proceed to contemplate the scene which meets us here, and over which most undoubtedly the Bible has thrown no veil— the scene, that is, of iniquity, oppression, injustice, misery, and vice. The reconciliation of this condition of things as a matter of fact with the belief in the rule of a great and righteous God, was the ever-present and vexing problem of the saints of old. This it was that tormented David and his fellow-psalmists, *Thus my heart was grieved, and it went even through my reins.*[1] This it was that confounded righteous Job, and to this problem the Old Testament presented nothing more than a partial solution. The book of Job itself was the nearest approximation to a solution. It was reserved for the Gospel to present the fullest solution yet proposed, and a solution which, as far as the present condition of things admits, is also entirely complete. It is not, however, a theoretical but a practical solution, the solution which is derived from the actual participation of the Lord of all in the evil to which He has

[1] Ps. lxxiii. 21, cf. Ps. xxxvii., etc.

subjected His creatures. But to this problem the saints of old had nothing they could bring, except their indomitable faith that a time would come when God would make His purpose plain, that He might be justified in His saying, and be clear when He was judged. Only here, observe, it was still man's instinctive sense of justice and right that was to pronounce God just. His notion of justice was not something radically different from and opposed to man's, otherwise man would never be competent to pronounce Him just, but it was the highest development of man's own moral sense to which when rightly and perfectly informed man himself would offer homage.

Then there enters in here another fact. We are placed for the present in an imperfect condition of things in which we have and can have only imperfect and inadequate information. If we knew the whole our verdict would be different from what it often is, not because the principles on which we should pronounce it would be altered, but because we should be better informed and have some ground to build upon. Did we know more, we should frequently not have to *wait* for a future readjustment of things to make them straight, but should see that they were far straighter than we supposed already. Were this information to be supplied now, such would be our judgment, and it would coincide with God's. But when the day of revelation comes this information shall be supplied, and then we shall confess that He is righteous in all His ways, and holy in all His works, then we shall lift up the chant of the redeemed, *Great and marvellous are Thy works Lord God Almighty, just and true are Thy ways thou King of Saints.*[1]

For the present then, as of old, we have nothing to sustain us, but what the saints of God in all ages have had—our faith. This faith, however, consists not so much in believing that a particular subversion of everything, a putting of bitter for sweet, and sweet for bitter will take place, of which we can form no definite idea because the foundation on which to form one has not been revealed, as in resting in the conviction that One who is perfect in knowledge and in judgment is dealing with us, that He can make no mistakes and cannot be party to a miscarriage of justice.

But, furthermore, there are two other considerations to sustain us. The first is that we are in *possession* of all the light that is shed upon this matter from the cross of Christ. This is a present and not a future light. Our Lord said that the Holy Ghost should convince the world about judgment, because the Prince of this world had been judged. The cross of Christ was the judgment of this world. It was the practical and present subversion of all things, it gave, therefore, once for all, that readjustment of all things which the popular notion relegates to the indefinite future. It put

[1] Rev. xv. 3.

everything in a new light, it assigned a fresh valuation to all that the world held precious, it showed the Divine estimate of pain, suffering, and death, it proved that the utmost degradation and rejection of man could coexist with infinite nearness and dearness to God. It threw, therefore, into all such humiliation and suffering, into every lot of trial and sorrow, and every passage of death, the possible element of dearness and nearness to God. *Thus the cross of Christ went very far towards anticipating the verdict of the judgment.*

But the cross itself was but part of a whole. The cross itself was nothing without the resurrection. It was the condition and the passage to the resurrection. It is the resurrection which itself shed glory on the cross. It is in the light of the resurrection, and in that alone, that we can interpret or understand the cross. Without the resurrection the cross is an unsolved mystery. But the two together are the prelude of the judgment, because God *hath appointed a day in the which He will judge the world in righteousness by that man whom He hath ordained, whereof He hath given assurance unto all men in that He hath raised Him from the dead.* Not only is the judgment based upon the resurrection, but the resurrection is the earnest of the judgment.

And from the analogy of the light which it throws upon the cross we can understand something of the nature of the judgment. It shall be the revelation of all mysteries, the solution of all problems. In the light of it we shall see light thrown on all that is most obscure; even every tangled path through the brushwood which hides the daylight will be glorified by the influx of Divine light and perfect knowledge, for then we shall know even as also we are known.

Surely, then, we may regard the judgment less after the manner of an irrevocable sentence, an unalterable doom, than as a vast accession of light and knowledge, in which we shall behold not only a part but the relation of the part to the whole; not only the appearances which confuse and distort the vision but the realities which will enable us to judge righteous judgment. Then not only the meaning of the problem will be revealed, but the result also of the discipline will be declared; then not only the complex machinery of the clock will be exposed to view, but the veil being withdrawn from its face, we shall be able to read the hour indicated on the dial-plate of eternity. We shall know not only wherefore the trial was, but also whereto it has led, and then man's judgment, which at present goes limping and halting after God's, will overtake and keep pace with it, and nature herself shall take up the chorus of rejoicing, and *the floods clap their hands, and the hills be joyful together before the Lord, when He cometh to judge the earth, and with righteousness to judge the world, and the people with equity.*[1]

[1] Ps. xcviii. 8, 9.

XXIII.

HE SHALL COME TO JUDGE THE QUICK AND THE DEAD.

We must all appear before the judgment seat of Christ, that everyone may receive the things done in his body according to that he hath done, whether it be good or bad.—2 COR. v. 10.

THERE is yet another aspect of the judgment to come, upon which I desire to dwell, before passing on to the next article of the Creed, and that is the aspect which was briefly mentioned at the close of my sermon on Sunday last, namely, that the judgment will be the declaration or manifestation of our truest actual self. This is really the most solemn and practical aspect of all, not, perhaps, the most startling and sensational, or, therefore, that upon which the popular mind is most willing to dwell, but by far the most tremendous aspect, and that which bears most directly on our personal and daily life.

For is it not an awful thought that it is impossible to separate the present moment from its ultimate issues in the world beyond the grave? What you and I are in the habit of doing day by day, of speaking from time to time, and of thinking moment by moment, all this is imperceptibly but inevitably moulding the form and fashion of that character which we must bear for ever. But is not this the case? It is certain that in this life we cannot shut off our existence as it were in compartments, so that one portion shall be wholly disconnected from another. The child is father of the man. The dispositions which are manifested and encouraged in childhood, the habits which are formed, the practices which are acquired in early youth, constitute a part of our future life. So certainly and undoubtedly is this the fact that we are all more or less aware of the importance and necessity of education and early training, but I believe that we are none of us sufficiently aware of it, or what is but a corollary of the same truth, of the prime importance of daily and hourly habit. It is well known that the most supple of our joints, if retained too long in the same position, will lose their suppleness and become rigidly fixed. And if it is so with the body, it is not otherwise with its counterpart, the mind or the spiritual character. The man who forms the habit of giving expression to the first thought that comes into his mind, or rather who continually does so till it insensibly becomes a habit finds, sooner or later, to his sorrow and pain, that this habit of expression has got the mastery of him, and he has lost, when he most requires it, the power of self-restraint. The mightiest tree in all the forest was capable, when a sapling, of being bent and directed to almost any extent, but left to its own spontaneous growth and to none but natural influences, it has followed the guidance of those influences, and become the inflexible, unalterable thing it is. Would that we could all remember what an allegory this is of human character and conduct. It is impossible but that the thoughts we think in our inexpressive secret hearts, the words we utter to our familiar companions, the manners we assume in our intercourse with our fellows and with the world should congeal and crystallise till they are beyond all control, and should stamp themselves upon our being and our life, till they give us what we call our character.

For character is but the result of habit, and it is this thought and the subsequent thought that judgment is but the manifestation of character, that the true and inevitable issue of character will be revealed in the judgment to come, that I want to lay before you this morning.

And you will at once observe that this is not necessarily a religious matter at all, but a most ordinary commonplace matter-of-fact affair which concerns us all alike. People, as a rule, dislike religion and religious topics; and the preacher who would be popular in the present day must avoid religion as much as he can, and discourse on any subject in which people take an interest. I have no intention, however, of avoiding religion, properly so called, but only at the present time of showing you that what you may probably regard as a purely religious subject, namely, the judgment to come, is not necessarily a religious subject at all. I want to make everyone feel that what he or she is at this present moment, is simply the result of habit. You have grown up in certain habits, have acted repeatedly in a certain way, and done certain things time after time, and these have become habitual; they have overlaid your nature till they have fitted and confined you like a habit, for the habit or garment which we wear on the body is but a figure and emblem of the habit which we adopt in our mental and moral being, and which becomes thicker and thicker till it disfigures and deforms our personal existence, and so shapes our character. I was told there were not ten people here who understood my sermon on Sunday last. Now if this was really the case, which I can scarcely believe, for I spoke as plainly as I could, why was it? Simply for this reason, that almost all people have got the habit of looking at religion and religious subjects in a kind of fictitious and unreal way, as though the things of the world to come were removed as far as possible from the things of this world. Now, I want to disabuse the people who come here of this habit, and especially I want to show you to-day that in all you think and speak and do you are, unconsciously it may be, but assuredly and inevitably, laying up a minute and imperceptible portion of that vast and immeasurable result which the day of judgment will reveal. Judgment is the declaration of character. The judgment to come will be the day of revelation; it will reveal our character. And character is like the coral reef. An insect so small as to be inconsiderable, if not imperceptible, as but for the brightness of its colour it often would be, is able in a succession of moments, each of which is inappreciable as it flies, to build up a vast accumulation of matter hard as rock, which is capable of withstanding the utmost fury of the raging mighty ocean, of forming a secure dwelling-place for man, and of shattering the proudest trophies of mechanical skill. The coral reef is the outcome of successive and continuous repetitions, each one of which is so small and inconsiderable that if taken alone it might be disregarded; but we cannot take them alone, each has a relation definite and indissoluble to every other, and all that we can estimate is the marvellous result.

It is so with character. In early youth an inability to appreciate the difference between truth and falsehood is manifested in a tendency, not, it may be to perpetrate an actual lie, but rather to look at things in a false light, to distort and to misrepresent them. This tendency is unchecked, perhaps it is unperceived by fond and inexperienced parents and teachers; or the habit, in spite of all their efforts, develops itself till the man enters into life with the character confirmed and fully set. Everything which concerns himself is regarded in this false light, is so represented and expressed, till without being able to say that in any given point the man has spoken or acted falsely, it is patent to all who have dealings with him that nowhere has he spoken or acted strictly in accordance to truth. Want of truthfulness is much more common than actual falsehood, for the one is capable of immediate detection and calls for immediate exposure, but the other is ingenious enough to elude detection and cannot be exposed. The consequence is that no character is so dangerous as this, because no man's conduct and no man's life can be proof against misrepresentation. More harm may be done by a few apparently undesigned and casual words than it is possible to undo by the undeviating conduct of many years. Surely, if anywhere, there must be a judgment here. It is impossible that the justice of the Searcher of all hearts and the discoverer of their intents can ultimately overlook iniquity so gross. The day of reckoning must come, and when it comes it will come with speed swiftly. But meanwhile the judgment is infallibly shaping itself and compassing its own ends. For what is the bare possession of such a character incompetent to distinguish actual truth from virtual falsehood, utterly unable to see the extent to which self enters into all matters of personal concern and interest, but in itself a very judgment on him who has it? Is it not more to be true and genuine as gold tried and purified seven times in the fire than it is to feel that every step one has gained is the result of craft, subtilty and cunning? And if as it often happens, the person so acting is not aware of his own inward duplicity and want of truth, is not this the sorest judgment of all and the surest earnest of the judgment that must be reserved for lying lips and for a deceitful tongue?

To take another instance, and one that is yet more common, though probably we have most of us been brought in contact with cases like the last. What a lamentable affliction is an evil temper, and yet how completely is temper (which is, if anything is, a defect of character) the result of habit. I take temper in its broader and more general sense, not in its restricted one, as applying mainly to anger, but as embracing the entire complexion of a man's inner self, in relation to persons and circumstances. What a curse—no less terrible than that of Cain,—does he carry about within him who has a heart at enmity with all the world, suspicious of His fellow-creatures, censorious as to their conduct, contemptuous of their opinions, unmerciful to their infirmities! What a harvest of dragons' teeth does not such a one sow for himself in all his intercourse with the world! What needless and insuperable barriers does he not throw in his own way to frustrate his efforts after good! No observation is more startlingly true and strikingly vivid than that of Thackeray. The world is a mirror, in which we see ourselves; smile and it smiles,—frown, and it frowns. And is it not a terrible judgment, terrible in the present, and yet more terrible to come, for a man to nurse within himself such a temper as this?

On the other hand, what an invaluable blessing is

the possession of a kind, a genial, a happy, and a cheerful disposition, which thinketh no evil because conscious of none within ; which is buoyant and equable, meeting the ever-recurrent waves of life like our largest and most skilfully constructed steam ships, at the angle of least resistance ; which is beaten back only to rise again more buoyantly, and which holds on its course undaunted and undeviating, well knowing that if all is sound within, no violence from without can injure.

This, then, be it understood, is what I call temper, not the inability to be ruffled into momentary anger or the sudden expression of transient warmth ; but the kind of disciplined nature which has the whole man well in hand, and is equal to either fortune because true to the central life.

Now though it is quite certain that the word just used, *nature*, has a good deal to do with each of these characters, it is not all. That indeed, is our consolation, that we can and do mould our characters. Would that we all remembered more than we do, that we each have a character to mould, and that the judgment will show to ourselves and to the world what we have done to mould it. This of course has a direct bearing upon the young, and upon all who are in any way connected with the education of the young ; but by no means only the young, for just as whatever our education may have been education proper does not commence till self-education has begun, so also is it with that discipline which must result in character. The old Latin proverb says, " The way to good manners is never too late." We have now each of us something to do with the formation of character, for we have each of us something to do with the acquisition of habit, just as we have something to do with the choice of our clothing.

And in illustration of this I cannot but observe how almost universally we see people's character strengthen as they get on in years. If in mid-life we have known them to be hard and sour, have we not seen that as age comes on that character of hardness and asperity developes and increases. The man who is fond of money in middle life, will become miserly in old age. The man who is vain in youth will become more and more so as the habit increases with his years, till even in old age there will be no concerns so interesting to himself, so usurping on the claims of others as his own, and self will be the centre of his centripetal system, round which he will revolve with undisturbed complacency, together with such lesser lights as he can attract within the circle of his influence. We must all have seen it many times ; the faults of character that we have lamented in others have become stronger and more conspicuous, not less so as the flight of time sped on. What a solemn lesson for all—for you, brethren, and for me, —for this is the law of human life ; habit passes into character and is the parent of character, and habit is but the aggregate of separate actions. Habits of carelessness are the consequence of indulged indifference to care: habits of sloth, of indulged tendency to indolence; habits of untruthfulness, of repeated disregard of truth, and the like.

And all this, you observe, is not called religion, it is something very different from religion. It has nothing to do with the soul, but it may and must have very much to do with the present bias and the ultimate issue of that spiritual being and essence which we term our self. Moment by moment the character of that self is formed. It is in process of formation now. You are forming it now. You are setting and shifting, perceptibly or impercebtibly the hands of that dial-plate, to use again the metaphor which I used last time, which is to indicate in eternity the result of your life here.

Surely a most solemn thought. *We must all be made manifest*, so the Apostle says, *before the judgment seat of Christ, that every one may receive the things done in the body according to that he hath done whether it be good or bad*.[1] Then, when the things are done here we have not done *with* them, we are to receive the issue and long result of them; the seed must bring forth its fruit, *for whatsoever a man soweth that shall he also reap*.[2] I speak not so much now of what is commonly understood by recompense, as of that inevitable product which human action cannot but beget, which is, apart from any further result, its recompense.

And it is this slow, sure, certain, and steady result,

[1] 2 Cor. v. 10. [2] Gal. vi. 7.

that, as it seems to me, people are indisposed to wait for, though they cannot escape it, in the present day,. They would not otherwise attempt to accomplish by spasmodic efforts what can only be the result of time. Character is the product of habit ; character is that which exists but is hidden now, and is to be revealed hereafter. Character is not produced in a day any more than a habit is formed in an hour. A life which has been habitually flowing in one direction cannot in a moment or a week be diverted into another channel, and be made to flow in an opposite direction. Not that I disbelieve in "conversion," real and genuine,—far from it; but I believe that St. Paul's character did not differ materially before and after his conversion, Otherwise he would not have said that he profited above many of his equals in his own nation, in the Jews' religion, being more exceedingly jealous of the traditions of his fathers [1]—there was the true Pauline character in germ and essence. But when he became a Christian his character was infused with another spirit, and came under the law of another influence, and this was the influence of faith.

And that, my friends, is the influence that we want to assist in moulding our character, as it is the influence which can alone regenerate us. We want a principle of new life. Who does not feel it ? The cry for exceptional and spasmodic agency which is so loud now,[2] is a proof of this. Religious London

---

[1] Gal. i. 14.   [2] The "mission" of 1874.

feels itself irreligious, and grasps at a hoped for remedy. There is but one remedy, and that is the application to the personal life and conscience of the death and resurrection of the Lord Jesus. This and this alone, taken into the heart as a vital and a vivifying principle, can suffice to give us life, and life is what we want. The power of the Holy Ghost operating upon and through faith can alone quicken and regenerate us.

And as there is nothing else which can do this and do it now, so there is nothing else which can give us confidence or hope in the future judgment. Only think of the awful revelation in being exhibited to the world, and to angels, and to men, as we really are, with all the blots, voluntary and involuntary, upon our hidden character that we are all privy to ;—the negligence, the indolence, the selfishness, the vanity, not to mention other and worse evils that infect and infest us, one and all;—if we have not learnt that there is One who has taken all this and more than all this upon Himself, and made it His own, in order that if we were willing and obedient we might eat the fruit of the promised land into which He has brought us, the fruit, namely, of His own perfect and spotless righteousness in which, and in which alone, we can stand just and accepted before God, and have boldness in the day of judgment, being assured that as He is so are we, if found in Him, not only in this world, but also in that which is to come.

XXIV.

I BELIEVE IN THE HOLY GHOST.

But the Comforter, which is the Holy Ghost, whom the Father will send in my name, He shall teach you all things, and bring all things to your remembrance, whatsoever I have said unto you. — JOHN xiv. 26.

WE pass on now, not only to another article, but also to a fresh division of the Creed: "I believe in the Holy Ghost." It is a very remarkable and significant fact that the phrase, "the Holy Ghost," which is used by our Lord in this place, is peculiar to the New Testament. Not only do the words, "the Holy Ghost," not occur in the ancient Scriptures, but so neither does the phrase which is obviously equivalent, "the Holy Spirit." Every one knows, of course, that the Old Testament speaks of the Spirit of God, as for example, *The Spirit of God moved upon the face of the waters*, and the like; and God Himself speaks of "My Spirit;" and the Psalmist says, *Take not Thy Holy Spirit from me;*[2] and Isaiah twice mentions *His Holy Spirit*,[3] and the Lord is called, chiefly by Isaiah, "*The Holy One of Israel*," and the like; but there is no phrase

[1] Gen. i. 2.   [2] Ps. li. 11.   [3] Isa. lxiii. 10, 11., cf. 14.

in the Old Testament answering to My Holy Spirit, or the Holy Spirit, or the Holy Ghost We must take careful note of that fact.

But now let us turn to the New Testament. We find the phrase, the Holy Ghost, or the Holy Spirit, occurring some seventy or eighty times ; and not only so, but it is used by our Lord, by each of the Evangelists, by the writer of the Acts, by St. Paul, by St. Peter, by St. John, by St. Jude, and by the writer of the Epistle to the Hebrews. What then, is the inference ? Clearly that a phrase so remarkable which is entirely new, which is peculiar to the New Testament, and to which there is no precise parallel in the ancient Scriptures, was used to denote a new fact, and was used in a sense which was also new. At all events, we cannot deny that the phenomena relating to this expression are altogether new.

And then further, along with these new phenomena we must notice the fact that the Gospel professed to come as an influence which was entirely new, which claimed to give men new life, which demanded of them a new birth, which was itself the very power of regeneration.

Also we must remember that the books known as the New Testament stand out from the rest of literature as an entirely new creation, as not only an attempt to produce something new, but also as literary productions distinct and separate from all others, not only in degree, but in kind. Or if it were to be claimed for the writings of the Christian fathers, for example, that they are separated from the books of the New Testament, not in kind, but only in degree, still this fact remains, that the impulse which gave these writings their existence was derived from the New Testament, which was itself an original production.

What then, again, is the inference? Clearly that a power which professed to be new, and which, undeniably, produced results so novel and so new, was itself as new as the results which it produced. In other words, that just as the language of the New Testament, in the particular mentioned, is evidence of a new spiritual fact, is clearly the first attempt to express a new spiritual conception, so the moral and spiritual facts which originated that expression were also new. The Holy Ghost had made Himself known to the writers of the New Testament in a way He had not made Himself known to the writers of the Old, and the revelation was witnessed to, and the fact confirmed by, the influence manifested in the language of the writers. This, as it seems to me, is a perfectly fair and legitimate conclusion, and one which no sophistry or ingenuity can set aside. Our Lord distinctly promised to send the Holy Ghost, His disciples distinctly claimed to bestow the gift of the Holy Ghost, the subsequent history of their actions, and the results of their teaching, and the phenomena of their language, show that the Holy Ghost was given and received as a new influence. And consequently this gift of the Holy Ghost was the greatest proof and confirmation of the mission of Jesus Christ, and of the promise He made to His disciples.

Thus the mere linguistic phenomena of the New Testament are, so far, collateral and corroborative proof of its character and its origin. The features are new, it speaks of something new, and it is itself an evidence of a power now for the first time in similar active operation.

I need only remind you of one remarkable passage in St. John to establish the correctness of what I say. When Jesus said, *He that believeth on Me, as the Scripture hath said, out of his belly shall flow rivers of living water*, the Apostle adds, *But this spake He of the Spirit, which they that believe on Him should receive; for the Holy Ghost was not yet [given] because that Jesus was not yet glorified.*[1] The word "given" is in italics. His words are, *The Holy Ghost was not yet*, that is, was not yet as a personal possession of believers.

It is, then, of this Holy Ghost that we are now to speak. The Holy Ghost in His distinct and individual existence is the special revelation of the New Testament. Very instructive it would be to run through all the passages in which mention is made of Him and His work, with a view to ascertaining exactly that which is told us of Him. But we cannot do this now. Any one who will take a

[1] John vii. 38, 39.

concordance, which, be it observed in passing, is a most valuable and instructive teacher, may do it for himself. All that is needful to observe now, is that the New Testament view of the Person and office of the Holy Ghost differs materially, because practically, from the theological view. The confusion which we get into by mental endeavours to conceive of one who is a separate, and yet not a separated person; of one who is three, and yet not three; who is one, and yet not one, and the like, is so great, at least,—I speak now from my own experience—as to be fatal to anything of the nature of simple earnest faith and fervent worship. Believe me, it is no part of Christian faith or practice to be able to have in one's mind a clear and lucid notion of the technical difference between the three Persons of the ever blessed Trinity, and of the distinct mode in which each works.

Let me quote here some words of an American writer, which seem to me most appropriate and true. "The Persons of the Godhead are not to be sepated one from another as to presence and place; as if one were with us here upon earth, and the other away from us up in heaven. Where the Son is, there the Father is in the Son; and where the Son is, and is revealed in any soul, there the Holy Spirit is as the revealer of the Son. So it comes to pass, that he who has the Son has the Father and the Spirit also. And he who is the temple of the Holy Ghost is the temple of the Triune God; and he who is in abiding union with Jesus, is in abiding union with God the Father, Son, and Holy Ghost."[1] Now this expresses, in a very clear and practical manner, what we may term the net result of that great mystery which, as many of us have been accustomed to regard it is, I am persuaded, a source of stumbling and offence to many.

My brethren, there are not three Gods, neither is God the Holy Ghost something which God is not, or which is not God. Neither as when we speak of the Spirit of God, do we speak of a distinct or separate part of God, which is more Divine, or less Divine than others, but just as the highest mathematical science may be called a transcript of the mind of God, because it expresses those eternal necessary laws by which the Divine mind governs the material universe, and guides the stars in their courses, but is not otherwise holy than as all that He doeth is holy and as the mental operations of the Divine mind must be holy; so also is the Spirit of God which is apparent in the writings of Paul and John, the highest operation and evidence of that fountain of holiness which is in God, and which is the special and the choicest characteristic of the nature of God. It is self-evident that the combination of a Newton, a Kepler, a Leibnitz, a La Place, a Pascal, and a hundred other chiefest mathematicians would not make one Isaiah ; and that, though when God gave those great lights to mankind, He gave transcendant

[1] Boardman, *The Higher Life.*

geniuses to whom He discovered the secret workings of His own mind, yet in giving them all, He did not so pour out the riches of His grace, or make bare His holy arm as when He gave to His chosen people the prophet Isaiah, and yet each was a gift of God, and each in His way was a revealer of God; but it was given to Isaiah to reveal that which no human intellect could discover, and to speak under the influence of a Being whose very existence, as we have seen, was but imperfectly revealed to him, but who was to be more fully revealed hereafter.

The Holy Ghost, then, is a different and special manifestation of the same God, and moreover He is that manifestation of God in which we are specially concerned as sinful creatures. As by the writer I have just quoted it has been well said, " The Father is all the fulness of the Godhead invisible. The Son is all the fulness of the Godhead manifest. The Spirit is all the fulness of the Godhead making manifest." And this is the office of the Holy Ghost to make manifest. When Christ promised to send the Holy Ghost, He promised to send a Spirit which should make manifest. And as this Spirit did not come historically till after Christ had gone, so, when He came, he did most clearly and conclusively fulfil what Christ had promised, for He made manifest to the disciples the meaning and intention of all that Christ had said and done. As a matter of fact, which there is no denying, He did teach them all things, and bring all things to their remembrance whatsoever He had said unto them. And if we will not admit this reasoning, then we must affirm that, the facts being what they are, the writers resorted to the clumsy shift of ascribing these promises to Christ in order to make more wonderful that which was already so wonderful that it could not be explained without them.

And, brethren, of all the names of the Holy Ghost there is no name so sweet as this of the Comforter. Even though it may not be the most exact equivalent of the Saviour's own word "Paraclete," yet being sanctioned by the usage of five hundred years, for it is used by Wicliff, and being supported by the *Tröster* of Luther's Bible, we may well cling to it. For when the Holy Spirit makes manifest to any one heart the purposes and the will of God towards him, then it is only to his comfort and to comfort him. Oh that people knew the comfort of true religion. That it was not something to make one timid and gloomy, fearful at every moment of doing something which would be visited upon us with unendurable severity, but a present possession of holy calm filling the soul with perfect peace. The Gospel is too often proclaimed as a threatened scourge, menacing chastisement for the smallest offences, and exacting payment to the uttermost farthing. For my part, I not only can see no Gospel in this, but I believe it is utterly opposed to that spirit of freedom and release which the Gospel was to bring in, and is wholly ignorant of that blessing of pardon, free and full and final, which was the special privilege of the Gospel. What evidence is there in a religion like this, the religion of servile fear, of the presence of the Holy Ghost the Comforter? None at all. The advocates of it must confess with the disciples at Ephesus, *We have not so much as heard whether there be any Holy Ghost*.[1] The article of the Creed, " I believe in the Holy Ghost " is indeed repeated as a charm or talisman, too precious to forego, but the meaning of belief in the Holy Ghost as in a person whose office it is to comfort, and in whom we can repose our trust is unknown. The Holy Ghost is an idol of the mind, not the precious experience and abiding possession of the heart.

"Oh," it will be said, " but you degrade the Holy Spirit of God into a mere subjective feeling." No, I reply, I do not. I do not identify any feeling of mine with the substantive existence of the Holy Spirit, but the substantive existence of the Holy Spirit is nothing to me unless He works in me, and produces an effect in me, and as far as His work in me is concerned, I cannot separate His work in me from the effect which that work produces. The work which it was said He should produce, was the work of comfort. He should strengthen and encourage and console ; surely, at all times, a most Divine work, and one altogether worthy of Him ; and if I find that work produced in me, as Christ said it should

[1] Acts xix. 2.

be produced, shall I turn round and deny it as the work of the Holy Ghost, and say it is only a subjective feeling of my own, which must be jealously watched and carefully repressed. Then what becomes of the work of the Holy Ghost, so far as that work is connected with comfort?

And now I beg you to observe, that if we are disciples of Christ, it is exactly this work which the Holy Ghost is to perform. The Lord says nothing here about making us holy, He speaks about giving us comfort. If we follow the guidance of His own words they will no doubt lead us right. The fact is when the Holy Ghost doth comfort then He maketh holy. He does not first make holy, and then comfort afterwards, because if so, who would be comforted? Are you so holy as to be able to take comfort because you are holy? I trow not. All such comfort, all such rejoicing is vain. But if you suffer the Holy Ghost to comfort you, if you will believe in His agency when He offers to comfort you, then you may trust in Him to make you holy. Depend upon it He will not come with comfort where there is a lurking spirit of unholiness, just as He will not come with comfort where there is a lurking spirit of unbelief, whether in the truth of Christ's Gospel or in the reality of His own agency; but if He comes with comfort, He will bring also the gift of personal holiness, He will come with the grace of sanctification.

It seems to me we have had rather too much

of the religion of the schoolmaster. Christianity was to be a kind of moral or spiritual policeman, perpetually parading up and down before our windows, and reminding of this which we ought to do, and of the other which we should not, and as a matter of fact, religion became a thing of doing and not doing. But surely the well-informed and responsible manhood of Christian life is not satisfied with this as any adequate expression of the mind of Christ in the Gospel. The Gospel is described by Him who first preached it as a healing of the broken-hearted, a deliverance to the captives, a recovering of sight to the blind, a setting at liberty them that are bound. I find, then, that spiritual emancipation is the grand characteristic of the Gospel, not legal restraint. I find that where the Spirit of the Lord is, the Holy Spirit, there is liberty. I find, then, that the Gospel, if it is to act with any power is to set us free; it is to give us peace, to make us clean within, to give us thankfulness in prosperity and cheerfulness in adversity—and this is the work of the Holy Ghost.

"I believe in the Holy Ghost," then, means very much more than "I believe that the Holy Ghost is the third person in the ever-blessed Trinity; that He is separate from the Father and the Son, and yet one with both, that He proceedeth not from one only but from both," and very much of the same kind, which is all very well if this sacred person were to have only a name and no local habitation in our own hearts; but if, on the other hand, He is only to be known by His agency, and only to be discovered by His fruits, then I say that we cannot separate His influence from Himself, but must seek to know Him through His hallowed influence on the heart.

This week is to be kept very generally in London as a week of special intercession for more abundant outpouring of the Holy Spirit, which is to be accompanied with special efforts to bring the indifferent and the ungodly within the range of His blessed operation. I am sure we shall all join in the most devout and fervent aspirations that these blessed objects may be attained, and shall earnesly pray that every effort which is made in the faith of Christ, and in dependence on the grace of God, may be blessed abundantly with success. It is a great thing when men so believe in the power of the Holy Ghost, and in the power of prayer, as to combine together in such a way as this, to ask for a larger outpouring of His grace. It is the one petition to which we know with absolute certainty that there is no limiting condition. *If ye then, being evil, know how to give good gifts unto your children, how much more shall your heavenly Father give the Holy Spirit to them that ask Him.*[1] Though there may be many characteristics in this movement, as it will be conducted, which may seem to us to be not according to knowledge, yet what are these but as the babbling and broken cries of children calling on their Father who knoweth what things

[1] Luke xi. 13.

they have need of before they ask Him, even if their language is imperfect and stammering. And be it ours, brethren, to pray also, that the cry may be heard even more than we or they can ask or think; that it may be answered, not according to our weak intention or our poor endeavours, but according to the grace and wisdom of Him who worketh all things after the counsel of His own will ; who giveth to all men liberally and upbraideth not, and is able abundantly to supply all our need out of His fulness in Christ Jesus.

XXV.

THE HOLY GHOST.

Likewise the Spirit also helpeth our infirmities : for we know not what we should pray for as we ought : but the Spirit itself maketh intercession for us with groanings which cannot be uttered. And He that searcheth the hearts knoweth what is the mind of the Spirit, because He maketh intercession for the saints according to the will of God.—ROM. viii. 26.

TO-DAY we pass on to the consideration of some of the other functions of the Holy Spirit in His relation to us, reserving for the following lecture the consideration of our duty in relation to Him. The aspect in which we were led to regard the Holy Spirit on Sunday last was that of a Comforter. There are two aspects to the inherent significance of this word comfort. One is that which is now probably the more common one of consolation, and it was this which chiefly occupied us before ; the other is that of strengthening, the giving of fortitude or strength, which will occupy us to-day. The Apostle is-speaking of the trials of the present state from which even the Christian is not exempt, and to which he is even more exposed than other men. He says, *That the whole creation groaneth and travaileth in pain together with us even until now*, that the burden of what has the appearance of a curse is laid upon external nature as well upon the beings who are made in the image of God ; but that for us who believe there is not only a present salvation in Christ, but also a future salvation through hope. And in addition to this anticipated redemption *the Spirit of God also helpeth our infirmities*, that is, not helpeth us to bear our infirmities (which it is the object of earnest resolution and of Christian discipline to lessen), but helpeth us to bear the present burden of deferred adoption or redemption of the body, by assisting us in relation to that burden, and making us strong to bear it.

You will at once see, then, that here there enters in the other office of the Comforter, not that of consoling, but that of giving strength. The Spirit itself helpeth our weakness to bear the burden laid upon us, by giving us Christian fortitude, and patience, and enduring courage. To St. Paul and to the Romans we cannot for a moment doubt that this was so, they had been made acquainted with the whereabouts of supernatural strength, with a fountain of Divine endurance, to which they had continual access through prayer and the Spirit's intercession. But how is it with ourselves? We have lately had the office of the Holy Spirit put put before us in a very marked and sensational, and even violent manner. His operation has been invoked in the whirlwind and the earthquake and, the tempest, rather than in the still small voice in which the prophet found Him. God forbid that we should limit the agency of that Spirit whose operation has been compared to the wind which bloweth where it listeth, and which can shatter the rocks and overturn the mountains when He pleaseth. God forbid that we should in any way discredit or discourage any attempts that are, or have been, made to overturn the mountains of difficulty and obstacle that interpose themselves but too fatally to the work of the Spirit in this place, and to break the rocky hearts of prejudice, indifference, and unbelief that exalt themselves on every side; but forasmuch as we have not all taken part in these special attempts, and as we would earnestly hope there are some here who do not need themselves to be the immediate objects of them, it is certainly allowable, and we would hope it may be profitable, to contemplate the Divine agency of the Holy Spirit in a somewhat different aspect. And bear with us, brethren, if, as in the presence of God, and by way of illustration, we speak for a moment of ourselves and of our own work. For almost sixteen years we have been preaching the Word of God in this place. We have devoted to that work the best of our power, our energy, and our time. We have earnestly desired and implored the Divine blessing on our labours. What has been the result as far as we can humanly judge? We do not know that one single soul has been won for God. The arrows, however sharp and winged they may have been, have been arrows shot in the dark. No great visible results have been produced. Empty seats have not been filled, communicants have not been increased, multitudes have not been added to our flock, still less added to the Lord. Such facts as these call for the most serious consideration and self-searching scrutiny. What has been the cause of a failure so apparent and so trying, if not so conspicuous? Has the message been at fault? Has Christ not been preached? Have the foundations of self not been shaken? Has the Holy Spirit not been invoked, or has the need of His personal agency been disparaged or overlooked? Has the preacher's matter been jejune, or his manner repellent? It is yours and not mine, brethren, to answer questions such as these. Is there any other fault near at home? Have we trusted to do by might and by power what can alone be done by the Spirit of the living God? I think not. Then where, brethren, has been the fault? God knows that we have tried to cut deep into the hearts and consciences of men. God knows that we have tried to get far beneath the surface, that we have tried to bring Christ into contact with the individual heart. If it has been all in vain, that, brethren, must rest with those who have heard us and with God. If there have not been, as some would say, many seals to our ministry, we can but take refuge in the confession of a greater than ourselves, and say, *I have laboured in vain, I have spent my strength for nought, and in vain; yet surely my judgment is with the Lord, and my work with my God.*[1]

And now the question arises, Is the work that is so needful to be done to be accomplished by other agency? Is the object confessedly to be to produce, by whatever means can be brought to bear, a great impression? Are additional inducements and attractions, whatever such can be devised, to be laid under requisition? Is the church to be filled with eager and expectant crowds by every conceivable expedient (and I can only say that I wish it could be filled, not for one day or one week, but for all days and every week) or is there anything else to seek after and to look for? I confess that if there is not, then the case is utterly hopeless; but this has ever been our hope. We have always been taught to believe, and we have tried to act on the belief, that visible results are fictitious and delusive; that it was wisest neither to look for nor to trust them ;—that the duty of the Christian, and more especially of the Christian minister, was to be regardless of results, to go on in independence of, and with indifference to them, believing assuredly that it was impossible to calculate or to gauge the effects and issues of the word preached ;—that being of the number of those who disdain to make the preaching of the Gospel the engine for attaching to themselves friends and followers, the true and the only course was to steer right onward, to bate no jot of heart or hope, but to

[1] Isa. xlix. 4.

leave all results and all consequences, all impressions, fruits, and seals to the day of judgment and to God. Whether or not this is right, brethren, time alone will show, but this I hold to be the chiefest practical duty, not only of the Christian preacher, but also of the every day Christian.

The tide, however, of popular opinion is plainly setting in the exactly opposite direction. The results and impressions which confessedly are not produced, if they are producible, by the ordinary means, must be forthwith and at once produced by all and by any means. Services must be multiplied, their character revolutionised, another method adopted, other machinery set in motion. Crowds must be gathered together, and a great visible, or at least apparent, effect produced.

Well, by all means let it be done ; let the churches be filled, let the streets be emptied. Let multitudes who have never thought on God and futurity if such there be, assemble themselves and be turned unto the Lord ; but I look at this matter in a practical light, and decline to look at it in any other. Whatever souls are thus brought to God,—for what are they thus brought ? That they may lead Christian lives. Very well, and for what purpose are you and I here now ? That we may learn to do the same. Precisely so, and for no other. If there is any one who comes here for any other I cannot help that. If, coming time after time to the wells of salvation, you have gone away without drinking of them, or without slaking your thirst I cannot help that. If, coming time after time into the very presence of the Crucified, you have not come into contact with Him, have not touched Him, I cannot help that. If by a different style of service, or a different style of preaching, or by anything else a different effect can be produced, by all means let it be produced. Only beware of this, that you do not mistake the spurious for the genuine. It is possible to go to church three or four times a day, it is possible to take the sacrament perpetually, and yet not to have that spiritual life within the heart which can alone make the presence in church of any value, or give any real virtue to the act of communion. It is possible to work the feelings and the imagination up to a great degree of tension, to superinduce a fervour of excitement, and yet not have that real thing within which the Gospel calls faith, which can alone save the soul.

And again, although it may be highly desirable that the vague generalities of any sermon may be reduced to the specialities of what is technically called the after-meeting, (what an extraordinary development of language, by the way, unheard of within the last few years or months), although it may be even desirable that there should in certain cases be direct spiritual converse between the preacher and his flock, and although many of our sermons may fall fruitless and ineffective, because the questions they may have suggested have not been asked, and therefore not been answered—yet

I should imagine that the only legitimate purpose and object of such intercourse, is to make all who seek for it independent of it. For I believe it to be a universal law of healthy, vigorous spiritual life, to be self-supporting, and self-dependent, as our Lord indicated, when He said, *He that believeth on Me, as the Scripture hath said, out of his belly shall flow rivers of living water.*[1] It is here, brethren, and it is well that you should know it, that there lies the radical vice of that practice of confession, which is openly, to the shame of Christianity in this nineteenth century, and in this reformed church, being introduced among us, but too commonly in the present day.

My brethren, we are not alarmists, but we say boldly, and with as much emphasis and weight as we can command, Men and women, fathers and mothers, husbands and wives of England, beware of the confessional! We say so, not to join in an ignorant popular cry against it, which is sometimes raised, but because the very principle it implies strikes at the root of that self-sustained and righteous independence and inalienable liberty of a pure and single-eyed conscience which is the necessary product of a true Christianity. We were informed by the leading organ of popular opinion yesterday, that the requisite machinery for confession is now in public operation, in a notorious church in London, as it is in Roman churches abroad.

[1] John vii. 38.

Surely the time has come to ask, Fellow-countrymen, and fellow-citizens, will you stand this ? Is it not the duty of every Christian minister to lift up his voice against it ? Is it not the duty of every Christian layman to echo and give effect and influence to that voice wherever and in whatever way he can ?[1] Public opinion, when once created and aroused, is a power that is irresistible.

But you will say to me, How have you fulfilled your promise, and how does all this bear upon the text? It bears upon it in this way, that whatever may be the throes and travail pangs, by which a soul is cast naked at the feet of Jesus, yet the living result of the Spirit's work in after life must be sought in calmness, quietness, and confidence, and not in the constant repetition of such stringent and stimulating methods of operation as have been referred to. To prepare to die may be the work of an hour, or of a moment; but to prepare to live must be the work of a lifetime. If you have not been really converted to God, that is your affair and no one's but yours. If you have, then your highest and unceasing effort must be to *live* as those who have been turned from darkness unto light, and from the power of Satan unto God.

And this I take it, you will not find easy. The atmosphere of everyday life is more chilling than

[1] Recent notorious events connected with *The Priest in Absolution* have furnished an instructive commentary on the observations in the text, which were written some years ago, and have shown them to be neither exaggerated nor uncalled for.—*Sept.* 1877.

that of the hour of prayer, and the hour of communion with Christ. It is easy to make one grand effort and subside ; it is not easy to make a lifelong effort of daily and hourly bearing of the cross, of daily and hourly government of the thoughts, the temper, and the tongue. Oh, how much easier it is to go to Church, and even (hard as some of you no doubt find it) to listen to a sermon, than it is to bear up with manful Christian fortitude against the inevitable rebukes of life; to go on in the path of duty, when the path of duty does not go on with you; to be true, patient, forbearing, hopeful, cheerful and resigned, to curb the biting sarcasm, or restrain the dubious jest ; to live habitually in the presence of God, and in the continual communion of the Holy Ghost. And yet, will anyone tell me, that less than this is the Christian life, and that anything which does not issue in this, as a lifelong habit, is worthy to be called conversion.

The function of the Holy Ghost, then, is to make us strong to bear the ills of life, the disappointments, frettings, worries, vexations, annoyances of daily and hourly existence. He or she who knows little of the ecstatic rapture of devotion, or of the luxury of a sustained effort of prayer, or of the sweetness of drinking in a fervent and impassioned discourse, may yet know something of the calmer and no less blessed influences of the Holy Spirit, who is the author of peace, and not of confusion, who is the lover of order, and not of disorder. He or she who would be sorely puzzled to take part in a so-called 'chain of prepetual intercession,' or to emulate those who made long prayers at the corners of the streets, may yet derive strength and encouragement from the thought that there is a Spirit who for believers maketh intercession with groanings which cannot be uttered. Yes, brethren, for believers, for the Holy Spirit is the very joy and crown of believers, of those who having by faith become personally and vitally united to Christ, have the earnest of the Spirit in their hearts. If you, being led by the Spirit of God, have the prescribed evidence that you are the sons of God, if you have received not the Spirit of bondage to repeated and continual fear, but the Spirit of adoption, whereby you can cry Abba, Father, then you may rejoice to think that prayer is the Spirit's own work, that it is a very real and not a formal thing, that it consists not in the repetition of stated formulas, but in the uplifting of the secret, silent heart to God, by a spontaneous, ever-recurrent, never wholly discontinued effort in which the imparted Spirit within holds its mystic converse with the central and fountain Spirit in heaven. Then you may take courage at the thought that if your heart is in union with the heart of God, which no will-worship, no compliance with external precepts will ever bring about, but which is the promised seal of the Spirit upon faith in Jesus, then He who is the Searcher of all hearts knoweth what is the mind of the Spirit—His own Spirit—in your heart, and that though through your manifold weakness, infirmity and ignorance you may know not what to pray for, nor know how to pray for it, as you ought, yet nevertheless there is a Spirit making intercession for you, though His language is inaudible, and His groanings cannot be uttered, nor His sighs expressed.

For, lastly, more than all, this Spirit intercedes, even as Christ intercedes, not that the will of God may be contravened and thwarted, but according to the will of God that it may be fully done. It is with God's own will that the Spirit moves in harmony, not in opposition to it; or as though if God's will left to itself were carried out, it would have a different issue to the will of the Spirit, or of Christ, for *He that searcheth the hearts knoweth what is the mind of the Spirit*, and that His aspirations and desires are, and can be, only for the more abundant and successful accomplishment of the good, and acceptable, and perfect will of God.

XXVI.

THE HOLY GHOST.

Grieve not the holy Spirit of God, whereby ye are sealed unto the day of redemption.—EPH. iv. 30.

NOT only is the clear revelation of the Holy Spirit of God the special glory of Christianity, but it is remarkable also that this revelation is accompanied with an equally clear recognition of corresponding duties which devolve upon ourselves in consequence. There is no more forcible statement of these obligations anywhere than that which is made in this place, which entreats us not to grieve the Holy Spirit.

The language is, in the highest degree, anthropomorphic, though it does not belong to an anthropomorphic age. Had it occurred in the ancient books of Moses, it might have been thus explained away; but it occurs at a time when, in the Christian Church, at least, the knowledge of God was in the very zenith of its brilliancy. In this respect, however, the earliest and the latest books of Scripture are in accordance, for Moses in old time had written, *It repented the Lord that He had made man on the earth, and it grieved Him at His heart.*[1] Now the revelation of St. Paul was higher than that of Moses, and yet he adopts precisely the same image.

It appears, then, that holy and true men, wherever their lot is cast, and whatever may be their outward circumstances, agree in this, that the wickedness of man is an occasion of grief and pain to God. We may speculate and philosophise about this as we please, in trying to find out how it is possible that God can be sensible to pain or grief; but here is the fact, if fact it is, or, at all events, here is the clear and unfaltering statement.

The waywardness, and wilfulness, and perversity of man's heart must either be regarded by God with indifference and unconcern, or with approbation, or with sorrow and grief, that is to say, if there is any reality in the nature and heart of God which at all answers to this human language. It is obvious that we cannot worthily speak of the Almighty. We can name His name, but higher than that our language cannot reach. Whatever we predicate of Him must be borrowed from the impoverished and scanty treasuries of earth, must therefore fall short of the true, if it does not suggest the false. Now, the true question is, What is the position of human language here? Does it suggest the false, or merely fail adequately to express the true? As far as we can at all trust the conclusions of our own mind, the

[1] Gen. vi. 6.

statement just ventured must include every possible aspect of the matter, and within the limits assigned the actual truth must necessarily lie.

But heart and conscience alike bear witness that God cannot regard the sin of man with approbation. God must be greater than man, and holier than man. Man cannot regard his own sin, or, at least, the sin of his fellow-man, with approbation, therefore it is clearly impossible that God can do so. The disapprobation man feels must be but the measure and not the multiple of that which is felt by God.

The only question, therefore is, whether man's sin is regarded by the Almighty with indifference and unconcern, or with sorrow and grief, always implying, of course, that these terms are used as only defective expressions of the truth.

And this question is a very fair representation of the issue between revelation and no revelation. If God has given no revelation to man in His Word, or has given us, in what we so term, a fictitious revelation, a revelation which is deceptive and illusory, then it is impossible to acquit the Almighty Judge of all men of absolute indifference and unconcern to all human action and to all matters of sublunary interest. And, as a matter of fact, this was how the heathen of old had become accustomed to consider that the gods did regard themselves and their actions, being not conscious of any valid reason to the contrary; but as a matter of no less certain fact, the writers of the Bible being conscious, as they were, of a special and direct revelation had learnt to look at this matter in a totally different aspect. They had been told by the Spirit which searcheth all things, yea, the deep things of God, that man's sin was to Him not merely an object of disgust and hatred, *that* the unenlightened conscience was only too ready to suspect, but yet more of grief and sorrow.

And, surely, if the shrinking from expected judgment is in any sense a revelation of God in the heart, an answer however wrong and imperfect to the voice of God without, which it certainly is, then the deep and energetic conviction that we find in the sacred writers of a different nature in God, which could not only rebuke and chasten, but much more could grieve and sorrow over, sin, was a higher, further, and truer revelation than the other, and one which, seeing it had historically not been aroused in the natural heart, had every just right and claim to be recognised as awakened by God Himself.

To Moses this conviction was vouchsafed in consequence of a redemption which had been commenced, and which he was assured would be completed finally. To St. Paul and the Ephesian Christians it was given in consequence of a redemption which had been accomplished in a Man, and had been communicated to themselves. Certain facts had taken place which had reduced to a tangible certainty the merely abstract truth that God cherished care for man. He had sent His Son with messages from heaven which bore on their very surface more of the stamp of the ideal heavenly than any others; He had laid down His life in defence and attestation of those messages, showing thereby that the messages were genuine and authentic; He had risen from the dead to show that He had personally the power to triumph over the enemies of mankind, and to cast out their inherent weakness, and to absolve them from their hopeless captivity to sin, and withal He had shed abroad upon them another Spirit which was identical with His own, and the like of which they had never experienced before. This was the Holy Spirit of the living God which had come upon them as a seal when they had surrendered themselves to the faith of Christ.

What is a seal? It is the recognised attestation of validity and good faith, it is the witness of truth, it is the pledge of security and of mutual obligation. The Holy Spirit was all this to these believers. He is all this to believers now. We do despite to the Spirit of Grace, when we suppose that the historic era of His operation has passed by. When we, with false modesty and delusive humility, suppose that a sign, which was vouchsafed at Ephesus, will not be given in London, that a pledge which was bestowed upon St. Paul will not be given to ourselves. These people believed in Jesus Christ as a living Man available to themselves and within their reach, who was to them the direct and palpable link which individually bound and united them to God. Each man saw in Jesus the Christ or chosen of God, in whom he personally could lay hold on God, could find God, could know God and retain God. Each man found that in Jesus he had the strength, the righteousness, the forgiveness, the favour, the goodness and sweetness of God. Each man felt that in touching Jesus, he touched God, that in grasping Jesus he passed into and became one with God. There was at once the abolition of sin, the realisation of pardon, the enjoyment of the grace of God. All this was to each man not a theory, not a fiction of the mind, but a felt reality, an experience. Each man took Jesus for this, and found all this in Jesus. He became to him the Christ, the fulness of God the manifested God. He was to them health, salvation, joy, peace, redemption, holiness, fulness of satisfaction, completeness of repose, assurance of acceptance and Divine favour, the certainty of Divine truth, as well as the promise of eternal life. Being all this to each Ephesian convert, Jesus became to him the source and fountain of a new gift, the bestower of the Holy Spirit of God. Each believer knew now that he was animated and actuated by a new spirit, the spirit of exuberant and abounding joy, the spirit of purity, and of unutterable sweetness in communion with God. This new and hitherto inexperienced flood of overflowing bliss in the realised presence of God and the assured favour of God, was to each believer the seal of the truth of Jesus. He who had thus attested Himself to the conscience of those who had yielded themselves to Him, who had given Himself to them in the fulness of His Christ glories and functions who had unreservedly surrendered themselves to Him, was and could be none other than the Christ, the chosen and promised One of God, who was Himself anointed with the Holy Spirit, that He might shed forth, as from a fountain in Himself, the gifts of the Holy Spirit upon His chosen ones. The reality of this gift was the seal of the reality of His claims, of the validity of His power to do that which they had believed He was able and willing to do for them. They knew now that the question, What is truth? which had so often seemed to perplex them, had virtually resolved itself to them. They had believed the offers of Jesus Christ, and the claims of Jesus Christ to be true, and lo, He had proved Himself to them to be the truth. Henceforth they would no more be like children, tossed to and fro, and carried about with every wind of doctrine, but being established in Him, would be established in the truth.

For the gift of the Holy Spirit was the pledge also of security. Having wandered so long in devious paths of error and folly, and having now returned to the Shepherd and overseer of their souls, they would wander no more. They had not yet come to the heavenly inheritance, they had a long march, a severe struggle, a desperate conflict before them, they had yet to take possession, though they had received the promise of possession. But He who had already done so much, would not leave His work half undone, He would accomplish that which was begun, He who was the redeemer, and had revealed Himself as the redeemer, would assuredly redeem. And the Holy Spirit was the harbinger and earnest of the still future day of redemption, He was Himself the very pledge and warranty of the perfect and manifested individual salvation which would assuredly come, but had hitherto not been so much as dreamt of, when death would be cast out, and this human personality would itself participate in the unseen but heavenly and eternal glories of the Lord.

This, undoubtedly was the position of St. Paul and of his disciples at Ephesus. There is no question about that. The only question can be how far our own position answers to it. We have lately been praying for the gift of the Holy Spirit,—that at least was the ostensible object of the late 'mission,' but if that object is to be attained, this is assuredly how the gift of the Holy Spirit will manifest itself. And there is no reason why it should not thus manifest itself to-day. I know there are those here who have not thus felt His influence ; I know there are those here who would deride it, who would regard it all as so much infatuation. No wonder preaching is useless when the ears are thus closed. Why, the archangel Gabriel himself could not open them!

But depend upon it, this is not infatuation, if the Epistle to the Ephesians is a reality, and it has been a reality for eighteen hundred years. Here is the written record of the Spirit's influence written in such a way as to stand for ever. It is no question whatever of authorship. It matters not one iota whether Paul wrote this letter,—I have no doubt he did ; or whether he sent it to Ephesus,—it very probably was sent there ; it *was* written, and it was read, and as it was read it was endorsed by the answer of the Spirit recognising His own work in the hearts of those who read it. If it is not endorsed in your hearts, I speak now only to the few, I trust, it is not endorsed because and only because the Spirit's assuring work is lacking there. You do not believe in Jesus Christ, and therefore you cannot shew the work of the Spirit written in your hearts. As long as unbelief in Jesus, who is the giver of the Spirit, lurks there, He will not, cannot, give the Spirit. You have not accepted Him, He has oftentimes been very near you, but you have not closed with Him, you have not reached forth your hand and grasped Him. You have not, as He was passing by, stealthily, shrinkingly, and yet confidently touched His garment. He is to you an unknown, because an untried Saviour, that is why you know nothing of pardon, nothing of holiness, nothing of sweetness, nothing of peace. You let the fatal—I had almost said the accursed—questionings of the intellect come between your soul and Him. You debate this, and argue the other, with your proud and self-confident intellect, and meanwhile the Saviour has passed by. " Oh, it was only a vision, nothing but thin air." He will not stand that sort of thing, He did not come to save such as you, for you decline to be saved, you laugh at His salvation.

There are two invisible elements in man, the intellect and the spirit, they are distinct and separate as the body and the soul are separate. You cannot tell where the two unite, anymore than you can tell where the body and the soul unite. That element in man, by which Christ's salvation reaches the central man, is not the intellect any more than it is the body. Christ's salvation cannot reach you through your body. There were many who touched the body of Christ who were not saved by Him. Christ's salvation must reach you, and reach you only, through the spirit. When it so reaches you, your intellect will be saved, and your body will be saved. You must lay aside your intellect if you would have your spirit saved, and when your spirit is saved, when Christ's salvation has reached you, as it can alone reach you through your spirit, then your intellect will acknowledge the Spirit's salvation in its own deliverance, and emancipation, for your intellect will thankfully accept Christ as the truth of God and the wisdom of God, and your intellect being enabled to expatiate on the truth and wisdom of God will rest content in the abundance of its joy.

And now, my dear friends, to press the matter one

step farther, as with a parting word, Why should it not be so with you? There is nothing overdrawn or exaggerated in what I have said. I have spoken of facts, of things that I know to be realities, and they may be realities to you. You may now, this very moment, if you will, be *sealed with that holy Spirit of promise which is the earnest of our inheritance until the redemption of the purchased possession unto the praise of His glory*.[1] Have you received the Holy Ghost since you believed? If not, then it is because your belief is a merely nominal belief. You have not taken Jesus as I have put Him before you, so as to make Him yours. You have not in Him received the fulness of God. You have not given Him your sins, your weakness, your timidity, your unwillingness, your reluctance, your temptations, your trials, your very self. You stand aloof from Him. You are like a man in a nightmare, who has something within his reach which he cannot reach, he longs to reach it, he seems to try to reach it, he upbraids himself for not reaching it, but he wakes and finds it gone. In this case, however, there is no nightmare, it is a waking reality, it is within your reach, and you may reach it if you will, you can reach it if you try. You may touch Him now if you will. There, did you touch Him then? oh ye faithless ones, how can ye be sealed unto the day of redemption? How can you be saved if you reject the Saviour when He offers to save you—when

---
[1] Eph. i. 13, 14.

He presents Himself within your reach, and you put Him by? Is not this to grieve the Holy Spirit of God, whereby you might be sealed if you only would? His seal is pardon, love, joy, peace, longsuffering, power of endurance, inextinguishable hope whose horizon is eternity and not time. But above all it is the fulness of assurance and satisfaction, the sense of spiritual completeness, of personal wholeness, which is imaged to us by what is said of her who felt in her body that she was healed of that plague.

I do trust there are some of you here to-day who will determine to prove and verify for themselves, ere the night close on them, the truth of what I have been saying. Do not believe it because I say it, but do not reject it because I say it. Test it for yourselves, and then you will know the truth of it. The issue is one in which the Almighty yearnings are specially interested and moved. God is not an indifferent spectator to the mental struggles of man, any more than a father is to the opening character of his child. What He desires is mutuality of surrender; He has surrendered Himself to you, He is now offering to do so again. Your part is to surrender, there is no other word that expresses it so well. Give it over, yield yourself a helpless and therefore a willing and an absolute surrender unto Him. You can do nothing else, but you can do this, and then you will know that He is the very joy of your heart, and that He will be your portion for ever.

XXVII.

THE HOLY CATHOLIC CHURCH.

Which is His body, the fulness of Him that filleth all in all.—
EPHESIANS i. 23.

"I BELIEVE in the Holy Catholic Church" is that article of the Creed which follows on from the one which we last considered, "I believe in the Holy Ghost." Its relative position in the Nicene Creed is the same, for there it succeeds the confession with respect to the Third Person of the Trinity, "Who spake by the Prophets," and the form it assumes is, "I believe one Catholic and Apostolic Church." From the combined confession of the two Creeds, then, we obtain these characteristics of the Church, that it is One, that it is Holy, that it is Catholic, that it is Apostolic. We will take these characteristics of the Church as they stand in order.

But first, with regard to the position of the article on the Church in both the Creeds. The Church is the creation of the Holy Spirit. The Church of Christ is the Spirit's work. As in the book of Genesis we are told that the Spirit of God moved on the abysmal and chaotic waters till it formed of them the order which now delights our senses and instructs our minds, so we are taught that the Holy Spirit in the new creation brooded on the face of the natural, confused and unformed mass of humanity, till there was produced that phenomenon of history which is apparent to the observation and philosophy of the believer and the unbeliever alike—the visible Church of Christ. This, we are led to infer, is the result of the Holy Spirit's operation.

Again, for the first time in the Creed, the expression "I believe" is applied to an object of which there can be no opportunity of doubt. The Church, as a matter of fact, exists. No one can call in question the existence of the Church of Christ any more than he can that of the Ottoman Empire or of the French Republic. There it is, account for the phenomenon and explain its existence as we may. The history of the Church must remain for ever, whether we are Christians or whether we are not, the most important chapter in the history of the world and the history of mankind that has ever been written. And it is impossible to conceive that any chapter more important can ever in the future be written.

The visible Church of Christ, then, is not, strictly speaking, an object of faith at all. It is an object of sight as much as the sun in the heavens, or the existence of man upon the earth. Every article of the Creed hitherto has made, in one way or other, a direct appeal to the faculty of faith. "I believe in God the Father," "I believe in Jesus Christ," "I believe in the Holy Ghost," and the like, each draws upon the exercise of the believing faculty, either as a matter of historic verity, or as an object transcending the apprehension of the ordinary powers to which the objects of sense appeal. But here it is different. The existence of the Church is not a thing to be believed, it is a thing to be seen.

And that, brethren, is a thought worth pondering. For the undoubted present existence of a fact so patent, inevitably and imperatively demands some explanation of its existence. What was its origin? There was a time when it was not. There are lands where it is not now. What was it brought the Church into existence in the past? What is it brings the Church into existence now? The Christian has an answer which may well challenge disproof, inasmuch as when all things are considered no other will be found satisfactory, which is, the being and operation of the Holy Spirit.

Although, however, the existence of the Church of Christ is an obvious fact, demanding an explanation of the enquiring and philosophic mind like any other fact, and as such is not strictly within the limits of things to be believed, yet there is an aspect of its existence in which it passes strictly and accurately within those limits. And for this reason it is that "I believe in the Holy Catholic Church," finds its place among the articles of the Christian Creed. And this aspect is its existence, independently of our observation, as an object of which the senses can take no cognisance. Most instructive, therefore, is

the occurrence of these words in the symbol of our belief, because by them the Church is taken out of the category of things to be merely seen, and placed with those others which either cannot be seen at all, or which, being patent to observation, like the life of our Lord Jesus Christ, appeal also, like Him, to other
✗ faculties than those of sight and sense for the full apprehension of their being.

We are not warranted, therefore, in taking the expression "I believe," when applied to the Church, in a sense different from that in which we take it elsewhere, as though its meaning were, "I believe, not only in the existence of the Church," which none can doubt, " but also in the absolute verity of all that the Church has taught : I believe, not only that the Church is One, Holy, Catholic, and Apostolic, but also that it is indefectible and infallible : I believe, not only in the Church as an organised and corporate society, but also as an authoritative teacher of absolute and indubitable truth." This, however accurately it may express the belief of many Christians, is unquestionably no part of the Apostles' Creed. We are not required to believe by the Scriptures of
✗ Divine revelation—we are not warranted in believing by the earliest Christian Creed—that God has committed to mankind any authentic, living, standard of infallible truth.

And a great blessing it is that we are not required to believe that, and that we are not charged with the responsibility of establishing an allegiance to it in the face of obstinate and awkward facts. Those who would claim for the Church any such function as this, must read into the word " believe " as it applies to this article of the Creed, a meaning quite different from that which it bears in every other instance. They must say, not merely "I believe in the Church," but " I believe the Church." " I believe," that is, " as infallible and incontrovertible, everything which has been propounded in the name of the Church, if only it comes with sufficient pomp and paraphernalia—if only it can make good its claim to be an article, which a respectable majority of people, calling themselves Catholic and Apostolic, have at any time believed."

Now this, I, for one, must emphatically protest against, and most distinctly do not believe. Any such view of the functions of the Church must result in one of two positions. Either we must believe that the Church has been continuous, unbroken and progressive from the first, that her existence has been maintained by an obstinate and persistent method of rejecting everything which interfered with her development in one direction as is the case with the Church of Rome, who has, in our own days, signally verified and illustrated her policy of development and progress by incorporating into her Creed ambiguous doctrine, declaring it infallible, and anathematising those who decline to accept it—or we must fall back upon the ideal Church of the first three centuries, before violent and unnatural attempts at outward unity had resulted in dismemberment and disorganisation, which is in fact equivalent to a confession that there is actually in the present no Church answering to our fond ideal of the past coupled with an ardent and impossible hope that eventually there may be.

Now in contradistinction let us rather say than in opposition to these two conceptions of the Church, we adopt the language of the Creed, and declare " I believe in the Holy Catholic Church." Consequently, as the first essential of the existence of the Church, as a reality not obvious to the senses, I believe in the *invisibility* of the Church of Christ. The Church is a spiritual body, having indeed an outward and visible existence, which cannot be denied, but by no means dependent upon the outward and visible limits of her existence for the truth and reality of her being. The real Church of Christ is not that which I see, whether in Rome, England, or Russia, but exactly that which I cannot see either here or there, but that which I believe exists, and the limits and conditions of whose existence are known to Christ alone. Thus the true and veritable Church of Christ, in which I believe, is a Church which I cannot see, and the limits of which I cannot define.

Oh, you will say, this is something very shadowy and indistinct; we want something palpable, something tangible, something which we can determine, so that we may be able to decide whether or not we ourselves are in it. Yes, my brethren, and it is that which I cannot give you, and which I believe Christ has not given you. The idea of "God the Father Almighty" must be something shadowy and indistinct, so must that of "Jesus Christ His only Son, our Lord," so must that of the "Holy Ghost." We are dealing with things which we believe, and not with things which we can see, *for we walk by faith and not by sight*.[1] It is analogous, therefore, to the rest of God's revelation that the Church of His Son is not only visible, which is a fact, but likewise invisible, and an object of faith not to be apprehended by the senses, but by the enlightened faculties of the spiritual mind.

And now observe the consequences of thus believing in the Church. We are for ever delivered from the responsibility of determining which is the true Church. How many anxious souls in these latter days have vexed themselves about this vexed question, and are still vexing themselves, Which and where is the true Church? Is the Church of England with her various crudities, anomalies, enormities, absurdities, contradictions, and scandals, a branch of the true Church? I confess that if I believed there was any mystical virtue in a visible Church, I should at once, and without the slightest hesitation, say No, she cannot be. If I am to have an outward and visible Church, compact and definite, then give me the Church of Rome, whose existence is not

[1] 2 Cor. v. 7.

merely on a piece of parchment, the result of a compromise between conflicting parties, and the creation of an act of Parliament which a vote of the House of Commons may at any time dissolve. But believing, as I am taught by the Creed to do, that the Church of Christ is an invisible and spiritual existence created by the operation of the Holy Spirit, I can regard with indifference any discussion as to the locality of the true Church, because I am well assured that the Church of England cannot shut me out of it, and that the Church of Rome cannot put me into it. The true Church is that which has the presence of Christ and the possession of the Spirit of God. And of this Church Christ Himself has said, *Where two or three*—the thing is unconditional and unlimited—*where two or three are gathered together in My name there am I in the midst of them ;*[1] and *If ye, being evil, know how to give good gifts unto your children, how much more shall your heavenly Father give the Holy Spirit to them that ask Him.*[2] And of this Church, St. Paul has said, that it is Christ's *body, the fulness of Him that filleth all in all.*[3] Wherever, therefore, there is the fulness of Christ, there is the true Church.

Again, by thus believing in the Church, we are for ever delivered from anxieties arising from the present condition of the outward Church. It is hardly possible to exaggerate the outward condition of the Church, take it where you will, in Greece, or

[1] Matt. xviii. 20. [2] Luke xi. 13. [3] Eph. i. 23.

Rome, or England, in conformity or nonconformity alike; and I, for one, do not grudge the utmost that the unbeliever and the adversary may choose to make of so promising and fruitful a theme. For my reply is, the home of the Christian is not here, and the Church of the Christian is not here. He is not dependent for his life upon the perfectness of organisation, or upon the right exercise of discipline, or upon the tradition of infallible doctrine, or upon any adventitious circumstance of the kind, but upon spiritual union with Christ. If he is one with Christ then he is one also with all those who belong to Christ; and one with them, even though in consequence of the various accidents arising from the inevitable imperfections of our present condition, there may be many impediments to the full realisation of this unity. Is not that Christian family one, of which the several members are devoted in their attachment to the father and mother, and among themselves, even though the sons may be dispersed in the four quarters of the globe, and the daughters may themselves have become centres of Christian homes in England or abroad. Thanks be to God, Christianity has revealed to us a centre of unity, permanent and indestructible, which is independent alike of time and place, and which, though gathering up into itself all the natural sentiments of the heart, is no mere matter of sentiment, but a reality centred in Christ.

And the Church is a Christian family, having

one Father unseen and invisible in heaven, and one Elder Brother, even Jesus who was crucified, dead, and buried, but is risen and ascended, not that He might be absent and govern by deputy, but that He might gather together all and bind them in one by His Spirit.

We have been led to dwell principally upon the essential and invisible constitution of the Church, because that must be not only of primary and fundamental importance, but because there is ever a tendency in our nature to forget it. If the Church is an object of faith and not of sight, then it is only by faith that we can belong to it. We cannot enroll ourselves among its members as we should in the case of some municipal or corporate body, for we one and all are members already of the visible Church of Christ. The only question is, whether that visible membership is the outward expression of an inward reality in ourselves; whether being nominal members, as we cannot help being, we are anything more, and sharers in an intrinsic unity which is indestructible; and this must be the work of the Holy Spirit. It is the office of the Holy Spirit to reveal Christ to the mind as the centre of unity and the source of life. It is the office of the Holy Spirit to bestow the gift of faith by which we are enabled to perceive Christ, and to behold in Him the fulfilment of our highest aspirations and the satisfaction of our deepest wants.

There can be no greater fallacy, or more fatal

error, than to confound Christ and His Church, to seek in and through the visible Church, or any form of it, or any function of it, what is only to be found in Christ Himself, and there is probably no mistake more commonly made in the present day. It arises from the want of experimental knowledge of the Spirit's work. When St. Paul says the Church is Christ's body, great honour, it is presumed, is laid upon the Church, as though to her were committed some of those functions which are the prerogative of Christ alone. For example, it is assumed that the Church has power to forgive sin and to impart Christ. But it is impossible that the Church, which is made up of fallible and sinful men, can be in her corporate capacity other than she is in her component elements. If every individual member of the Church is defectible and defective, the Church herself cannot be indefectible and infallible. She becomes possessed of the attributes of her Lord, His perfection and holiness, in proportion as she appropriates those attributes by faith; and the faith of the Church is neither more nor less than the aggregate of the faith of her several members. The Holy Spirit dwells in the Church because He dwells in every member going to make up the Church; but He does not dwell in the Church apart from the way in which He dwells in each several member, for if so there would be some members in whom He dwells and does not dwell at the same time, which is absurd.

If we would be members of Christ's true, real, and invisible Church, we must be filled with the Holy Spirit, the Spirit of promise which is given in answer to prayer; then we shall know that it is with individuals as it is with the Church of Christ, that they are filled with Christ in proportion as they are emptied of themselves. For it is the office of the Holy Spirit to *burn up the chaff with unquenchable fire;*[1] to consume what is of self and is not of God, and to fill with all the fulness of Christ. And as the state of fulness and the state of vanity cannot coexist, so, if we are filled with Christ through the Spirit, there will be no room for the emptiness of self, but self, and the things of self, will be swallowed up, and then we shall know by experience, the only safe guide to the spiritual meaning of Scripture, what is the meaning of the Apostle's language, as applied to the Church, by having that language realised and fulfilled in our own condition, for, being *filled with all the fulness of God*,[2] we shall be able to understand practically how the Church also can be the very substance and body of Christ by becoming *the fulness of Him who filleth all in all.*[3]

[1] Matt. iii. 12.   [2] Eph. iii. 19.   [3] Eph. i. 23.

XXVIII.

THE HOLY CATHOLIC CHURCH.

Which is His body, the fulness of Him that filleth all in all.—
EPHESIANS i. 23.

HAVING dwelt in the former lecture on the significance of the position which "the Holy Catholic Church" holds among the other articles of the Creed, we pass on now to dilate upon the terms of that article itself, and first with regard to the Church's unity. That the Church is one is not expressly told us in the Apostles' Creed, but it is implied: for the Holy Catholic Church admits of no second any more than other ideas which are in in their nature single. We speak, for example, of the sun, the moon, the earth, and the like when we do not contemplate any repetition of the object in either case; so the Church implies the one Church.

Now this again, it must carefully be borne in mind, is an object of belief. I believe that there is one Church and that there cannot be more. But then it is a unity that is co-existent with endless divisibility: as the body hath many members so also is Christ, each member has its own collection of nerves, tissues, vessels, and the like, which are characteristic of its peculiar organisation. Each member has its own appropriate mode of action, which cannot at will be changed for any other. In like manner we find a frequent recognition of this principle of divisibility in holy Scripture. St. Paul continually alludes to the many *churches of Christ*.[1] He speaks of *all the churches of the Gentiles*[2]; he speaks of the *churches of Macedonia*,[3] of the *churches of God in Judea*,[4] of the *churches of Galatia*,[5] and the like. He implies that his own sphere of labour was distinct from that of Peter.[6] St. John, also, in the Revelation, speaks of the seven churches of Asia, and does so in terms that shows them to have been independent of one another as regards practice, character, and the like. All this seems to imply not only that the body of Christ has many members, in the sense of being composed of many individuals, but that it has also, like the natural body, many groups of members, as the head, the hand, the foot, each of which is possessed of an independent system of organisation, and is of necessity committed to an independent mode of action : the head cannot act like the hand, nor the hand like the foot.

And from this, brethren, I derive a most important inference,—that the Church of Christ was from the first constituted on a basis of variety and independence quite as much as on one of uniformity. It is perfectly absurd to suppose that in a society

[1] Rom. xvi. 16; 1 Cor. xi. 16. [3] 2 Cor. viii. 1. [5] Gal. i. 2.
[2] Rom. xvi. 4. [4] 1 Thess. ii. 14. [6] Gal. ii. 9.

made up of members from various nations so distinct as the Jews and the Greeks, there should have been one mode of thought, or even one habit of practice in minor things : nothing but a perpetual miracle could secure such a uniformity as this. And whatever may have been the practice of the early churches of the New Testament, which we can see differed widely from our own, the writings of the New Testament contain clear evidence of a considerable diversity of thought among the writers, as, for example, in St. Paul, St. John, and St. James.

I believe, then, in the unity of the Church, and by no means in its uniformity. I believe that its essential unity is not and would not be secured by any amount of uniformity, less or greater. I believe, that its unity is entirely distinct from and independent of its uniformity. And it is this essential, invisible, inevitable unity of the Church which constitutes the Church an object of faith. Suppose, now, we were to substitute for such a unity, a visible, or at least a professed, uniformity, like that of the Church of Rome, what then would be the meaning of this confession, " I believe in the Holy Catholic Church "? It would simply mean, "I believe in that outward, dull, monotonous uniformity, predominating at Rome, which I hold to be an essential characteristic of the true Church, and which I see, or at least the profession of which I see, obtains wherever the authority of Rome prevails " : that is to say, an object of faith would be at once exchanged for an object of sight, and the exercise of the spiritual faculty of faith degenerate into the dogged retention of an opinion. The unity of the Church, then, is something I am taught to believe, which is deeper than anything external which appears to contradict it.

For example, the unity of the Church is deeper and wider than the principles and practice of any one church, with regard to that which should be the symbol and token of unity, namely, the rite of Communion. A circular was sent me the other day, in which mention was made of "all the churches in full communion with the Church of England." I began to think what those churches could be, and, as far as I can determine, they seem to be pretty fairly limited to these three—the Episcopal body in Scotland, the Irish Church, and the Episcopal Church in America. All the reformed churches abroad are excluded, all the Nonconformists in England are excluded, all non-Episcopalians in America are excluded, and the two great sections of the Kirk of Scotland are excluded; while obviously the Greek Church and the Church of Rome are not included. Now here is a spectacle of realised Christianity, or rather, here is a living example of Christian disunion. Clearly the terms of communion do not constitute unity; and for any one who does not believe in the essential unity of the Church, despite all the outward marks of disunion, such a spectacle as this can only make the heart ache, while it is enough to quench love, to extinguish hope, and to paralyse effort.

But we may illustrate this underlying unity yet further. For example, persons of all communions, I suppose, believe that the Holy Communion is a bond of union between the living and the dead ; there the Church on earth meets with the Church in heaven around the table of the common Lord : and yet the outward disunion is apparent ; there are physical barriers which we cannot pass, and surely these physical barriers are not less than any which can be interposed by the arrangements and ordinances of internal organisation. In short, every Church or community of Christians is compelled for the purposes of internal economy to ordain precepts and regulations which it has no right to impose upon or require of other bodies ; just as every Christian family has a right to prescribe internal regulations for its own observance, which it has no right to impose upon any other family, still less upon the community at large. The mistake is, when the outward observance of these rules and regulations is confounded with adherence to internal and essential unity. If the Kirk of Scotland is not in communion with the Church of England that is an accident of family organisation ; it no more disproves the fact of both bodies being in communion with their common Head, and if so in unseen communion with one another, in spite of themselves, than does the circumstance of one Christian family dining at one hour of the day and another Christian family dining at another show them to belong to different kingdoms or even to different counties, or than the fact that some individuals of either family are to be found in the nursery and some elsewhere shows that they cannot be regarded as common members of the same family. I am not aware that if any Nonconformist or any member of any Christian Church on earth presents himself at the table of the Lord I have any right to withhold from him the symbols of Christ's body and blood; and I doubt very much whether any Christian Church on earth would have any other than an ecclesiastical right to censure any member who, believing in the actual unity of the body of Christ, puts that belief into practice by joining in the act of communion with any other Christian body than that to which he happens to belong himself; and sure I am that no Christian body has any right to impose as terms or conditions of communion any others than those which it would regard as conditions also of salvation. Now the conditions of salvation are these, and none can dispute their authority. *Believe on the Lord Jesus Christ and thou shalt be saved*,[1] and they are none other than these. We may not substitute for them belief in the Thirty-nine Articles, or the Westminster Confession, or the Athanasian Creed, or anything else, and so neither may we make the acknowledgment of one or other of these formularies the condition of communion. That you or I may, as a matter of accident, habit, or preference, communicate only in the Church of

[1] Acts xvi. 31.

England, by no means shows us to be not in communion with other churches, any more than does the fact of the communion service of the American Church differing from that of our Prayer-book, necessarily deprive a member of that Church of the privilege of communicating with ours when he happens to be sojourning among us.

So much, then, by way of showing that the essential unity of the Church is not affected by organic differences in the mode and practice of communion among the Churches. As many members differing organically and in principles of action go to make up one body, so also many Churches differing organically and in principles of action go to make up the one Church, which is bound together in union with Christ, the Head, by the unseen principle of faith in Him, and by nothing else.

The next characteristic of the one Church is, that it is Holy. This also, I believe, although, as in the case of its unity, I cannot see it. Nay, more, as I should distrust the holiness of that man whose holiness was too obstrusive and over-apparent, so I am not staggered in my belief in the real and sincere and substantial holiness of the Church by the manifold contradictions of holiness which are only too patent and manifest. You cannot find the perfect Christian any more than you can find the perfect Church. You cannot find the ideal Christian any more than you can find the ideal Church. The ideal and the real differ here as painfully as they do elsewhere, in this routine and prosaic world. It is a great gain to be able to regard the two as distinct, and not to be dismayed if we find the real falling short of the ideal; to be able to accept the real as we find it, and yet at the same time to retain our belief in the ideal. The Church is holy in reality and truth, but all the members of the Church are not holy; they are *called with a holy calling*,[1] and *called to be saints*,[2] but they do not all fulfil their calling. Which of us, let me ask, would be willing that the holiness of the Church should be estimated by his own personal standard of holiness, and if we do not fulfil our own ideal, need we be very greatly dismayed if others fail to realise it too? Here, again, our safety lies in holding fast to the ideal, and believing in One whose realised holiness is the holiness of His Church. The command is, *Be ye holy, for I am holy*[3]; but those very writings, like the first Epistle of St. Peter, which dwell most forcibly on the holiness of the Church, insist also most emphatically on the practice of holiness, as though such exhortations were, even in those cases, not superfluous. There will ever be a want of correspondence and conformity between the ideal and the actual, at least, so long as the visible Church is exposed to the trials and temptations of this lower world. While, therefore, the holiness of the Church is an article of the faith which is calculated to allay our apprehensions at the spectacle of the unholiness

[1] 2 Tim. i. 9.   [2] 1 Cor. i. 2.   [3] 1 Pet. i. 16.

of particular Christians, just as the belief in the indestructible unity of the Church is the only remedy for dismay at the present spectacle of the Church's disunion, so also is it calculated to stimulate our personal efforts after holiness, because it is a great help to action to know that the highest ideal is not an unreality. This is how St. Paul employs the marvellous elevation of thought to which he has raised his converts in the fifteenth chapter of his first Epistle to the Corinthians, when, after saying, *Thanks be to God, which giveth us the victory* (over death and the grave) *through our Lord Jesus Christ,* he goes on to say, *Therefore, my beloved brethren, be ye stedfast, unmovable, always abounding in the work of the Lord, forasmuch as ye know that your labour is not in vain in the Lord.* I can meet the actual unholiness of my brethren in the world with the greater equanimity when I believe in the realised holiness of the seven thousand uncontaminated ones whom God has reserved unto Himself. I can aspire after higher attainments of inward holiness in myself when I know and believe that there is One in whom is no sin, and that those who belong to Him are, in His sight, and therefore in reality and truth, holy as He is holy. This is the natural consequence of believing in the Holy Church, which, in the midst and by reason of surrounding unholiness, we cannot see.

Again, the Church is catholic, that is, universal : surely there is no word in the English language which has been more grossly abused than this ; and may we not add that from the very fact of its being so un-English, and therefore not understood, it has become a symbol for all sorts of associated ideas with which it has nothing whatever to do. The word does not occur in Scripture ; note that, I beseech you, and then determine for yourselves the value of the supposed mystical advantages of what is called catholicity. The only approximation to it is found in Acts iv. 18, where we read, *And they called them and commanded them not to speak " at all"* [καθόλου], *nor teach in the name of Jesus.* The position of the analogous expression here is in singular, may we not say ominous, contrast to the use hereafter to be made of its derivative, " catholic." We fall back, however, not upon its subsequently developed meaning, but upon its natural significance as indicated by the place in Scripture just quoted, which is that of *überall*, everywhere, the Church which is universal. As a matter of undeniable fact, the Church is far more catholic now than ever it was, when it first adopted the name ; but yet even now the significance of the name is as nothing to what we believe it will be, when the apocalyptic vision has been realised, and all the kingdoms of the world have become the kingdoms of our Lord and of His Christ. This is the Catholic Church in which we believe, the Catholic Church of the future, not the Catholic Church of the past, any more than the Catholic Church of the present. We believe in the Holy Catholic Church of God's intention and design, not in some visibly defined body which must first originate a meaning for the term "catholic," and then establish its claim and exclusive right to the conditions and qualifications of the term which it has originated. No such Catholic Church is found in Scripture ; no such Catholic Church, then, can claim to legislate for that society which came into existence fresh from the hands of its founder long before the epithet was invented. Certainly those who are the most inclined to take their stand upon the supposed merits of this term are the least mindful of, and the most opposed to its natural and intrinsic meaning. What can be less catholic than to circumscribe the boundless and unrestricted significance of the term, and to make it synonymous and identical with Roman. If I believe really in a *Catholic* Church, *that*, from the nature of the case and the very necessities of language, cannot be a Roman church in which I believe. Verily, in her jealous assumption of this term, she bears unimpeachable evidence against herself to her post-Scriptural, post-Apostolic, and therefore post-Christian origin and growth.

Lastly, the Church is Apostolic, though this term is derived from the Nicene and not from the Apostles' Creed, but we need not hesitate thankfully to accept it. The Church of Christ was planted and watered by apostles, whose work is known and registered in the writings of the New Testament, and whose very existence and conduct is unexplained and unaccountable if it does not rest upon the person and teaching, and word and work of the Lord Jesus. Every investigation of the being and existence of the Church must take us back eventually to the apostles of

Christ; for example, the Church of the present century rests upon, is derived from, cannot be accounted for, but by presupposing the Church of the last century. The Church of the last century leads us back to the Church of the seventeenth, and so on till we come to the second, which in like manner leads us back to the first, where we find, established by unexceptionable pedigree, the very writings and monuments of the first preachers of Christ, who received their commission from Christ. Here we are face to face with the very men who were commanded by those in authority *not to speak at all, nor teach in the name of Jesus.*

That is the apostolic origin of the Church; and we who have bowed the knee to Jesus on His sapphire throne to-day[1] are, in virtue of the faith of that act, one with the apostles who first proclaimed His name, and one with those who by faith accepted their proclamation, and one with those behind the veil who believed in Him to the saving of the soul, and one with those beneath the altar who were slain for His testimony, and still cry "O Lord, how long?" and one with all those of every communion and of every clime, of every age and of every church, who receive their life from and acknowledge Him, and one with each other and with Him whom they and we receive and believe; for this is what we mean and say when we confess, "I believe in the Holy Catholic Church."

[1] Preached on Trinity Sunday.

XXIX.

THE COMMUNION OF SAINTS.

I am the vine, ye are the branches.—JOHN xv. 5.

AS the "Holy Catholic Church" derives much of its true significance from the fact that it follows after the article about the Holy Ghost, so likewise is it further illustrated by the article "on the Communion of Saints" by which it is immediately followed.

I tried to show in the last lecture that the true unity of the Church was that which underlay all apparent and outward disunion. The true recognition of this truth seems to me to present the only remedy that can be found for this open disunion, and at the same time to reveal a source of real consolation, such as no other conception of the Church can promise or present. Nor only so, for a union of this nature points us at once to a power above nature, creating and causing it. He who gathers up in Himself the most discordant elements, and gives them a union with one another in their union with Him, which before they had not and could not have, has done a work which is at once worthy of God and impossible for man : and this is the work of Christ as it is manifested to us in the communion of saints, which we proceed now to consider.

This also is an article of belief; and if there is any justice in the position already adopted, and any truth in the sentiments expressed, this also must be something the cognisance of which is not derived from the senses. We do not see the communion of the saints, we only believe in it ; we cannot see the communion of saints, we can only believe in it. The two great thoughts, then, are—the communion subsisting between the saints, and the character of those between whom it subsists. Furthermore, it is this communion which is the prerogative of the Holy Catholic Church, and the result of the operation of the Holy Spirit,—which is to be found only in the Holy Catholic Church, and in which the special and peculiar character of the Holy Church of Christ's mystical body consists.

Now, in order to understand wherein the special character of this communion consists, let us look for a while at the nearest resemblances to it. No doubt, in the old world, there was something analogous to it in the mutual interest which was felt by those who enjoyed the privileges of Roman citizenship. There is something, as it always seems to me, very striking in that incident in the twenty-second chapter of the Acts, where a Roman officer who commanded the garrison in the castle of Antonia, which overlooked the temple, suddenly discovers that the prisoner whom he had in his power and was about to scourge is a Roman citizen. *As they bound him with thongs, Paul said unto the centurion that stood by, Is it lawful for you to scourge a man that is a Roman, and uncondemned? When the centurion heard that, he went and told the chief captain, saving, Take heed what thou doest: for this man is a Roman. Then the chief captain came, and said unto him, Tell me, art thou a Roman? He said, Yea. And the chief captain answered, With a great sum obtained I this freedom. And Paul said, But I was free born.* There we see the Christian prisoner at once set at a great advantage above the Roman officer, who only had by purchase what was Paul's by birth; but it is manifest that the magic talisman of that word *Roman* citizenship has at once established a bond of union and sympathy between the chief captain and his prisoner which had not been felt before.

And this is a fair specimen of what the adventitious circumstances of similar nationality and the like are capable of producing. Frequently, to belong to the same country, or the same county, or the same city, or the same university, or to have been educated at the same school is the cause of a union which lasts as long as life lasts; and whether or not this is so, all are aware of the subtle links of association which under any circumstances may be thereby created. To have undergone the same experience, to have lived in the same place, to have visited the same scenes at home or abroad, to have engaged in the same pursuits, to belong to the same society or the same club, to have filled the same office, to have served in the same campaign, to have taken the same journey, to have sailed in the same ship,— these and a hundred other things at once open out channels of communication, avenues of interest, and create links of association and connection between one mind and another, and not seldom between one heart and another, which, but for these things would have been left closed, or never have existed.

But, perhaps, of this kind there is nothing more potent than the accidentally discovered link of community of friendship. We are thrown across this man and that man in the journey of life, and we presently find that he is a friend of a friend of ours, and is known to some one whom we know, and at once there is a new principle of concern awakened, a new motive for intercourse, or kindness, or friendship, or the like, established. We are conscious of the subtle bond of common relation to a common object, and are at once affected thereby. Yet more is this the case where there is community of sentiment. The influence of a common idea, a common opinion, a common endeavour, and the like, is perhaps the most potent operative principle in bringing men together who were before totally unknown, or had not the slightest interest in one another. To be members of the same political party, of the same church party, of the same school of art, philosophy, or science, is to have a basis for intercourse and friendship established which, but for such an excuse, had not existed. All this, however, while it reveals an undoubted and a very deep-lying principle in human nature, is also a token of its weakness and defect. Why should I feel and surrender myself to an interest in that man because he happens to be a conservative or a liberal, a high-churchman, a low-churchman, or a broad-churchman, a geologist, a botanist, or an antiquary, for whom, on merely personal grounds, I should have no interest whatever? Simply because there is in one or other of these things a principle of possible communion between us which otherwise would not exist. When, in youth, we are commencing a new study or a new language, what an element of joy it is to meet with some one who has engaged in it already, and is competent to be our companion and guide along the road, and in after years the philologer finds pleasure in the society of philologers, the mathematician in that of mathematicians, and the like; but all this is special, and therefore I think that society itself teaches us that the more truly a man is a man of culture, the more truly he is independent of any of these specialities. The mere mathematician and mere botanist may have little in common, but no two men of real culture, whatever their specialities may be, can fail to derive pleasure from their intercourse with one another. And all this leads us up to the truth which had revealed itself to the Roman poet of old, *Homo sum, humani nihil a me alienum puto*—" I am a man, and regard nothing that is of human interest as alien from myself." The real bond of union between us is, after all, our common humanity. "One touch of nature makes the whole world kin." It is this which gives the novelist, the poet, the dramatist, his power, and it is nothing else. It is this which alone can give the preacher or the speaker any power over his hearers. He who is not a true man himself can have no access to the hearts of men, nor does he deserve to have. Now, the communion of saints is a communion established on this broad basis of a common humanity. If it were not for the natural truth which lies hid in the maxim of Terence just referred to, the communion of saints would have been an impossibility. As it is, Christ has taken this basis and reared upon it the edifice of the communion of saints. He has revealed Himself as the true vine, of which His disciples are the branches. He has presented to us, in Himself, the true and root principle of humanity, the perfect ideal of man. He has shown us what man was designed by God to be. He has revealed, in Himself, the original stock, essence or principle of humanity, so that, as it was accidentally, and yet most truly, said of Him, Ecce Homo, *Behold the man!*[1] so he says of Himself, Homo sum, *I am the true Man*, the true Vine, the original Son of the Father, who alone was made in the express image and likeness of the Father, the subdued human and humanised bright-

[1] John xix. 5.

ness of His Divine and unapproachable, incommunicable glory.

Here, then, in Him, is the natural and the supernatural basis of the communion of saints. If we admit, as we must admit, that He is the truest, the greatest, the loftiest, the most perfect, the most human, also the most Divine man that history presents to our contemplation, then we can preceive without effort, that it is only just, and right, and natural, that He should be the foundation stone of a new edifice of humanity, and that He also in Himself should be the centre of a new union among men, who are raised by their recognition of the Divine in Him, to a new dignity and degree of manhood. In Christ then, and the Christian communion of saints, we have the fulfilment of the two qualifications which we have seen our common nature demands. The broader the basis, the truer the union. We are not united by those things which distinguish us, but by those things which we have in common, though we commonly prize ourselves most for the things which we have, which others have not, such as wealth, station, and talent. Yet it is not these things which constitute our greatest glory, but on the contrary, those things which are common to us all, the power of feeling or of doing a kindness, the perception of goodness, justice and truth, the natural affections of the heart, by which we are capable of love for one another, whether it be our wives, our parents, or our children. What mother is not touched by the spectacle of motherly love, in another, however far removed from herself in position, or however degraded. And this is the Divine link of humanity, this is the glory of womanhood. Rightly and wisely did the old painters dwell with unwearied assiduity on, and continually repeat, that loveliest and most Divine, because most human of all subjects,—the mother and her child. These were the commonest of all objects, and yet the most glorious of all—the perfection of self-sacrifice, the unsullied purity of love, the spotless innocence of infancy, the very original form of a recreated humanity. Christ thus gathers up in Himself all the commonest and most characteristic features of our humanity. He is the meeting-point of the highest and the lowest, because in Him there is that which alone is common to both, and therefore the glory of both. His basis of union is coextensive with the widest limits of the family of man. Oh that we could make men see this in Christ, for then indeed we should make them Christians.

Thus, then, Christ fulfils in Himself the desire for breadth, which our nature demands. But He also fulfils in Himself that other qualification which it no less requires. For He appeals likewise to the instinct in man, which demands only the best. It is the highest goodness, the highest truth, the highest beauty which is found in Christ, for in Him is revealed the point in which the human is merged in the Divine, the point where man touches God.

Thus while Christ says, Because I am truly man, I regard nothing that is manly, nothing that is human, as alien from Myself, and thus appeals to universal man, His character is essentially such that it appeals only to the highest in man, and to that in which men are like unto God. It can only be therefore as men are won to Christ, that they can love Christ, and find their centre in Christ. Men do not commonly love the highest, but only what they think to be the highest. The love of the highest is a specialty, just as mathematics or geology is a specialty, and the specialist prefers his specialty, just as the Christian prefers Christ. And thus as geology or philology is a bond of union between geologists and philologists, so is Christ a special bond of union between Christians, between, that is, those who have been taught to see in Christ the greatest glory of humanity, and the greatest good of man. For such there is established on the old, the world-wide, and the natural basis of humanity, a new bond of union in the love of the highest humanity, and the worship of the perfect man. This is the principle of the earthly communion of saints, of those who have become holy through their union with the Holy Man, who have thus been grafted into and made branches of the true vine. Between all such, there is not only the natural bond of union, which even in a heathen could lead him to esteem nothing human as alien from himself, but also that talismanic principle of union which discovers a new motive for interest, a fresh attraction for sympathy, in attachment to the same person, in admiration for the same character, in pursuit of the same object, in possession of the same idea, in devotion to the same sentiment.

As all true patriots, whatever their political creed, are equally loyal to the constitution and the crown, and are necessarily drawn together when the safety or honour of either is threatened, so all true Christians, whatever their individual sentiments, or their denominational creed, are mutually drawn together, and sympathetically united in love and allegiance to their common Lord. There is a magic, talismanic power in the name of Christ, and in the name of Jesus, who is the Christ, which like the touch of nature that makes the whole world kin, convinces every Christian of a community of origin between all who love the Lord Jesus Christ in sincerity, of an origin that cannot be broken by the accidental severance of the Churches, any more than those who are united in a common friendship or bound to a common friend can be severed by the flight of time, or by the billows that wash divided continents.

The communion of saints, then, is a communion which they have with one another, through their union with a common centre and common object of love. Just as any point on the circumference is united by an invisible line to the centre, and may so be united with any other point by a line passing through the centre, or by two lines meeting in the centre, so also is the union of the saints in Christ. He is their invisible Head, to whom they one and all are joined by invisible bonds of faith and love ; and as nothing can separate between Christ and those, whom He calls His own, so nothing can separate between those who belong to Christ, because they are united one with another, by being one and all united to Him. They are, as He says, all several branches of the true vine, which is Himself. They all derive their life from Him, as the sap flows through the branches of the vine. One branch differs from another branch : as in any one tree there are no two branches similar, no two leaves alike, so in the true vine there are many members of various characteristics, various conditions, various capacities, but all possessed of a general likeness, as the leaves and branches of the vine are like one another, but distinct from the leaves and branches of the oak.

And there is one special and peculiar feature in the communion of those who are holy as Christ is holy, which is, that the communion is not confined to this living world. As the communion is not to be detected by the sight, so neither is it limited to the world of sight. The friends whom we have lost yet live in Christ. As when they were here our communion with them was not dependent on anything we found here, but on the union that we found in Christ, so now that communion cannot be broken because we find them no longer here. Their communion is where it was, and ours is where it was, before we lost them; our communion was not one which we found in them, but one which they and we alike found in Christ, and it is one we may find there still. They have passed beyond the circumference of our ken, and their circle is a larger one than ours, but it is concentric with ours, for the centre of both is Christ. Nothing can separate them from Christ, and nothing need separate us from Christ, and nothing can separate us from them if we do not separate ourselves from Christ. If we abide in Him, and He abides in us, then we are branches of the true vine, and being branches of the true vine the communion which we have with Christ is the measure of the communion we may have with them in Him, a communion which is an object of faith now, and shall be one of reality and fact hereafter.

XXX.

THE FORGIVENESS OF SINS.

In Whom we have redemption through His blood, even the forgiveness of sins.—COL. i. 14.

"THE forgiveness of sins" may be regarded as the distinctive tenet of the Gospel. No other religion has made the same daring proclamation of the remission of sins that Christianity has made. Every religion that has instructed or deceived mankind has professed to deal with sin and with the consciousness of sin in some way or other which has of course been assumed to be efficient and effectual, and consequently the necessary inference has been suggested that the sin has been forgiven. And it is obvious that all these methods of dealing with sin, if they were really effectual, must have depended upon one of two things for their efficiency—the discovery of man or the revelation of God. If they depended on the revelation of God, then, as the methods of dealing varied in various religions, the revelation of God would vary and be inconsistent which is not conceivable; if they depended on the discovery of man, then the question would arise, Which religion had discovered the truth or made the true discovery? and then, of necessity, all other religions would be worthless, and, in proportion to the strength of their claims, would be deceptive.

Now we may certainly say that there was a strong point of contrast between Christianity and all other religions, that the forgiveness of sins was not left by it to the ingenuity of an inference, but was declared as a fact. Here then, at once, there would be an additional ground of accusation against Christianity if there was not therein an additional evidence of its truth. But in point of fact, Christianity not only contrasts with all other religions in respect of its declaration of forgiveness, but also in respect of its denunciation of sin, and of the far greater and more intense conviction of sin which it produces in the conscience.

And here is the strength of Christianity. It first of all accuses man as a sinner and reveals his sin. It declares plainly, not only that the natural conscience was warranted in the estimate it had formed of sin, which was sufficient to justify the worst misgivings and misapprehensions that had been expressed in the more terrific forms of sacrifice, but also that these misgivings and misapprehensions were short of the mark. Christianity, that is, revealed a sin that the natural conscience had not discovered, and to which it did not spontaneously plead guilty. In this consisted its charge against mankind, its indictment against man.

And here we are dealing with facts which it is simply impossible to deny. The deeper consciousness of sin brought in by Christianity is a patent fact, to which literature, morals, social life and the conscience itself alike bear witness. We may join issue with Christianity on this ground, that its estimate of sin is an undue and exaggerated estimate, but that such is its estimate admits of no doubt whatever. And therefore it is that Christianity anticipates a ground of objection to itself, because as its distinctive mark is the freedom of its declaration of forgiveness it virtually declines to deal with those who are blind to the necessity for such forgiveness. Christianity offers pardon to those who feel the want of it; if there is no felt want of pardon the offer of pardon becomes a nullity. But it is no proof of the unreality or invalidity of the pardon offered to confess to a consciousness of no need for it. That there is no such consciousness may itself be a radical and primary defect. Christianity affirms that it is. *If ye were blind ye should have no sin: but now ye say, We see, therefore your sin remaineth.*[1] When the Pharisees questioned our Lord's authority, which is precisely what men do now-a-days, He asked them the previous question, What was the authority of John's baptism?[2] Now John's baptism was a baptism of repentance for, or with a view to, the remission of sins. If, therefore, they had not accepted that baptism as authoritative, if they had not quailed under a sense of sin, they were not competent judges of Christ's authority which professed to give a re-

---
[1] John ix. 41. [2] Matt. xxi. 24 sq.

mission of sin that implied a prior repentance. And so it will ever be. Those objections to Christianity are of no avail that betray in the objector an ignorance of the true evil of sin. We may boldly say, as the Gospel itself says, that it is not for such. It comes professing to forgive; its profession cannot apply to those who acknowledge that they have nothing to be forgiven.

And this is really a fair question that we may reasonably put to all objectors to supernatural religion in the present day, How do you propose to deal with sin? And the answer would be, We do not propose to deal with it at all. We say that sin is a misconception. Sin is the appearance of imperfection in that which, regarded in a broader view, is a vast and perfect whole. In the wise and cultivated man there should be no such thing as sin. Failing and infirmity there may be, for it were absurd to seek for perfection and entirety in the imperfect and the partial; but sin presupposes a relation between the finite and the infinite, which is impossible and unreasonable. Very well, then, be it so; let us grant that the relation between the philosopher and the deity, if he admits so superannuated a conception, is perfectly smooth and satisfactory. Then, I ask, What about crime? because crime is a fact, and a very awful fact, and crime is not something distinct from sin, for sin is the cause of crime, and though you and I may not be criminals, yet there may be, and there is, in us that which is of the nature of crime, namely, sin, and we do not acknowledge the absence of the same nature in the philosopher. Is it possible, then, that this sin which is liable to outbreaks, so tremendous as those of our prisons and police-courts, can be a misconception resolvable into a mental error on our own part? I think not.

But we may go nearer home. We will assume that you have not sinned lately, that there is nothing in your life now for which you need shrink from the severest scrutiny; but has it always been so? You will hardly ask us to believe that. You can hardly believe it yourself. You can hardly say that you have never sinned. There must be something in the area of the past that you would wish otherwise, that you would gladly forget, perhaps have forgotten. With respect to this you must either be self-condemned, or you are self-forgiven. If you are self-condemned, then *there* is the evidence of sin; if you are self-forgiven, then the reality of sin is not disproved, but it appears that instead of an external fountain of forgiveness, the source of your forgiveness is within; but unless your sin is merely against yourself this is of small avail. You can have no power to forgive that which is a sin, not against yourself, but against God. If your sin has really been against God, then the fact of your being self-forgiven does not prove that you are God-forgiven. You may have forgotten your sin, but it does not follow that God has forgotten it. And all speculations as to its forgiveness must be vain, unless there is some way of getting at, or of receiving an authoritative declaration from God on this matter.

So far, then, as to the fact of forgiveness, supposing there is the acknowledgment of sin to be forgiven; but, then, observe that the condition of sin according to the Gospel is something very different from the mere overt act of sin. It may not be that you are guilty of sin now, but it by no means follows that you are not sinful; the very ignorance and denial of sinfulness may be your sin. The root-sin of the Gospel is a negative and not a positive sin. *When the Comforter is come, He shall convince the world of sin, because they believe not in Me.*[1] The condition of man, irrespective of his acts, is one of sin. This is the allegation of the Gospel. If man denies it, all we can do is to leave him alone with his conscience, and to pray for him; if he responds to it, then we can proclaim to him the forgiveness of sins. And in evidence of the reality of this forgiveness, and of the authority on which it rests, we can say, that as the depth of the consciousness of sin produced by Christianity was greater than nature could or did attain to in any other religion, so the certainty and the adequacy of the forgiveness offered being greater than nature could attain to or conceive of too, is an evidence of the validity of the offer. For if we reject this forgiveness as Divine, we must either deny the reality of sin, and therefore the need of forgiveness, or else we must forgive ourselves, which is obviously

[1] John xvi. 8, 9.

something very different from God forgiving us, or else we must be content to rest in the bare presumption that we have been forgiven, or shall hereafter be forgiven. Now, in direct opposition to each of these points, the Gospel declares, in distinct and emphatic language, that *we have redemption through His blood, even the forgiveness of sins.*[1] It is plain, then, that the Gospel offer of forgiveness is linked in some special and intimate way to the death of Christ. This is plainly affirmed in the text, and it is corroborated by our Lord's own words, *This is My blood of the New Testament which is shed for many, for the remission of sins.*[2]

Thus, then, the Gospel assurance of forgiveness appeals at once to the senses, and is such as cannot be called in question, and admits of no dispute. That the blood of Christ was shed, is a fact of history which nobody denies, or can deny. If His death had anything to do with man's forgiveness, then man is as surely forgiven as he may be sure and cannot doubt that Christ died. This, then, is the root-question : granted the death of Christ which we must all grant, was His death a death for the remission of sins? It is not a question of the fact, but only of the interpretation of the fact. The message of the Gospel is not merely that Jesus Christ died, which is the message of history—of the historian Tacitus—as well as the Gospel, but that Christ died for *sin*, for that which is the cause of crime, and is perpetually breaking forth into crime,

[1] Eph. i. 7; Col. i. 14.   [2] Matt. xxvi. 28.

for that to which the conscience of universal man, except only the philosophers, for thousands of years has borne spontaneous witness, for that which, in the individual heart, is continually asserting itself, continually accusing or excusing its presence, and equally in either way, calling aloud for condemnation.

And this is not only the message of the Gospel, that Christ died for sin, but His death is likewise the evidence of the Gospel message. For as long as we have these words of Christ, *This is my blood that is shed for the remission of sins*, it is impossible to deny that He taught that His death was a death for sin, and that He died in attestation of the truth of what He taught. This, then, being so, we must either admit that He taught what was false and died for what was false, or we must accept His death as the inseparable crown and culmination of His teaching, and therefore as a death for sin. But if we accept Christ's death as a death for sin, and the remission of sin, then the sins for which He died are remitted and forgiven, and then we may believe in the forgiveness of sins, not as an invention of priests, not as the self-deception of the naturally lax and self-forgiving, self-indulgent heart, not as the mere presumption of nature and of human speculations on the general amiability and benevolence of the Divine Being and character, but as the very voice of God to the sin-stricken heart, proclaimed to a guilty but repentant world, and ratified so that none can question it in the blood of His own Son.

And this, verily, is the message of the Gospel to a sinful world, and to a world which acknowledges its sin. *In whom we have redemption through His blood, even the forgiveness of sins.* If we have it *in Him*, then we have it, not out of Him, apart from Him, independently of Him. If God forgives us by Christ, then we may be quite sure He does not and will not forgive us in any other way. The consistency of the Divine conduct would be impaired and violated were He to do so. Christ would not have shed His blood for the remission of sins if sins were to be, or might be, remitted without His shedding of blood. Christ must, in His life, teaching, and death, cease to be the exponent of the will of God ; or God must, as St. John says, be made a liar if, after the death of Christ as a death for sin, it were to be in any way probable or possible that sin should be forgiven independently of Him. Whatever the mysterious relation may be between the death of Christ and the forgiveness of sins, as to the reality, validity, and actuality of the relation, there can be no possible room for doubt. So neither can there be any question as to the finality of this relation, for if *we have* redemption through His blood, then we do not wait for it : it is a present possession, not a future or conditional or contingent promise. It is not something to come, but something already come, not something to be given, but something already bestowed ; not something to be had, but something already had—through the past, historic, never-to-be-repeated, solitary act of the shedding of His blood.

And so the possession of this forgiveness is direct and immediate through Christ, not from Christ through others, whether persons or things, ; it is distinctly not through the sacraments or through the priest in such a way that but for them it would not have been through Christ. The Christian, we are assured, is a priest unto himself. We have the authority of St. John for saying so, for he tells us that Christ *hath made us priests unto God and His Father*:[1] and if He has made us priests unto God and His Father, He must have made us independent of a priest to come between us and Himself; for if we have not yet accepted Christ as our priest He has not yet made us priests unto God and His Father. If the order is—first the priest, then Christ, then the priesthood unto God the Father, all we can say is, that the first term in the series is here entirely omitted, and the position of the Christian described at a point ulterior to it, where, having Christ for his priest, he is in that sense and so far a priest unto himself, because himself made a priest unto God and the Father.

In fact, we have redemption in Him, He is the source and centre of it; we go to Him for it, and find and receive it in Him; for we believe that He died for the remission of sins, and that the redemption which we have in Him is the remission of sins, involves and implies and includes the remission of

[1] Rev. i.

sins. Unless every barrier is broken down between ourselves and Christ, unless there is immediate contact between ourselves and Christ, we have not that in Him which is to be had alone in Him. To say that we have contact with Christ through the priest, or in the sacraments, is to imply that we have a special contact in and through them, which differs from ordinary contact; or a contact which we cannot otherwise have, which is to establish an additional machinery of mediation between us and Christ, independently of, and over and above His mediation between us and the Father which, so far as this machinery is necessary or indispensable, is thereby shown to be defective and incomplete. Whereas, on the contrary, the priesthood and the sacraments exist solely and only to proclaim and to manifest Christ : in proportion as they discharge their office they accomplish their work, and Christ is proclaimed and manifested ; in proportion as they fulfil their office, they are lost in Him, on the principle that, as *He must increase, I must decrease*,[1] not in the discharge of my functions, but in their relative importance and necessity in the eyes of them who most thankfully receive them unto edification. There can be no room for the priest and the Saviour in the believer's presence. As the priest fulfils his office, and his office is effectual, the Saviour becomes the priest, and takes his place. The sacraments do not give us a participation of Christ, which but for them we could not have, but, having become partakers of

[1] John iii. 30.

Christ by faith in Him, the sacraments assure us of that participation, and demonstrate it to the senses. But the sacraments cannot convey to the spirit a participation which cannot reach the spirit through the senses but must come to it through faith. To partake of the sacrament is not necessarily to partake of Christ, but we may partake of Christ in the sacrament by faith ; and so partaking of Him, the sacrament will confirm our faith, assuring us through the senses of the reality of that participation, and demonstrating to the reason that the act in which we have engaged is the counterpart and derivative of, and in fact identical with the act of Him who, in the same night that He was betrayed, took bread and blessed and brake it in the upper room and said, *This is My body which is given for you ;*[1] *and who likewise after supper took the cup, when He had given thanks, and said, This is My blood which is shed for you for the remission of sins ; do this in remembrance of Me.*[2] Thus remembering and believing in Him to the saving of the soul, we have, as a matter of fact and a realised present possession, that *redemption through His blood* which is *the remission of sins ;* and *though we see Him not, yet, believing in Him* and in the remission of sins through Him, *we rejoice with joy unspeakable and full of glory.*[3]

Oh, my dear brethren, will you not so believe ?

[1] Luke xxii. 19 ;
[2] Luke xxii. 20 ; Matt. xxvi. 28.
[3] 1 Pet. i. 8.

XXXI.

THE RESURRECTION OF THE BODY.

So also is the resurrection of the dead. It is sown in corruption; it is raised in incorruption: it is sown in dishonour; it is raised in glory: it is sown in weakness; it is raised in power: it is sown a natural body; it is raised a spiritual body. There is a natural body and there is a spiritual body.—1 COR. xv. 42-44.

IN the article which announces or implies the distinctive promise of the remission of sins, in the clear emphatic and authoritative manner in which the Gospel proclaims it, we may perhaps say that we have taken leave of those doctrines which can be regarded as peculiar to Christianity. "The resurrection of the body," it is plain from the New Testament, was a doctrine in vogue among the Jews at the time of our Lord, for otherwise the Sadducees would have been deprived of the very reason for their existence as deniers of it. By some, it has been supposed that the doctrine of the resurrection was adopted by the Jews as a foreign belief, and derived by them from the ancient Persians. Our Lord, however, declared plainly, that the belief in a resurrection was implied in the words addressed by God to Moses, *I am the God of Abraham, and the God of Isaac, and the God of Jacob, for* he said, *God is not a God of the dead, but of the living*,[1] and any one who believes that He has in the words of the Old Testament something more than the unaided and untaught utterances of men, will have no difficulty in recognising the germs of a similar belief in various parts of it. Whether or not, however, other religions have apprehended or taught the doctrine of a resurrection to come, certain it is that no religion has spoken out upon this subject, in the same open, and unmistakable way that Christianity has. Whatever other religions may have taught, or not taught, there is, and can be no shadow of doubt that Christianity has taught, distinctly and emphatically, the doctrine of the resurrection of the dead. It may be worth observing therefore, that in whatever degree this doctrine is common to other creeds besides that of Christendom, it ceases to be a doctrine for which Christianity alone can be held responsible. If the human mind, outside the pale of Christendom, has clung to this belief, and thought it reasonable, it can hardly be alleged as a ground or evidence of unreasonableness against Christianity.

Assuming, therefore, that the doctrine of a resurrection has entered to any extent into the national beliefs of mankind, what does that fact teach us? It teaches us either that the belief must have been arrived at by the unaided effort of the reason, or that it must have been imparted from without. It must have been the result of a deep instinct, or of a definite

[1] Matt. xxii. 32; Mark xii. 26, 27; Luke xx. 37, 38.

act of revelation imparting it to man. Now what is there in reason calculated to lead us to this belief? It is unquestionable, that to a certain extent, nature herself seems to speak of a resurrection. When in returning spring, the aspect of the world is changed, and the earth awakens from the deep sleep of winter to clothe herself once more in the habiliments of life and gladness, is not the very word we use to express it, resurrection? When "the jolly hours lead on propitious May," we see, as it were, the resurrection of nature. She was dead and is alive again. And yet the flowers and the leaves, the foliage and the fruit of each returning season are not the same as those of last year, they are a new series connected with the former one only as one link of a chain is connected with another, by the order of succession, and yet more intimately by derivation. All that we can say in this case is, that the result is similar, but it is not the same. The law of nature is reproduction, repetition, the multiplication of individuals after the same type, but not the preservation of the individuals. So also is it with the generations of the human family. One generation succeeds another. The aspect of man upon the earth now is very much what it was a hundred or a thousand years ago; but the individuals are not the same, though they are in this case the representatives and derivations of their predecessors. It hardly seems, therefore, that these analogies of nature are adequate to suggesting the doctrine of a resurrection in any real sense. If this is all that could be learnt from nature, it would hardly account for the belief in a resurrection. To say that resurrection is nothing more than endless repetition, infinite reproduction of the type, is to fall far short of what would seem to be its natural and necessary meaning. If then the belief in a resurrection had really been attained, it would seem that it must have come from other sources. When a son stands over the open grave of his dead father, and professes his belief in the resurrection, he does not, cannot mean that the father is risen again in himself, the son—that would be a truism, and an obvious fact. Whatever nations have held the faith of a resurrection, must have meant by it much more than this. But it does not seem that nature could teach them much more, or therefore lead them to the doctrine of a resurrection. Surely to whatever extent they held that doctrine, it must have been the result of a deep irrepressible inextinguishable instinct: and therefore the inculcation of the Divine, just as the mother's love, is taught by God, or else it must have been the remnant of an original Divine revelation.

And though considering the extent of its hold upon the human mind, it cannot be said that the doctrine of the resurrection is contrary to reason, yet it would be absurd to say that it is not a doctrine above and beyond reason. So manifestly is this the case, that it is well-nigh impossible that the belief can have been derived from reason, and it must almost necessarily point us to revelation.

What then, is it, that we learn from Revelation? A seed is cast into the ground and dies, but after it has died it springs up again, not as it was before, but another " body " : the same, inasmuch as the "body," a plant derived from one seed, is different from that derived from another seed, but not the same inasmuch as the plant is different from the seed. Here, then, we get the great law of the preservation of individuality in and through dissolution. *That which thou sowest, thou sowest not that body which shall be, but bare grain, it may chance of wheat or of some other grain, but God giveth it a body as it hath pleased Him, and to every seed his own body.*[1] That which is raised is the same and yet not the same; and so also is the resurrection of the body, which is the same inasmuch as it is not another as the son who succeeds his father is another, but yet not the same, for it is sown in corruption, and raised in incorruption.

A profound mystery, my brethren, for the simple reason that everything which transcends the limits of our experience must be mysterious until we have experienced it, but therefore for that very reason a truth, which, if a truth, can only be derived by revelation from the source of truth. St. Paul must have been as ignorant as you or I on this matter of the resurrection, and as incompetent to arrive at any knowledge about it, except so far as that knowledge was imparted to him by the Most High.

In the statement of Scripture, then, about the

[1] 1 Cor. xv., 37, 38.

resurrection, we seem to have got more than reason could have guided us to, and therefore that which reason cannot understand. By reason alone we could not have got so far; no wonder therefore, if being where we are, we find our reason baffled.

But let us gather up what Scripture has taught us on the matter.

First, then, the resurrection of the body is something distinct from the resurrection of the spirit. It is clear not only from this chapter, but from others, that there were those in the Apostle's time, who had made the two convertible. The notion of a resurrection of the body was a stumblingblock to them, as it is to us, and they tried to elude it by dwelling on the resurrection which takes place by faith in Christ. If St. Paul is orthodox on this matter, it is perfectly certain they were not. He taught distinctly that there is a resurrection of the body. And in fact the body is an integral part of the human entity. We cannot have a man without a body, any more than we can have a flower without petals, or a fruit without substance. If therefore there is to be a resurrection of the man, there must be a resurrection of the body.

But how, if the body is dissolved into its component elements, which are scattered to the four winds, and become portions of other beings, beasts, fishes, birds and plants, and are destined again to return to corruption, in never-ending succession? Here is the very point at which reason, having been led thereto by faith, turns back in dismay, faint and dizzy at the prospect before her.

And it is manifestly hopeless to render her position more secure. We cannot do it. Reason must wait, and stay herself upon faith, but she has certain principles to cling to, one is the preservation of the individual, or of personal, identity. As a matter of fact, we know that this preservation is maintained under circumstances no less staggering to the processes of reason and the efforts of the understanding. There is not one particle of the same substance or matter in your body, or in mine, now that there was ten years ago, and yet our identity is preserved, and in many cases our appearance even is but little changed. We know that we are the same, our friends recognise us as the same. Is not this a mystery? Can you account for it? Can I? Can anyone? Take again the law of growth. A child is born with a very small body, it is preserved with great solicitude and care, through a variety of accidents and dangers, and it gathers bulk—where from? —till by slow degrees the child has become a boy, and the boy has become a man, and then the process of growth which has continued, perhaps for twenty years or so without intermission, suddenly stops, but why? Can any one tell? The only reason we can give is, that these things are so, because they are so; but "O most lame and impotent conclusion!" But it is, however, perfectly obvious, that of the child who has thus become a man, no vestige has remained at various successive stages of his growth. Every particle has become dissolved, over and over again, has passed into other beings and the like : is there no mystery here? And yet this is a patent fact before our own eyes, occuring in thousands and tens of thousands of instances, in fact in every instance. And shall we say that the preservation of the individual and of personal identity, in and through death, after a visible dissolution has passed upon the body is a thing impossible? Why impossible? What do we know about the possible or the impossible? In the vocabulary of the Almighty, the word impossible is not found; inconceivable it may be; unintelligible it is; incredible, but for certain considerations it might well be; but impossible! nay we must know a little more about the limits of the possible before we dare say that. When it is a known fact then, that the actual body of every one of us has already been the subject of a certain resurrection many times, shall we refuse to believe that there is yet another and a greater resurrection reserved for it, which may or may not have a greater or less analogy with those which have already occurred, but which, unlike them, shall be its final resurrection. On the conditions of this resurrection it were vain to speculate. We can only suppose that the body shall be a body still, though no longer corrupt, dishonourable or weak, it shall be a body, even as the body of the risen Christ was a body which bore the marks of the nails and spear; but it shall not be a natural or psychical, but a spiritual or pneumatical body, that is to say, it shall not be an animal body, but it shall be a spiritual body More than this we know not and cannot find out, and what perchance even this may mean we dare not guess.

But two other relative thoughts Scripture seems to give us. As we have seen, our Lord deduced the doctrine of the resurrection from the words spoken to Moses in the memorable declaration, *God is not the God of the dead, but of the living*, implying surely, therefore, that Abraham, Isaac, and Jacob were yet alive in God, and also, as it seems to me, in some sense risen, if we are to preserve the validity of His argument, otherwise, how would their being alive in God prove the resurrection ? If God was the God of Abraham, Isaac, and Jacob, and thereby the God of the living and not of the dead, then those of whom He was the God were living, and in communion with Him ; their mortal bodies had turned again to their dust, but they were not dead, and the bodies which had died and turned to dust did not constitute them. We do not wish to dogmatise on a matter of such profound obscurity ; but, verily, the thought appears to be suggested by the words of our Lord, that, after all, we may have erred in mixing up the notion of *time* with the *fact* of the resurrection, in relegating that resurrection to a point beyond a vast and unlimited gulf of time.

The resurrection is a condition which is independent of time, and not measured by time, nor modified by time. *Thy brother shall rise again*, said Christ to Martha. *I know that he shall rise again in the resurrection at the last day*,[1] was her reply, mixing up the condition of the resurrection with an indefinite conception of future time; but Jesus said unto her, in ever memorable words, *I am the resurrection, and the life: he that believeth in Me, though he were dead, yet shall he live: and whosoever liveth and believeth in Me shall never die. Believest thou this?*[2] If the body is essential to the integrity of man, though particular parts or accidents of the body are not essential to the identity of the individual, we know not what change has passed upon the man when the being with whom we held personal and spiritual converse has passed away and left us nothing but the husk of his visible and lifeless clay. *Thou sowest not that body that shall be, but bare grain;* and, *That which thou sowest is not quickened except it die;*[3] but out of the body so sown, though the *when* and the *where* we know not, any more than we know the *how*, there cometh forth a body the same, yet not the same; the same as regards personal identity, but not the same as regardeth accidents; for, *It is sown in corruption;* but, *it is raised in incorruption:* the verbs are impersonal verbs without a subject, σπείρεται ἐγείρεται. *It is sown in dishonour, it is raised in glory: it is sown in weakness, it is raised in power: it is sown a natural body, it is*

[1] John xi. 23, 24.
[2] John xi. 25, 26.
[3] 1 Cor. xv. 37, 36.

raised a spiritual body.[1] *There is a natural body, and there is a spiritual body.* Does not this, and similar language, suggest the thought that the resurrection *is* the change of the natural body into the spiritual body, and if this was already a fact to Abraham, Isaac, and Jacob, as our Lord's language seems partly, at least, to hint, may it not also be a fact to all those who are *heirs with them of the same promise?* [2] What if this was that very mystery which the Apostle would show the Corinthians, *We shall not all sleep, but we shall all be changed, in a moment, in the twinkling of an eye, at the last trump.*[3]

But this brings us to the other thought of which I spoke, that though the language of our Lord and St. John seems to point us to an actual and present resurrection, which becomes a reality to those who believe in Christ, whether in life or in death, yet there is also another aspect which seems well nigh to have cast out the other from our popular belief, which is that of a final and general resurrection, at a definite but unknown point of future time, *When the sea shall give up the dead which are in it; and death and hell shall deliver up the dead which are in them.*[4] How far such expressions are to be interpreted literally, we do not presume to say. It might seem that the truth they teach is the preservation of every single responsible human agent in his integrity in the safe custody of God till the day of final reckon-

[1] 1 Cor. xv. 42—44.
[2] Heb. xi. 9.
[3] 1 Cor. xv. 51, 52.
[4] Rev. xx. 13.

ing, and only this; but, at all events, the day is hastening on which shall declare it, and already the *Lord of Hosts mustereth the host of the battle.*[1] That there shall be a great gathering at the last, when the Lord comes to make up His jewels, from all times, nations, and languages, none can doubt. How far that gathering has even yet been prepared for in the invisible world we know not. In the obvious obscurity of Scripture we cannot say. This only we know, that if Jesus is the resurrection and the life, then to believe in Him is to be risen from the dead now, and to live for evermore, to have the *promise of the life that now is, and of the* endless *life to come*,[2] and then to die is to fall asleep in, and to live again in Him. *For if we believe that Jesus died and rose again, even so them also which sleep in Jesus will God bring with Him.*[3] *For to this end Christ both died, and rose, and revived, that He might be Lord both of the dead and living.*[4] Even so be it, Amen.

[1] Isa. xiii. 4.
[2] 1 Tim. iv. 8.
[3] 1 Thess. iv. 14.
[4] Rom. xiv. 9.

XXXII.

THE LIFE EVERLASTING.

For God so loved the world that He gave His only begotten Son, that whosoever believeth in Him should not perish but have everlasting life.
—JOHN iii. 16.

WE come now to the issue of all practice, and the end of all belief—the "life everlasting." This, according to the words of our Lord just read, was the purpose for which He was given to the world, that we might have eternal life. We say that we believe in the life everlasting. What do we mean by it? Strange to say, there is perhaps nothing which is at once so intelligible, and yet so hopelessly unintelligible, as this same life everlasting or eternity of existence.

The belief in immortality is an instinct. Is there any one of us whose heart, when questioned narrowly, does not assure him in accents unmistakable, albeit inaudible, that he cannot die; that there is in him an indestructible essence, an unquenchable spark, which is independent of change and unrelated to time, and which therefore must be unaffected by and superior to death? There can be no question but that a very large induction, based upon the experience of the vast majority of mankind, confirms this statement. It is not that in earlier and later times there have not been those who have grudged and endeavoured to wrench from man his birthright of immortality, but not only the great majority of thinking men have arrived at the conviction that man is immortal, but, what is even more to the point in such a case, the popular belief of by far the larger portion of mankind has instinctively declared in favour of such a conviction. Indeed, the immortality of man, or as it used to be called the immortality of the soul, was a doctrine familiar to many nations and to many beliefs long before Christianity was first preached. To acknowledge this, which is an unquestionable fact, is not at all to detract from the glory of our Saviour Jesus Christ, who, St. Paul says, *abolished death and brought life and immortality to light through the gospel.*[1] Here, however, as was observed in the last lecture, we must distinguish carefully between the immortality of man and the deathlessness of the individual. The immortality of the soul is a Pagan and a very chilly doctrine, as well as a shadowy and a very vague doctrine. The thought of the former inhabitants of the world being reduced to the condition of insubstantial disembodied spirits is a notion calculated, I should imagine, to give but little comfort to any one. It is the notion which the irrepressible instinct of the human heart, when left to itself and unaided is likely to beget. It is the net result of the heathen poet's belief which

[1] 2 Tim. i. 10.

he cannot get rid of, *Non omnis moriar,* " I shall not wholly die." It is the witness to that instinct, the evidence and token of it. Even this notion, however, vindicates to a certain extent the immortality of the separate man, the deathlessness of the *ego* or the I.

But it is obvious that the notion of the immortality of man is perfectly well susceptible of a very different meaning, only then it becomes the expression of a fact, and not the utterance of a belief. It is obvious that man is immortal. Any one who has stood in the magnificent amphitheatre at Verona must have felt the presence of this fact. Man is immortal in his works ; the pyramids of Egypt and the ruins of Rome alike attest it. There is the abiding evidence of the existence of men who have long passed away. Even greater than such evidence is the witness of literary monuments, *Exegi monumentum ære perennius*: " I have reared for myself a monument more durable than bronze " was the proud consciousness of the Roman poet, which is that also of all who, like him, have produced works that cannot die. This, however, is and can be the heritage only of a few. It bears witness to the immortality of certain men, but not to the immortality of man. It is the glorious achievement of select exceptions, not the inalienable birthright of the many and the all.

But man is immortal in his race. The *genus homo* does not die. One generation passes away, but another takes its place. Man is perpetually dying and being buried, but he is likewise perpetually rising again from the dead. Phœnix-like, from the ashes of the dead there comes forth the inextinguishable hope of an undying futurity, though it is the futurity of succession, and not of the separate and solitary *one*. The Christian doctrine of the life everlasting is something more than the eternity of the type, it is the deathlessness of the individual. It is not that I am immortal, because the race to which I belong cannot die, and because I belong to it, but it is that I am immortal because death cannot ultimately extinguish me. The doctrine has been proclaimed of late that Christianity does not predicate the immortality of man in the abstract, but only of those whom it invests with immortality through faith in the Redeemer. With reference to this doctrine, I can only say that I do not go to Christianity to learn whether or not I shall die, but to the scrutiny of my own heart. I learn there, and thousands besides me have learnt the same, that there is that in me which death cannot touch.

And I should say that the very fact of man being able to debate such a topic as that of his own immortality is an unmistakable proof of the immortality which he debates. Who told thee that thou wast immortal? Didst thou dream it of thyself? If so, whence came the dream? How was it that such a dream could take possession of thee, nay, could visit thee at all, if from the nature of the case thou wast incapable of immortality? It is like the thought of God. How came that thought into the mind of man ? How did the thought stamp itself indelibly on the language of man unless because it was the expression of a fact. Human language expresses only those things which need to be expressed. The existence of a word for God in all the languages of man as a primary, elementary, and necessary thought, and not as an artificial or refined necessity, is surely no small proof of the fact which man felt compelled to acknowledge and express.

I take it, then, that this immortality of man's nature is a primary truth which Christianity assumes and does not inculcate. The immortality of man is involved in the fact of his moral superiority no less than in that of his marvellous power of contemplating himself as a whole, from a point external to himself. If man is responsible, there must be a time and place, or something that answers to a time and place, for him to give an account. Let those who like take refuge in the thought of annihilation, of total extinction after death ; there is, after all, I presume, something to be annihilated, something to be extinguished ; this is clearly not that which we see annihilated, which we see touched by the icy hand of death ; but what is it ? If we say that it is annihilated, how do we arrive at the knowledge that it exists to be annihilated ? Surely it is a cumbrous operation first to call it into existence and then to annihilate it, better by far to deny its existence ; but then, what need for its annihilation ? Surely man's consciousness, his sense of responsibility, his perpetual tendency to reach forth into worlds unknown, are all so many undeniable indications of a capacity which he has in virtue of his being, which Christianity does not, and has not given him, but to which it only appeals. And annihilation is nothing better than a cowardly way of baulking the inevitable inference which forces itself upon the conscience and will not be put by.

On the other hand, however, there are two great difficulties connected with this matter of immortality which, as they are not invented by Christianity, so neither are they solved by it. The first is, that if man is eternal with reference to futurity, he must, or may be eternal with reference also to the past ; which brings us face to face with the mysteries of previous existence, a doctrine which has oftentimes been held, and of which there may have been a trace in the words, *Master, who did sin, this man, or his parents, that he was born blind?*[1] but upon which our Lord, with characteristic indifference to such abstract and idle questionings, has thrown no light in His reply. Certain it is, that the testimony of human consciousness on this point is incomparably less distinct than it is on the other of immortality, and the notion of pre-existence is probably nothing more than the logical penumbra of the doctrine of immortality. There appears to be nothing inconceivable in the notion of the Almighty Creator calling into existence in time and in the world of matter beings whom

[1] 1 John, ix. 2.

He has endowed with the capacity of eternal existence; but however this may be, we cannot refuse to believe in man's immortality simply because to do so would oblige us, if so be it were to oblige us, logically, to believe also in his pre-existence. His responsibility, which is the condition of his existence here, has reference to the all-golden present, and not to a past of which, as far as we are concerned, nothing whatever is known, but which clearly is as though it had never been. This is a matter on which I do not pretend to pronounce. I personally do not believe in it, I only say that, supposing the logical consequence of accepting the doctrine of immortality were to be the belief in pre-existence, this would not constitute a valid reason for rejecting that doctrine.

But we pass on to the second difficulty. And this is the stupendous magnitude of the thought, and the terrible oppressiveness of the attempt to realise it. Towards the end of the London season, there are two words which frequently suggest themselves, which, happily, have no equivalents in our language, but which are expressive of conditions unhappily too common among us; one is *blasé*, the other is *ennui*. It is sad, indeed, when the continued stroke of affliction and suffering has made us weary of life; but it is sadder far when the repeated draught of pleasure has wrought the same preternatural effect; when we have drunk to the fill of the sweet wine of amusement and society till we are fain to put the cup from us with disgust, when we have enjoyed so much that we can enjoy no more. It is not all of whom this is true, but is it not true of some? If, however, to be weary of the hours and moments as they fly is the experience of some in this life, what is not the very thought itself of a life which knows no change and can have no end? Fortunately, imagination itself fails to apprehend the conception, she sinks under it, baffled and crest-fallen. To live for ever; it is a solemn, an awful, an overwhelming, and oppressive thought, and one which, in its positive aspect, we dare not realise, and cannot hope to appreciate; but, happily, this is hardly the aspect in which we need to apprehend it. *He that believeth in Me*, saith our Lord,[1] *shall never die*, and that, I imagine, is appreciable. Miserable as life, whether from a surfeit of pleasure or from excess of pain, sometimes is, there is a deeper, because an unknown misery yet in death. We quail before the notion of death, we shrink from the prospect of dissolution and the thought of dying. It is still, under all circumstances, "life and fuller life we want," and not annihilation, or any form of death.

And this is what Christianity has to give us, this is the assured promise of faith in Christ, that whosoever—the insignificant no less than the distinguished, the fool no less than the reputed wise, the poor man no less than the mighty rich; not the select or the favoured few, whether among the philosophers, or the fashionable, or the blameless and the moral, but that

[1] 1 John xi. 26.

whosoever—high and low, rich and poor, great and small, one with another, all and everyone alike who believeth in Jesus, may not perish but have everlasting life. It is not the Christian Creed which gives this life but faith in the Christ who gives it, that faith in Him as the living centre which carries with it the radiating, subsidiary and subordinate faith in the various articles of the Christian Creed.

And here we must for a moment contemplate the alternative, for there surely is an alternative to be contemplated. St. John, the apostle of love, does not hesitate to say so : *He that hath the Son hath life he that hath not the Son of God hath not life.*[1] If man's birthright in virtue of his constitution is immortality ; if he is endowed with an inextinguishable spark of life, what will not, must not, that life be apart from Christ. *He that hath not the Son hath not life.* The language is itself stamped with the mark of the eternal, for it is studiously and conspicuously independent of time—it is couched in the terms of an unqualified and interminable present ; it expresses an unfailing condition which, from moment to moment, from year to year, from century to century, is unalterably true, which, perhaps, since the words were first penned, was never so capable of being apprehended, or likely to be apprehended, as it is now. But can we limit their significance to the present life or the present state of being ? I

[1] 1 John v. 12.

think not. Wherever and in whatever state man is, if he hath not the Son of God, though he may last for ever, yet he hath not life. It is an awful thought, verily, but it is a thought, the truth and awfulness of which we see around us. Christianity gives us no light on the necessary problems of our being : it does not tell us what our history in the past has been, nor even whether or not we have a past ; it does not tell us what our future shall be ; it does not help us in the slightest degree to grasp the thought of that immortality which our very nature bears witness to, and the thought of which we cannot suppress because it is our nature. Christianity does not rend aside the thick veil of uncertainty and perplexity which envelops us on every side and intercepts our view. But Christianity knows perfectly well what it offers, and is perfectly distinct and clear about what it has to give. It has life, eternal life, to give. This life, despite man's natural inextinguishable immortality, he does not possess. Christianity comes to him, telling him he does not possess it, and he knows that he does not. It comes to him and says, *God so loved the world that He gave His only begotten Son, that whosoever believeth in Him should not perish :* therefore, whosoever believeth not is perishing, doth perish, is dead while he liveth, will continue dead as long as he so liveth, for what is true at any given moment of a particular condition, is true at any given moment as long as that condition is unaltered, must be true for ever if the condition remains for ever unaltered—*should not perish* as all without Christ are thus perishing, *but have everlasting life*.[1]

Then what of those who know not Christ and have never heard of Him? Nay, from the very nature of the case, the statement applies not to them; it applies only to those who, by the presence and the preaching of Christ, have been made conscious, or at least have been assured, of their great want, of their lost condition without Him. Of these no one needs to continue perishing, as, without Him, he must perish. Belief in Christ, or rather Christ, upon his belief, will give him eternal, everlasting life—that is to say, a life which is devoid of death, which is independent of change; though verily we know not what changes may be reserved for it, changes manifestly here many and various, touching oftentimes the very apple of the eye, penetrating even to the quick, and piercing to the dividing asunder of the joints and marrow; but changes possibly also hereafter: does not the very word αἰώνιος, æonian, pertaining to cycles of ages, serve to suggest as much? It shall give an everlasting life which is out of the reach of change, which looks down unmoved upon the flux of time and change beneath, enduring and surviving all. About this life there is and can be no mistake to the possessor. He knows that his heritage by faith in Christ is a distinct, palpable, substantive possession, which he had not before he believed, and which he holds only upon condition of

[1] 1 John iii. 16.

belief. Nor can others question its influence and effects, however stoutly they may deny its reality. There is such a thing as Christian peace, which is the result of Christian faith; there is such a thing as Christian joy, which springs out of Christian peace; and there is such a thing as Christian hope, which no prospect of death can quench, and for which the stolid indifference of blank materialism can offer but a miserable substitute, which can in no way be confounded or compared with it.

This is everlasting life; not the infinite prolongation in an eternally protracted time of the life we naturally live here, but the super-addition to our natural life of another condition and capacity of existence, which gives scope for the infinite development of all the existing powers, and calls into operation other faculties, energies, and perceptions which, but for its influence, had otherwise lain dormant or had not existed—the communication to the spiritual nature of man of that new life of love, which is the endowment of those who have learnt to believe that God is love, and to find strength in the thought that He has encouraged them unreservedly to trust His love, inasmuch as He has called them to the fellowship of the Son of His love, and given them in Him the free promise of all things else. *For this is life eternal, that they might know thee, the only true God and Jesus Christ whom thou hast sent.*[1]

[1] John xvii. 5.

www.ingramcontent.com/pod-product-compliance
Lightning Source LLC
Chambersburg PA
CBHW020739020526
44115CB00030B/606